variety
entertainment
and
outdoor
amusements

Recent Titles in
American Popular Culture
Series Editor: *M. Thomas Inge*

Film: A Reference Guide
Robert A. Armour

Women's Gothic and Romantic Fiction: A Reference Guide
Kay Mussell

Animation: A Reference Guide
Thomas W. Hoffer

variety entertainment and outdoor amusements
A REFERENCE GUIDE

Don B. Wilmeth

American Popular Culture

GREENWOOD PRESS
Westport, Connecticut ● London, England

Library of Congress Cataloging in Publication Data

Wilmeth, Don B.
  Variety entertainment and outdoor amusements.

  (American popular culture, ISSN 0193-6859)
  Bibliography: p.
  Includes index.
    1. Amusement—United States—History.   2. United
States—Popular culture.   3. Music-halls (Variety—
theaters, cabarets, etc.)—United States—History.
I. Title.   II. Series.
GV1853.2.W54   790'.0973   81-13417
ISBN 0-313-21455-7 (lib. bdg.)   AACR2

Copyright © 1982 by Don B. Wilmeth

Library of Congress Catalog Card Number: 81-13417
ISBN: 0-313-21455-7
ISSN: 0193-6859

First published in 1982

Greenwood Press
A division of Congressional Information Service, Inc.
88 Post Road West
Westport, Connecticut 06881

Printed in the United States of America

10 9 8 7 6 5 4 3 2 1

To my mother and father,
for their faith
and unswerving support

Contents

Preface

The objectives of this guide are threefold. The first is to provide brief historical overviews of major forms of American variety entertainment and outdoor amusements, including in the final chapter showboats and tent shows, two prominent traditional American institutions that featured variety entertainment. Because of the ongoing popularity of stage magic and its prominence as an entertainment form in various variety forms, a separate chapter has been included. The second objective has been to evaluate briefly the available literature, including graduate theses and periodicals, collections, and organizations relevant to each chapter topic. Last, a checklist of major sources discussed in each chapter is provided.

This guide to resources is not meant to be exhaustive. The choices reflect my own biases and judgments. Nonetheless, an attempt has been made to offer a balanced selection for each chapter, to suggest representative sources (and among them, the better and most recent ones available), and thus to stimulate more meaningful research and thoughtful study in this important area of American popular culture. I trust that I have included the majority of the most useful and illuminating sources. In virtually every instance sources have been personally examined before inclusion. Although I am certain that such a requirement has necessitated the exclusion of some excellent sources, such a process should also give the user of this guide greater confidence in the assessments.

I am aware of the many exclusions in this guide, both in terms of topics and sources. I am also conscious that some users will not find the area, topic, or source that they expected in this volume. I apologize for such frustrations. My original intention was to be as inclusive and exhaustive as possible; it soon became evident that a separate volume could be produced on any one of the forms included in this study or on the dozens that I finally determined had to be excluded. It seemed more useful, in the final analysis, to provide the user of this volume with more detailed coverage of the major forms of traditional American variety entertainment and outdoor amusements, including the circus, than to attempt to produce a guide that would be so wide-ranging as to be almost amorphous.

The missing area that I regret the most is popular theater, although in defining the scope of this volume and determining its title, such an exclusion is certainly justifiable. Still, the very nature of popular entertainment makes the elimination of any aspect regrettable. I must confess that I have compromised somewhat by providing some discussion of popular theater in both the opening chapter and in the final chapter and have suggested additional bibliographical sources that would aid the user of this guide in seeking sources on popular theater.

In order to use this guide most productively, then, it should be understood that the prime concern has been with entertainment or amusement that exists or has existed without the prerequisite of a full-length, well-developed "book" or script. The only exception to this rule will be found in the chapter on the musical revue and musical comedy. It seemed appropriate, however, to include these topics because of their popular appeal and, in the case of the musical comedy, because this uniquely American form represents the culmination of earlier American variety traditions. However, the focus of chapter 10 on the musical revue and the early musical theater is on the formative period, prior to what we consider the emergence of the modern musical, although the historical overview brings the picture up to the present. Revues are included because of the great effect they had on other variety forms and because of their similarities to earlier spectacles and aspects of variety.

As much as is possible, the chapters are arranged to reflect the evolution of forms. Major outdoor amusements are covered in chapter 2; each form is discussed in order of origin, beginning with the fair and concluding with the modern-day theme park. This is followed by two related chapters, one on the American circus and another on the Wild West exhibition. Chapters 5 to 10 form another group of related topics. Each of these chapters focuses on one major form of variety entertainment, beginning with the dime museum and concluding with the musical revue and early musical theater. Admittedly, there is much overlapping of these forms and a strict chronology is impossible and perhaps not desirable. The final two chapters are independent of chronological considerations. Chapter 11 focuses on stage magic and its unique place as an entertainment form, and chapter 12 discusses the showboat and the tent theater as two distinctively American methods of presenting entertainment to otherwise largely inaccessible areas in America's heartland before the days of improved transportation.

I have not tried to make any sharp divisions between outdoor amusements and staged variety entertainment, other than in the ordering of chapters explained above. In general, each of the major forms discussed depends on a series of acts or specialties, including the circus and the Wild West show. The most obvious forms of outdoor amusement have been grouped into one chapter, although several of these forms, for example the carnival or amusement park with midway attractions, could be categorized as variety because of the dependence on compartmented entertainment. Indeed, it would be just as feasible to organize a number of the forms discussed as outdoor amusement under the general heading of environmental entertainment. The dime museum could easily fall into such a category as well. Such choices simply indicate the unique nature of popular entertainment and the problems involved in coming to grips with such diverse forms as vaudeville, theme parks, and Wild West exhibitions. Some of these problems are discussed in more detail in chapter 1.

All forms of amusement included in this guide were presented by professional showmen for profit. Clearly a guide to minor forms of American popular entertainment would be welcomed to supplement the major forms included here. Peripheral forms not covered in this guide, such as rodeos, roller derbies, professional wrestling, balloon ascensions, ice shows, puppetry, and so forth, are important facets of American popular culture and demand greater attention. The wealth of information on folk forms and ethnic entertainment in the United States, closely related to the more obvious and well-known forms dealt with in this guide, suggests another area of American popular culture that must be given more serious consideration. However, since my concern is with forms involving professional show people, folk forms do not easily fall into my present purview. Likewise, many of the other peripheral forms (rodeo and wrestling, for example) are designated as sports or contests, although the entertainment value is obvious to most of us. Indeed, most professional, spectator sports are becoming more "show biz" oriented each year. Rock concerts today draw millions of people yearly, but a clear perspective on their significance as aspects of American popular culture is not easy to ascertain, although some tentative conclusions could certainly be drawn. The whole range of popular music is, of course, closely related to the topics covered in this guide, and some attention has been given to sources of this music in several chapters. The currentness of contemporary rock concerts and spectator sports suggests another criterion that has conditioned the scope of this guide. Selection has been made in large part on the basis of forms that provide clear perspective upon examination and assessment. As a consequence, most forms included in this guide date at least from the nineteenth century. Also, the emphasis throughout has been on live per-formance or active participation on the part of the patron. In a few in-stances, forms presented by professional showmen, such as early optical or mechanical amusements (included in chapter 5), seemed appropriate for inclusion. Perhaps somewhat arbitrarily, but also because of other guides in this series, I have omitted film, other than early predecessors, although entertainments that have continued beyond the advent of cinema and the introduction of mass communication are carried to their demise or brought up to the present, as in the case, for example, of the circus and the amuse-ment park. The emphasis also has been on those entertainments that were intended as money-making operations, presented to a largely broad-based, unsophisticated audience, another reason for excluding amateur folk forms. Not all forms covered, it should be added, appealed exclusively to working-class or lower-middle-class audiences but several developed a broad middle-class audience, or, in the case of the revue, an upper-class audience as well.

The historical summaries in each chapter are perhaps not totally new or original, although a strong effort has been made to include as much current thought and up-to-date historical research as possible. On the other hand, I accept complete responsibility for the judgmental commentary in the bibliographical essays. My overriding concern in each chapter and particularly in the historical sections has been to synthesize, summarize, and present in an objective and straightforward manner the work of others far more expert on specific major entertainments than I am. As a result, my indebtedness to others is immense. The core of this work began as two chapters in volumes 1 and 2 of the *Handbook of American Popular Culture,* and, although this work retains only faint resemblances to those initial efforts, I am deeply grateful to the editor of that series, M. Thomas Inge, and to Greenwood Press for giving me the opportunity to explore more fully the area of American popular entertainment in this longer guide. Of the many authorities whose work became the basis for much of this guide, I would be remiss if I did not single out, in no particular order, the following: Marcello Truzzi, Brooks McNamara, Ralph G. Allen, Robert C. Toll, Sarah Howell, William Green, Patrick Easto, George Speaight, David Hammarstrom, Joe McKennon, Ray B. Browne, Helen Augur, Lila Perl, Milbourne Christopher, Don Russell, William Brasmer, Mary Calhoun, Julian Mates, Shirley Staples, John E. Kasson, Charles Pecor, John Allwood, David Burg, Tim Onosko, Earl Chapin May, Stuart Thayer, Neil Harris, William W. Appleton, John DiMeglio, Parker Zellers, Joe

Laurie, Douglas Gilbert, Gerald Bordman, Cecil Smith, Robert Baral, Sally Banes, William L. Slout, Philip Graham, Jere C. Mickel, and Paul Bruce Pettit. There are, undoubtedly, others that have been omitted, and I trust the listing of their work in the various bibliographies will atone for any unintentional oversight.

Although I accept all responsibility for the contents of this guide, an effort of this sort would be impossible without the advice, suggestions, and support of a great number of individuals. Without the aid of the following colleagues, friends, and former students I would not have been presumptuous enough to take on this project: A. H. Saxon, Robert Toll, Brooks McNamara, Ann Costello Landensburg, Ralph Allen, Virginia M. Goss, Julie Barlow, Trish Sandberg, William Green, Marcello Truzzi, John Lucas, Leslie Fiedler, Monica Allen, George Speaight, Laurence Senelick, Susan Marcus, Barbara S. Pook, Thomas Garrett, John Degen, Tom Parkinson, Sharon Grodin, Elizabeth Lawrence, Andrea A. Fox, Jonathan Gyory, Charles H. McCaghy, Matt Sussman, Mrs. Neil Schaffner, Larry D. Clark, Amy Cahners, Shirley Staples, Michael B. Dixon, Stephen Archer, Cynthia Jenner, Shaun Curran, and many others. A special word of thanks must go to Elizabeth Coogan and the Brown University Interlibrary Loan Department for the enormous effort made on my behalf. Without this service this project would have been impossible. In addition, the staffs of the Rockefeller Library and the Harris Collection of American Drama at Brown graciously gave me their enthusiastic assistance and helped me track down a number of obscure sources. During my search for sources I was privileged to work in a number of public and private collections. A number of very pleasant days was spent in the private magic collection of H. Adrian Smith, the country's leading magic bibliophile. Liz Fugate, drama librarian of the University of Washington, Seattle, and a good friend, located a number of items for me on the Wild West exhibition. Robert L. Parkinson of the Circus World Museum Library in Baraboo, Wisconsin, was most helpful, as were the staffs of the Performing Arts Collection at Lincoln Center, the Dallas Public Library, and the various branches and central library of the Providence Public Library. Louis A. Rachow, as usual, made me feel at home in the Walter Hampden-Edwin Booth Theatre Collections and Memorial Library at The Players in New York.

Finally, my thanks go to Pam Enos for assisting with the typing of the manuscript and to my wife Judy for her willingness to read my awkward prose and for suggesting ways to unscramble some of my more garbled sentences. In her defense, however, I should say that there was only so much she could do. Nevertheless, the narrative segments are far better than they would have been as a result of her critical but sympathetic eye.

variety
entertainment
and
outdoor
amusements

CHAPTER I

Amusing the Million:
General Introduction to
Popular Entertainment

As a boy growing up in south Texas, far from the mainstream of the American theater of the 1940s, despite infrequent road shows and the yearly visit of the Metropolitan Opera Company, I was stagestruck early because of showmen who appeared in forms of entertainment designed to appeal to a broad strata and to make money—popular entertainments that did find their way to the heart of the Lone Star State. Furthermore, most of these amusements were acceptable to my family on moral grounds. For many generations of Americans, such amusements provided their only entertainment diversions. A traveling circus, carnival, variety show, medicine show, or storefront dime museum made indelible impressions on relatively unsophisticated Americans throughout the hinterlands. Even large segments of urban centers hungered for entertainment of a nonalienating sort, especially during the nineteenth century when rural migrants and foreign immigrants were moving into major American cities in great numbers. For the new city dweller the more elite forms of entertainment failed to mirror successfully their needs, concerns, and anxieties in a sympathetic or integrating manner. So, millions of Americans turned instead to amusement parks, variety shows, dime museums, and other unpretentious, easily accessible amusements. It is revealing that between 1870 and 1910, the years of greatest growth for virtually all forms of live, popular amusements and entertainment centers, the "new middle class" grew almost eightfold, from 765,000 to 5,609,000, or from 33 percent of the population in 1870 to 63 percent in 1910.

In the nineteenth century, then, the climate was ripe for live entertainment to prosper. Prior to the late eighteenth century, it was not possible for variety entertainment or outdoor amusements to attract large audiences, for it was necessary that there be a more concentrated society and the incorporation of the majority of the population into that society in order to foster popular amusements. In this country, with the rise of technology and the rapid expansion of the frontier during the nineteenth century, Americans found increased time for leisure activities and developed a hunger and need for amusements to fill what was for many a dreary and difficult existence. As cities grew and Americans were concentrated into cohesive urban or near-urban units with common social, economic, and cultural characteristics, a huge market for entertainment was created. As more Americans moved into rural or frontier areas, another market exploded for the itinerant showman and entertainments that could move with relative ease into heretofore untapped territory. In the city variety, amusement parks, and seaside resorts were especially prosperous; rural areas depended more on small circuses, medicine shows, tent shows, and small-time variety for amusement.

Popular entertainment brought to both rural and urban audiences a common ingredient that assured success—a vital and appealing alternative "theater" that satisfied the needs and desires of the ordinary man. Professional showmen quickly perceived what would be accepted and consciously attempted to appeal to the majority by creating entertainment that was neither complex nor profound but readily comprehended. In the case of major outdoor amusements, the showmen even encouraged active participation. Thus the forms of amusements discussed in this guide, with the exception of minor offshoots, were those that became popular in the sense that the majority of people liked and approved of them, and one reason for their acceptance was because they deviated little from standards and conventions. Hundreds of professional troupes and individual performers emerged during the mid-nineteenth century to provide a variety of amusement forms, some new, some adaptations of earlier forms, but all aimed at a new audience seeking diversion. Urban centers developed theaters, "palaces" of entertainment, and large outdoor amusement areas. Rural America supported traveling troupes, in the form of circuses, repertoire companies playing town halls, opera houses, or even in tents; chautauqua troupes performing under the guise of religion or culture; and variety companies of all sorts and descriptions.

Most of these forms declined in popularity during the first half of this century, replaced by less expensive and more accessible forms of entertainment such as films, radio, and television. As a result, the tendency has been to think of these former entertainments as somewhat crude, inferior, and unworthy of serious attention. In reality, despite much mediocrity that doubtless permeated these live amusements, the show people involved in popular entertainment had unique abilities. We are now beginning to admit that the art of the performer and the actor is not limited to the legitimate stage or the more elite forms of entertainment. The late Kenneth Tynan has illustrated this idea in *The Sound of Two Hands Clapping* (New York, 1975) in which he discusses what he calls "High Definition Performance or HDP"—that quality shared by authentic stars (great athletes, sportsmen, bullfighters, and conversationalists, as well as stage performers). This is the same quality shared by great showmen, whether they be vaudeville comics, circus aerialists, or burlesque strippers. Tynan defines this rare star-quality ingredient as the artist's ability "to communicate the essence of one's talent to an audience with economy, grace, no apparent effort, and absolute, hard-edged clarity of outline." Certainly the vaudeville team of Smith and Dale possessed this ability in their Dr. Kronkite routine, which they repeated thousands of times. Even Chang and Eng, the original Siamese twins, who displayed themselves to curious audiences in the nineteenth century in an almost balletic routine, had most of these qualities. And even the greatest of the carnival pitchmen, who were out to fleece the chumps, were impressive and convincing performers with their hyped spiel.

As Ray B. Browne, scholar of American popular culture, suggested recently, nearly all Americans have been active participants or "closet" appreciators of popular entertainment. Furthermore he concludes that the blood flow of a nation cannot be charted without studying popular entertainment. A careful and thorough look at American popular entertainment can reveal many attitudes of our past society. Today, most of us get our entertainment from machines—radios, tape decks, stereos, TVs, and motion picture projectors. It is worth repeating that before mass media pervaded the nation, average Americans crammed into theaters, auditoriums, halls, tents, and parks to get their excitement, adventure, and escapism from live performers and showmen. First and foremost, people went to such amusement areas to enjoy themselves, even at the so-called cultural institution known as the chautauqua. But show business was not just meaningless fluff. Perhaps more than any other facet of American life, show business, as explored in this guide, was created of, by, and for average Americans. Professional showmen developed forms, features, styles, and material out of their intimate relationship with their patrons. As popular forms entertained they reflected and spoke to the patrons' deepest concerns, desires, and needs, though often unconsciously. No one had to take such amusements seriously, which meant that they could deal with the most serious, most troubling subjects possible without threatening or irritating anyone. As Robert C. Toll points out in *On with the Show,* whenever new public issues or problems surfaced, show business dealt with them, often with new entertainment forms centered on the new concerns.

In the foreword to my bibliographical guide, *American and English Popular Entertainment* (Gale Research, 1980), Brooks McNamara, a leader in the field of popular entertainment at New York University, describes the problems he experienced in researching the medicine show for his superb book *Step Right Up*. He points out that "it soon became clear that medicine showmen had not been much inclined to write about their exploits, except in a mellow old age, when the main events of their careers often took on a somewhat romantic glow." In fact, he goes on to say, "all of the early books and articles on the shows were the most casual sort of journalism, relentlessly anecdotal and fanciful in the extreme." Yet, as he explains, often they contained all there was to be found about some event or personality central to his research, and he soon discovered that by careful cross-checking, a source could often provide revealing material about both the facts and the spirit of a long-vanished American form. McNamara's difficulties illustrate just one of the stumbling blocks to the serious study of American popular entertainment forms.

Unquestionably, there are legitimate difficulties in investigating variety entertainment and outdoor amusements, but research of the past decade has now taken these forms out of the closet and illustrated that live amusements created by professional showmen for profit and aimed at a broad, relatively unsophisticated audience are worthy of serious attention. Slowly we are overcoming this previous oversight and coming to grips with investigatory difficulties. Fewer scholars of American popular culture look upon popular amusements with what was once an anticommerical bias or relegate the forms to the garbage heap because of the lack of a strong literary base. The recognition that most of these popular forms lack a strong literary base and depend more significantly on the performer and the audience than a written text is revealing in itself and suggests the need for new or different but meaningful analytical methods. The student of popular entertainment must contend with one additional hurdle, a both bothersome and rewarding problem indicative of the rich and complex nature of these popular forms. Throughout history popular forms have appeared, merged, mutated, disappeared, and, in some cases, reappeared in new guises, and all the while these forms have been virtually ignored by scholars and historians.

Few of the stumbling blocks outlined above are insurmountable. It is encouraging, in fact, that in the 1970s and early 1980s the study of popular entertainment has begun to emerge as viable components of theater, social, and cultural history. As old biases break down, such forms as circus, vaudeville, and burlesque have come to be seen not merely as part of some primitive substratum of theater but as significant kinds of cultural expression, well worth the time and trouble required for close investigation. It is significant to note that in recent years a large number of doctoral projects listed annually in *The Theatre Journal* fall into the general category of popular entertainment or popular theater. During the past decade conferences on various facets of popular performance have been held in England and the United States. In this country, the Conference on the History of American Popular Entertainment, held at the New York Public Library at Lincoln Center in 1977 and cosponsored by the American Society for Theatre Research and the Theatre Library Association, legitimized such study once and for all. Important journals, such as *Theatre Quarterly, The Drama Review,* the *Journal of Popular Culture, Educational Theatre Journal* (*The Theatre Journal*), and *Theatre Studies* have focused attention in this area with entire issues devoted to the discussion of popular material. It is now commonplace for the more scholarly theater journals to include essays devoted to topics that once were considered inappropriate for their pages. The indicators are clear. A new field of research has finally begun to come of age and the field of American popular culture will be enriched as a result of more serious investigation into popular entertainment forms.

SURVEY OF GENERAL SOURCES

As Brooks McNamara has suggested, one should not be too quick to decry the mediocrity of sources on variety entertainments and outdoor amusements. Although many of the better sources might be called "good bad" books—chatty autobiographies and memoirs, undocumented histories and the like—the attention paid to the whole range of popular entertainments has changed drastically in recent years, and several excellent sources are now available. No longer are forms like vaudeville, burlesque, the amusement park, and popular theater considered insignificant because they are not abstruse, profound, or complicated. Social scientists and humanists are going beyond the primary function of these forms, and discovering other values, including the reflection and expression of aesthetic and other needs of a large population base, as well as the creation of effective satire and politically motivated comment. If taken seriously, most major forms of American popular amusements can be seen as something more than idle forms of mass diversion; they are important manifestations of psychic and social forces at work in American culture.

A thorough investigation of any form of American popular entertainment should leave no stone unturned; the construct of this guide has followed that idea, so that old and new sources, documented and popular histories, memoirs and biographies, collections and serials are included in order to present a balanced resource. Underscoring the new-found significance of popular entertainment as a legitimate area of study is the attention paid the subject by scholarly journals and organizations, as well as in graduate theses and sociological studies. These too have been incorporated in this guide as they were deemed most useful.

Several publishers have begun to focus attention in this area. The Center for the Study of Popular Culture at Bowling Green State University publishes significant books under the aegis of the Bowling Green State University Popular Press and issues the important *Journal of Popular Culture,* which periodically includes articles on popular entertainments. Archon, an imprint of The Shoe String Press, has established a series on popular entertainments under the initial editorship of A. H. Saxon; Scarecrow Press has recently published a number of important reference books cited elsewhere in this guide in the general area of popular entertainment and promises more; and Greenwood Press has expanded their publications in this field appreciably in the last few years, including one of the better general sources on the subject, *American Popular Entertainment,* edited by Myron Matlaw, and my own glossary of argot, slang, and termininology entitled *The Language of American Popular Entertainment.* Although not particularly germane to the subject of this guide, their publication of *Puppetry Library,* compiled and edited by George B. Miller, Janet S. Harris, and William E. Hannaford, Jr., is indicative of the scope of recent Greenwood publications. This particular volume is an extremely helpful annotated bibliography based on the Batchelder-McPharlin Collection at the University of New Mexico.

In 1971 *Theatre Quarterly* (published in London) devoted an issue to "People's Theatre," including essays on melodrama, equestrian drama, and American vaudeville. *The Drama Review,* the single best source for essays dealing with the influence of popular entertainments on the avant-garde, published an issue in 1974 devoted to "popular entertainments," containing good articles on popular scenography, commedia dell' arte and the actor, stage magic, and other relevant topics, among them an excellent introduction to the study by Brooks McNamara, which lays out a sensible categorization of forms. The *Educational Theatre Journal* followed in 1975 with an excellent issue featuring articles on early American musical theater, burlesque, revue, and pantomime. Specific essays relevant to this guide from these special issues have been cited within appropriate chapters. As basic sources, however, these issues are worth attention in their entirety.

Although serious scholarly research is relatively new in the field of popular entertainment, a number of comprehensive bibliographies are now available, and more are on the way. As a very basic beginning place, John H. Towsen's "Sources on Popular Entertainment" provides a reasonably good guide to general sources, including a list of basic research tools, libraries and museums, organizations, performer training, and a select bibliography. An even more complete guide is Don B. Wilmeth's *American and English Popular Entertainment: A Guide to Information Sources,* the only one-volume, annotated bibliographic guide to major forms of popular entertainment available, with sections on organizations, periodicals and serials, and libraries and museums, along with over two thousand annotated sources. My select bibliographical guide entitled "American Popular Entertainment: A Historical Perspective" first appeared in 1977 and in 1979 was reprinted in *American Popular Entertainment,* edited by Matlaw. One of the most thorough reference sources incorporating fifteen thousand sources on most aspects of the circus and outdoor entertainment (and other related topics) remains Raymond Toole-Stott's four volume *Circus and Allied Arts, A World Bibliography,* discussed in more detail in chapter 3. Supplementary bibliographical sources on popular theater are discussed in chapter 12. The basic trade magazine for all forms of show business remains the weekly, *Variety.* This magazine and *Amusement Business* are the major sources for studying variety entertainment, the circus, and outdoor amusements. Other useful periodicals and serials are *Billboard, The Drama Review, Journal of Popular Culture, The Theatre Journal, New York Clipper, New York Mirror, Nineteenth-Century Theatre Research, Spirit of the Times, Theatre History Studies,* and *Theatre Quarterly.* Serials of specific use are discussed in each chapter where appropriate.

A definitive, comprehensive history of American popular entertainment has yet to be written, although several volumes published in the last few years, combined with several older sources, provide a satisfactory perspective. The proceedings of the Conference on the History of American Popular Entertainment were collected into a superb volume, edited by Myron Matlaw. *American Popular Entertainment* provides twenty-six excellent essays on all aspects of the subject, from the opening overview by Monroe Lippmann ("Notes from an Old Girl Watcher") to the summing up by Ray B. Browne. Specific essays from this collection have been cited in appropriate chapters throughout this volume. Although less relevant to this guide than the Matlaw volume, the published proceedings of two English conferences on various aspects of Western popular entertainment and theater should be mentioned: *Western Popular Theatre,* edited by David Mayer and Kenneth Richards, and *Performance and Politics in Popular Drama,* edited by David Bradby, Louis James, and Bernard Sharratt. Two additional recent sources focus more specifically on American forms. Robert C. Toll's *On with the Show* is the only recent attempt to chronicle major American forms of entertainment with some semblance of documentation and despite organizational and emphases problems, this volume is a generally excellent introduction to these major forms. It also contains an excellent bibliographical essay and a comparative chronology showing the parallel between the evolution of American society and American show business. Joseph and June Bundy Csida's *American Entertainment: A Unique History of Popular Show Business,* an attempt to fashion a history of American popular entertainments from the files of *Billboard,* suffers by trying to do too much but is still a fascinating smorgasbord of information on all aspects of entertainment—from vaudeville to film and the circus to rock concerts (although burlesque and carnival, which received scant attention by *Billboard* over the years, is also given similar treatment here). Also recommended is a recent double issue of *Theatre Studies* edited by Barbara A. Kachur and devoted to popular North American Theatre.

Two older sources are also recommended, basic surveys: Samuel McKechnie's *Popular Entertainment Through the Ages* and Gilbert Seldes's *The 7 Lively Arts*. The former, although originally published in 1931, offers a good introduction to major entertainment forms (with a focus on Europe), such as mimes, minstrels, strolling players, fairs, commedia dell'arte, Punch and Judy, pantomime, and music hall and thus provides a good background to European roots of American entertainment. Seldes's collection of essays was the first attempt by an American to justify and defend popular forms and as such is still stimulating. Though only of peripheral interest, Marian Hannah Winter's *The Theatre of Marvels* is an interesting analysis of selected types of popular entertainers with a chapter on America between 1790 and 1860.

Of the various one-volume encyclopedic-style reference books, there is room here to single out only three of the most recent: *Performing Arts: A Guide to Practice and Appreciation* (consultant editor, Michael Billington), *The Entertainers,* edited by Clive Unger-Hamilton, and *The Encyclopedia of World Theatre* (general editor, Martin Esslin). Though the first two were originally published in England, their kaleidoscopic panoramas are surprisingly universal, with an unusually large amount of coverage given to American forms and performers. *Performing Arts,* a handsomely designed and illustrated volume, though frequently flawed with inaccuracies or contradictions, can prove helpful if a judicious use is made of the contents; *The Entertainers,* arranged chronologically, includes a large number of American popular performers, though coverage is brief and superficial. *The Encyclopedia of World Theatre,* though uneven in its coverage, does include entries on most popular forms and many performers. *The Oxford Companion to the Theatre,* though not a recent publication, includes overviews of most major forms and a few performers as well (a fourth, expanded edition has been promised for years).

In addition to McNamara's introduction to the special issue of *The Drama Review* mentioned above, a number of other essays postulate ways to approach a study of popular entertainments, including McNamara's "The Scenography of Popular Entertainments," which provides a good framework for studying the architecture and design of popular forms, including circuses and outdoor forms. Heinrich Richard Falk's "Conventions of Popular Entertainment: Framework for a Methodology" and David Mayer's "Towards a Definition of Popular Theatre" provide two additional points of view. Mayer's essay is less a definition than a posing of questions and possibilities but is nonetheless useful and stimulating for further consideration of so large and amorphous a category of forms. Maurice Gorham's *Showmen and Suckers: An Excursion on the Crazy Fringe of the Entertainment World* explores the relationship between the showman and the sucker, a condition that prevails in many of the amusement forms discussed in this guide. Another special nature of the entertainments covered in this guide is their language. Although a number of specific sources are covered elsewhere in relation to specific forms, two basic glossaries cover most of the forms included in this volume: *The Language of Show Biz*, edited by Sherman Sergel, and my *The Language of American Popular Entertainment*. The latter is a more exhaustive collection of argot, slang, and terminology (over 3,000 entries) and includes an introductory essay. The most complete guide to popular entertainment discography is Brian Rust's *The Complete Entertainment Discography From the Mid-1890s to 1942*. A very perceptive and recent study of the music of popular entertainment forms is Charles Hamm's *Yesterdays: Popular Song in America*, which covers minstrelsy, the birth of Tin Pan Alley, vaudeville, and early musical theater; an older source, covering much the same ground, is Sigmund Spaeth's *A History of Popular Music in America*. Other sources on popular music are discussed in chapter 10. Recommended reference sources and surveys of black entertainers are Henry T. Sampson's *Blacks in Blackface* (especially in musical forms) and Langston Hughes and Milton Meltzer's *Black Magic*. Additional sources on black performers can be found in chapters 7, 8, 9, and 10. A reasonably good, though not always accurate, survey of early itinerant performers is Richardson Wright's *Hawkers and Walkers in Early America*.

The many studies of popular culture relevant to those forms covered in this guide are too extensive to cover in depth, but a few are too essential or representative for exclusion. Constance Rourke's *American Humour* and *The Roots of American Culture* are especially important for their analysis of American comic stereotypes in the nineteenth century. Jesse Bier's *The Rise and Fall of American Humor* is less significant but still a good study of nineteenth-century American popular culture, as is Carl Bode's *The Anatomy of American Popular Culture, 1840-1861*, Ezra Bowen's *This Fabulous Century, Prelude, 1870-1900*, Russell Crouse's *It Seems Like Yesterday*, Oliver Jensen's *The Nineties*, Meade Minnigerode's *The Fabulous Forties, 1840-1850, A Presentation of Private Life*, Lloyd Morris's *Postscript to Yesterday*, Bellamy Partridge and Otto Bettmann's *As We Were: Family Life in America, 1850-1900*, Martin W. Sandler's *This Was America* (turn of the century), Arthur W. Schlesinger's *The Rise of the City, 1878-1898*, Bayrd Still's *Mirror for Gotham*, Mark Sullivan's *Our Times, The Turn of the Century,* and *Reflections of a Decade, 1901-1910* (essays from the pages of the *Saturday Evening Post*). Norman Cantor and Michael

Werthman's anthology, *The History of Popular Culture,* includes a useful section of essays entitled "Popular Entertainments and Recreation." Foster Rhea Dulles's *America Learns to Play* remains the best general introduction to early American popular entertainment and includes much more than show business in its coverage of how Americans made use of their leisure time. Russel Nye's *The Unembarrassed Muse* is also an excellent general introduction to the popular arts and includes a good section on popular theater. Of the numerous sources on American culture during the early twentieth century that also include entertainment in the context of the period, the following are representative, useful overviews: Allen Churchill, *Remember When;* Fon W. Boardman, Jr., *The Thirties, America and the Great Depression;* Lewis Atherton, *Mainstreet on the Middle Border;* and Robert Baral, *Turn West on 23rd; A Toast to New York's Old Chelsea* (coverage from the nineteenth century). The eight-volume series *The American Culture,* edited by Neil Harris, provides excellent background for a study of American popular amusements.

American variety entertainment, theater and to a lesser extent outdoor amusements depend a great deal on general histories for investigation. It is necessary to exclude most of these here; a list of bibliographies on popular theater can be found in chapter 12 and should lead the user of this guide to most general and many specific sources. Two major histories, however, are essential for the student of American popular entertainment: G.C.D. Odell's fifteen-volume *Annals of the New York Stage* and T. Allston Brown's three-volume *History of the New York Stage.* Odell's remains the standard history through the 1893-1894 season and is written with charm, accuracy, and impressive scholarship; Brown, a theatrical agent and historian, was a devotee of popular entertainment, and his work contains histories of over four hundred New York theaters, opera houses, music halls, circuses, and other places of entertainment. Brooks Atkinson's *Broadway,* though less detailed, is a more up-to-date overview of New York entertainment from 1900 to 1974. Edward Marks's *They All Had Glamour,* although not limited to popular entertainment, is an amusing source for lesser known theater and musical artists, as is his companion volume, *They All Sang.* Allen Churchill, the author of numerous theater studies, offers a survey of Broadway from 1900 to 1919 in *The Great White Way* and during the revue era and the birth of the modern American musical in *The Theatrical Twenties. A Book About the Theatre* gives an interesting perspective on popular entertainments by an important early American theater historian, Brander Matthews, as do George Jean Nathan's *Encyclopaedia of the Theatre* and Laurence Hutton's *Curiositites of the American Stage.* In *America Takes the Stage,* Richard Moody traces the development of romanticism in American drama and theater from 1750 to 1900 and deals prominently with the stage Yankee and blackface minstrelsy. Garff B. Wilson includes adequate but superficial coverage of popular forms in his survey history of the American stage, *Three Hundred Years of American Drama and Theatre.* Mary C. Henderson in *The City and the Theatre* provides background on New York and its places of entertainment from 1700.

Of the many other sources on popular theater or popular culture that include useful information on variety entertainment or outdoor amusement, including the circus, the following should be mentioned: Ann Banks, *First-Person America* (interviews with showmen); Daniel J. Brown, "Footlight Favorites Forty Years Ago: A Stroll Up Old Broadway"; Henry Collins Brown, ed., *Valentine's Manual, 1927: New York in the Elegant Eighties* and *In the Golden Nineties;* Jack Burton, *In Memorium—Oldtime Show Biz;* William Cahn, *The Laugh Makers* (minstrelsy, circus, vaudeville, and revues); Samuel B. Charters and Leonard Kunstadt, *Jazz: A History of the New York Scene* (variety, seaside resorts, the black entertainer); A. W. Davis, "Past Days of Minstrelsy, Variety, Circus and Side Shows"; Michael Marks Davis, Jr., *The Exploitation of Pleasure* (survey of early twentieth-century entertainment in New York, including penny arcades, burlesque, vaudeville, and so forth); Agnes DeMille, *America Dances* (useful survey chapters on various periods); Ruth Crosby Dimmick, *Our Theatres To-Day and Yesterday* (amusement industry in New York, 1731-1913); Richard Henry Edwards, *Popular Amusements* and *Christianity and Amusements* (social and moralistic investigation of most popular forms); Robert Grau, *The Stage in the Twentieth Century;* Abel Green and Joe Laurie, Jr., *Show Biz from Vaude to Video;* Marsden Hartley, *Adventures in the Arts* (bemoans the passing of popular traditions as of 1921); Rollin Lynde Hartt, *The People at Play* (burlesque, amusement park, dime museum, biograph show, and minor forms); Judge William E. Horton, *About Stage Folks* and *Driftwood of the Stage* (essays on all aspects of nineteenth-century American entertainment); Reese D. James, *Cradle of Culture, 1800-1810: The Philadelphia Stage* (excellent list of popular attractions); Stephen Jenkins, *The Greatest Street in the World—Broadway;* John J. Jennings, *Theatrical and Circus Life* (useful older source); Donald C. King, "A Historical Survey of the Theatres of Boston" (vaudeville, burlesque, and dime museums); John Lahr, *Notes on a Cowardly Lion* (more than a biography of Bert Lahr; insights into burlesque, vaudeville, revues, and other areas); James D. McCabe, Jr., *Lights and Shadows of New York Life* and *The Secrets of a Great City* (both revealing nineteenth-century sources on all entertainment forms in New York); Richard Maney, *Fanfare* (thirty-three-year career of a press agent); Ward Morehouse, *Matinee Tomorrow* (popular entertainments and New York theater from 1900): George Jean Nathan, *The Popular Theatre* (revue, vaudeville, and musical theater) and *The World of George Jean Nathan,* edited by Charles Angoff; C. L. Pancoast, *Trail Blazers of Advertising* (techniques used in show business); Louis Sobol, *The Longest Street* (last days of vaudeville and burlesque); Bernard Sobel, *Broadway Heartbeat* (revue, vaudeville, and burlesque, plus chapters on Florenz Ziegfeld and Earl Carroll); Marshall and Jean Stearns, *Jazz Dance* (all major forms and general history of blacks in show business); Jesse Frederick Steiner, *Americans at Play;* Robert Lewis Taylor, *The Running Pianist* and *Niagara* (the former is a collection of essays on various topics dealing with vaudeville, the circus, and medicine shows; the latter is a novel set in the Niagara Falls region with frequent atmospheric use of showmen's exploits); Miriam Young, *Mother Wore Tights* (life of Myrtle McKinley, a "Floradora" girl, but useful for entertainment at the turn of the century, dime museums to revues); and William C. Young, *Famous Actors and Actresses on the American Stage* (225 performers, including many known primarily for their work in popular forms). The preceding listing is not meant to be exhaustive, but simply suggests the enormous number of sources available in the general areas of this guide. It must be underscored that frequently sources cited in other chapters also deal with more than one form or tradition but have been placed where, in the estimation of the compiler, they are most relevant and useful.

BIBLIOGRAPHY

BOOKS AND ARTICLES

Atherton, Lewis. *Mainstreet on the Middle Border.* Bloomington: Indiana University Press, 1954.
Atkinson, Brooks. *Broadway.* Rev. ed. New York: Macmillan Co., 1974.
Banks, Ann, ed. *First-Person America.* New York: Alfred A. Knopf, 1980.
Baral, Robert. *Turn West on 23rd; A Toast to New York's Old Chelsea.* New York: Fleet Publishing Co., 1965.
Bier, Jesse. *The Rise and Fall of American Humor.* New York: Holt, Rinehart, and Winston, 1968.
Billington, Michael, consultant ed. *Performing Arts: A Guide to Practice and Appreciation.* New York: Facts on File, 1980.
Boardman, Fon W., Jr. *The Thirties. America and the Great Depression.* New York: Harry Z. Walck, 1967.
Bode, Carl. *The Anatomy of American Popular Culture, 1840-1861.* Berkeley and Los Angeles: University of California Press, 1959.
Bowen, Ezra, ed. *The Fabulous Century. Prelude, 1870-1900.* New York: Time-Life Books, 1970.
Bradby, David; James, Louis; and Sharratt, Bernard; eds. *Performance and Politics in Popular Drama.* Cambridge and New York: Cambridge University Press, 1980.

Brown, Daniel J. "Footlight Favorites Forty Years Ago: A Stroll Up Old Broadway." In *Valentine's Manual of Old New York,* edited by Henry Collins Brown. New York: Valentine's Manual, 1922.

Brown, Henry Collins, ed. *Valentine's Manual, 1927: New York in the Elegant Eighties.* Hastings-on-Hudson, N.Y.: Valentine's Manual, [1927].

_____. *In the Golden Nineties.* Hastings-on-Hudson, N.Y.: Valentine's Manual, 1928.

Brown, T. Allston. *History of the New York Stage, From the First Performance in 1732 to 1901 in Encyclopedic Form.* 2 vols. 1903. Reprint. New York: Benjamin Blom, 1963.

Burton, Jack. *In Memorium—Oldtime Show Biz.* New York: Vantage Press, 1965.

Cahn, William. *The Laugh Makers: A Pictorial History of American Comedians.* New York: Bramhall House, 1957.

Cantor, Norman I., and Werthman, Michael S., eds. *The History of Popular Culture.* New York: Macmillan Co., 1968.

Charters, Samuel B., and Kunstadt, Leonard. *Jazz: A History of the New York Scene.* Garden City, N.Y.: Doubleday and Co., 1962.

Churchill, Allen. *The Great White Way.* New York: E. P. Dutton, 1962.

_____. *Remember When.* New York: Golden Press, 1967.

_____. *The Theatrical Twenties.* New York: McGraw-Hill, 1975.

Crouse, Russell. *It Seems Like Yesterday; With Numerous Illustrations from Contemporary Sources.* Garden City, N.Y.: Doubleday and Co., 1931.

Csida, Joseph, and Csida, June Bundy. *American Entertainment: A Unique History of Popular Show Business.* New York: Billboard/Watson Guptill, 1978.

Davis, A. W. "Past Days of Minstrelsy, Variety, Circus and Side Shows." *Americana* 8 (June 1912):529-47.

Davis, Michael Marks, Jr. *The Exploitation of Pleasure. A Study of Commercial Recreations in New York City.* New York: Department of Child Hygiene of the Russell Sage Foundation, 1911.

DeMille, Agnes. *America Dances: A Personal Chronicle in Words and Pictures.* New York: Macmillan Co., 1980.

Dimmick, Ruth Crosby. *Our Theatres To-Day and Yesterday.* New York: H. K. Fly Co., 1913.

Dulles, Foster Rhea. *America Learns to Play. A History of Popular Recreation 1607-1940.* New York: Appleton-Century, 1940.

Edwards, Richard Henry. *Popular Amusements.* New York and London: Association Press, 1915.

_____. *Christianity and Amusements.* New York: Association Press, 1915.

Esslin, Martin, ed. *The Encyclopedia of World Theatre.* New York: Charles Scribner's Sons, 1977.

Falk, Heinrich Richard. "Conventions of Popular Entertainment: Framework for a Methodology." *Journal of Popular Culture* 9 (Fall 1975):480/128-481/129.

Gorham, Maurice. *Showmen and Suckers: An Excursion on the Crazy Fringe of the Entertainment World.* London: Percival Marshall, 1951.

Grau, Robert. *The Stage in the Twentieth Century.* New York: Broadway Publishing Co., 1912.

Green, Abel, and Laurie, Joe, Jr. *Show Biz From Vaude to Video.* Garden City, N.Y.: Permabooks, 1953.

Hamm, Charles. *Yesterdays: Popular Song in America.* New York and London: W. W. Norton and Co., 1979.

Harris, Neil, ed. *The American Culture.* 8 vols. New York: George Braziller, 1970-1973.

Hartley, Marsden. *Adventures in the Arts.* Introduction by Waldo Frank. New York: Boni and Liveright Publishers, 1921.

Hartnoll, Phyllis, ed. *The Oxford Companion to the Theatre.* 3d ed. London, New York, and Toronto: Oxford University Press, 1967.

Hartt, Rollin Lynde. *The People at Play: Excursions in the Humor and Philosophy of Popular Amusements.* Boston and New York: Houghton Mifflin Co., 1909.

Henderson, Mary C. *The City and the Theatre.* Clifton, N.J.: James T. White, 1973.

Horton, Judge [William E.]. *About Stage Folks.* Detroit: Free Press Printing Co., 1902.

_____. *Driftwood of the Stage.* Detroit: Press of Winn and Hammond, 1904.

Hughes, Langston, and Meltzer, Milton. *Black Magic, A Pictorial History of the Negro in American Entertainment.* Englewood Cliffs, N.J.: Prentice-Hall, 1967.

Hutton, Laurence. *Curiosities of the American Stage.* New York: Harper and Bros., 1891.

James, Reese D. *Cradle of Culture, 1800-1810: The Philadelphia Stage.* Philadelphia: University of Pennsylvania Press, 1957.

Jenkins, Stephen. *The Greatest Street in the World—Broadway.* New York: G. P. Putnam's Sons, 1911.

Jensen, Oliver, ed. *The Nineties.* New York: American Heritage Publishing Co., 1967.

Jennings, John J. *Theatrical and Circus Life; or, Secrets of the Stage, Greenroom and Sawdust Arena.* St. Louis: Herbert and Cole, 1882.

Kachur, Barbara A., ed. "The Popular North America Theatre." *Theatre Studies* No. 24/25 (1977/78-1978/79):1-169.

King, Donald C. "A Historical Survey of the Theatres of Boston." *Marquee* 6 (3d quarter 1974):5-22.

Lahr, John. *Notes on a Cowardly Lion.* New York: Alfred A. Knopf, 1969.

McCabe, James D., Jr. *The Secrets of a Great City: A Work Descriptive of the Virtues and Vices, The Mysteries, Miseries and Crimes of New York City.* Philadelphia: Jones, Brothers, and Co., 1868.

_____. *Lights and Shadows of New York Life; Sights and Sensations of the Great City.* Philadelphia, Cincinnati, Chicago, and St. Louis: National Publishing Co., 1872.

McKechnie, Samuel. *Popular Entertainments Through the Ages.* 1931. Reprint. New York: Benjamin Blom, 1969.

McNamara, Brooks. "The Scenography of Popular Entertainments." *The Drama Review* 18 (March 1974):16-25.

Maney, Richard. *Fanfare: The Confessions of a Press Agent.* New York: Harper and Brothers, 1957.

Marks, Edward Bennett, as told to Abbott J. Liebling. *They All Sang: From Tony Pastor to Rudy Vallee.* New York: Viking Press, 1934.

_____. *They All Had Glamour: From the Swedish Nightingale to the Naked Lady.* New York: J. Messner, 1944.

Matlaw, Myron, ed. *American Popular Entertainment.* Westport, Conn. and London: Greenwood Press, 1979.

Matthews, Brander. *A Book About the Theatre.* New York: Charles Scribner's Sons, 1916.

Mayer, David. "Towards a Definition of Popular Theatre." In *Western Popular Theatre,* edited by David Mayer and Kenneth Richards. London: Methuen and Co., 1977.

Mayer, David, and Richards, Kenneth, eds. *Western Popular Theatre.* London: Methuen and Co., 1977.

Miller, George B., Jr. et al. *Puppetry Library.* Westport, Conn. and London: Greenwood Press, 1981.

Minnigerode, Meade. *The Fabulous Forties, 1840-1859, A Presentation of Private Life.* New York: G. P. Putnam's Sons, 1924.

Moody, Richard. *America Takes the Stage.* Bloomington: Indiana University Press, 1955.

Morehouse, Ward. *Matinee Tomorrow.* New York: Whittlesey House (McGraw-Hill), 1949.

Morris, Lloyd. *Postscript to Yesterday. America: The Last Fifty Years.* New York: Random House, 1947.

_____. *Incredible New York.* New York: Random House, 1957.

Nathan, George Jean. *The Popular Theatre.* 2d ed. 1923. Reprint. Rutherford, N.J.: Fairleigh Dickinson University Press, 1971.

_____. *Encyclopaedia of the Theatre.* New York: Alfred A. Knopf, 1940.

_____. *The World of George Jean Nathan.* Edited by Charles Angoff. New York: Alfred A. Knopf, 1952.

Nye, Russel B. *The Unembarrassed Muse: The Popular Arts in America.* New York: Dial Press, 1970.

Odell, George C.D. *Annals of the New York Stage.* 15 vols. New York: Columbia University Press, 1927-1949.

Pancoast, C. L. *Trail Blazers of Advertising.* 1926. Reprint. New York: Arno Press, 1976.

Partridge, Bellamy, and Bettmann, Otto. *As We Were: Family Life in America, 1850-1900.* New York and London: Whittlesey House, 1946.

"People's Theatre." *Theatre Quarterly* 1 (October-December 1971), Entire issue.

"Popular Entertainments." *The Drama Review* 18 (March 1974), Entire issue.

"Popular Theatre." *Educational Theatre Journal* 27 (October 1975), Entire issue.

Reflections of a Decade, 1901-1910. Indianapolis: Curtis Publishing Co., 1980.

Rourke, Constance. *American Humour: A Study of the National Character.* New York: Harcourt, Brace and Co., 1931.

_____. *The Roots of American Culture.* Edited by Van Wyck Brooks. New York: Harcourt, Brace and Co., 1942.

Rust, Brian, with Debus, Allen G. *The Complete Entertainment Discography from the Mid-1890s to 1942.* New Rochelle, N.Y.: Arlington House, 1973.

Sampson, Henry T. *Blacks in Blackface: A Source Book on Early Black Musical Shows.* Metuchen, N.J. and London: The Scarecrow Press, 1980.

Sandler, Martin W. *This Was America.* Boston and Toronto: Little, Brown and Co., 1980.

Schlesinger, Arthur M. *The Rise of the City, 1878-1898.* New York: Macmillan Co., 1933.

Seldes, Gilbert. *The 7 Lively Arts.* Rev. ed. New York: Sagamore Press, 1957.

Sergel, Sherman Louis, ed. *The Language of Show Biz.* Chicago: Dramatic Publishing Co., 1973.

Sobel, Bernard. *Broadway Heartbeat: Memoirs of a Press Agent.* New York: Hermitage House, 1953.

Sobol, Louis. *The Longest Street.* Foreword by Jim Bishop. New York: Crown Publishers, 1968.

Spaeth, Sigmund. *A History of Popular Music in America.* New York: Random House, 1948.

Stearns, Marshall, and Stearns, Jean. *Jazz Dance.* New York: Macmillan Co., 1968.

Steiner, Jesse Frederick. *Americans at Play.* New York and London: McGraw-Hill, 1933.

Still, Bayrd. *Mirror for Gotham.* New York: New York University Press, 1956.

Sullivan, Mark. *Our Times, The Turn of the Century.* New York and London: Charles Scribner's Sons, 1926.

Taylor, Robert Lewis. *The Running Pianist.* Garden City, N.Y.: Doubleday and Co., 1950.

_____. *Niagara.* New York: G. P. Putnam's Sons, 1980.

Toll, Robert C. *On with the Show: The First Century of Show Business in America.* New York: Oxford University Press, 1976.

Toole-Stott, Raymond. *Circus and Allied Arts, A World Bibliography.* 4 vols. Derby, England: Harpur, 1958-1971.

Towsen, John H. "Sources in Popular Entertainment." *The Drama Review* 18 (March 1974):118-22.

Unger-Hamilton, Clive, ed. *The Entertainers.* New York: St. Martin's Press, 1980.

Wilmeth, Don B. "American Popular Entertainment: A Historical Perspective." *Choice* 14 (October 1977):987-1 004. Reprint. In *American Popular Entertainment,* edited by Myron Matlaw. Westport, Conn. and London: Greenwood Press, 1979.

_____, ed. *American and English Popular Entertainment: A Guide to Information Sources.* Detroit: Gale Research Co., 1980.

_____. *The Language of American Popular Entertainment: A Glossary of Argot, Slang, and Terminology.* Westport, Conn. and London: Greenwood Press, 1981.

Wilson, Garff B. *Three Hundred Years of American Drama and Theatre.* 2d ed. Englewood Cliffs, N.J.: Prentice-Hall, 1982.

Winter, Marian Hannah. *The Theatre of Marvels.* Preface by Marcel Marceau. Translated by Charles Meldon. New York: Benjamin Blom, 1964.

Wright, Richardson. *Hawkers and Walkers in Early America.* 1927. Reprint. New York: Frederick Ungar Publishing Co., 1965.

Young, Miriam. *Mother Wore Tights.* New York: Whittlesey House, 1944.

Young, William C. *Famous Actors and Actresses on the American Stage.* 2 vols. New York and London: Bowker, 1975.

SELECT PERIODICALS AND SERIALS

Amusement Business. Nashville, 1961- .
Billboard. Los Angeles, 1894- .
The Drama Review. New York, 1955- .
Educational Theatre Journal (The Theatre Journal). Washington, D.C., 1949- .
Journal of Popular Culture. Bowling Green, Ohio, 1967- .
New York Clipper. New York, 1900-1918.
New York Mirror. New York, 1879-1922.
Nineteenth-Century Theatre Research. Tucson, Ariz., 1973- .
Spirit of the Times. New York, 1856-1902.
Theatre History Studies. Grand Forks, North Dakota, 1981- .
Theatre Quarterly. London, England, 1971- .
Variety. New York, 1905- .

CHAPTER 2

Outdoor Amusements

FAIRS AND CARNIVALS

As might be expected, the first fairs in America were market fairs in the European tradition. The Dutch government decreed only a few years after its settlement on Manhattan Island in 1625 that two fairs be held annually: a fair for the sale of cattle on October 15 and one for the sale of hogs on November 1. The first known cattle fair was held in 1641 in the territory which is now the Manhasset-Port Washington area of Long Island. By the 1650s the Dutch in New Amsterdam were holding kermis fairs, common in the Low Countries of Europe. These early examples of fairs in North America emphasized trading but also included pure entertainment—puppet shows, tightrope dancing, clowning, strolling fiddlers, and other amusement provided by itinerant performers. In addition, participants created their own fun with various contests (like catching the greased pig), races, cudgeling bouts, whistling and grinning, and competitions.

During the seventeenth century, the fair tradition spread throughout the colonies: Southern fairs were frequently major social events; early New England fairs were more decorous than those of the South or the Middle Atlantic region due to the prevalent Puritan influence. New England's first cattle fair, held in New Haven in 1644, was strictly for business. New Englanders, in fact, eschewed fairs, weekly markets in the towns, and the traveling Yankee peddler. But unlike the legitimate theater, which was condemned on moral grounds, these traditions were not outlawed because of the overriding needs of the numerous small, isolated farming communities. In time, however, these early fairs died out with colonial America.

With the Revolution over and an independent nation established, the need for improved agriculture became all too obvious and was made even more evident by scientific advancements. To foster potential advances, agricultural societies were formed as early as 1785 in Philadelphia and 1791 in New York. Rural festivals were held called "sheepshearings" and these, combined with the early activities of the agricultural societies, established the basis for the modern American fair.

By 1809 the exhibitions on farming by these various groups were combined with market fairs in a few states. The major thrust, however, came when Elkanah Watson of Pittsfield, Massachusetts, decided to show Americans advanced farming methods and exhibited in 1807 a pair of Merino sheep imported from Spain. His efforts were met with an enthusiastic reception and on October 1, 1810, he organized a more ambitious exhibition, featuring a music band and a procession displaying stock, plows, and the like. This was the first of the Berkshire County Fairs; it was followed in 1811 by the formation of the Berkshire Agricultural Society, the first of the so-called "practical societies." Slowly the number and amount of prizes increased, and attendance grew. Women were encouraged to attend the fair, compete, and win prizes along with the men. The American county fair had been born and soon rural America was rife with fairs of the "practical societies."

From the entertainment standpoint, Watson's pioneer effort made a great impact in New England. The fair was beneficial to the farmer, even if it did provide a once a year social and entertainment event as well. The evolution of the American fair from Watson's early efforts to the present has been steady. After a brief lull in the spread of fairs in the 1820s and 1830s, with the invention of new farm implements, most notably Cyrus McCormick's reaper, demonstrated in 1831, and John Deere's steel plow, developed in 1837, the local fair experienced another growth spurt. As international trade grew, new technology increased productivity, prices sky-rocketed, and farmers experienced a golden age in American agriculture. As state governments began to prosper, interest in agriculture on a statewide basis became prevalent, and with this surge came the state fair. The first state fair took place in September 1841 in Syracuse, New York. New Jersey soon followed with its first state fair at New Brunswick. Between 1849 and 1854, state fairs were established in Michigan, Pennsylvania, Ohio, Wisconsin, Indiana, Illinois, and Iowa. By 1868 there were 1,367 state, county, and district fairs held every year.

Today, state fairs are held in virtually every state, along with several regional fairs in which several states consolidate efforts. The total number of fairs of all sizes and varieties today is in excess of 3,200, from small county fairs to the giant State Fair of Texas in Dallas. The value of these fairs in terms of the development of scientific farming is unassailable; it is still an important place for trade and healthy competition. For years the local fair was the only break in the monotony of the lonely and isolated life of the farmer. And, for the professional showman, it provided a fertile opportunity for selling his wares and exploiting a captive audience.

It is virtually impossible to separate the traveling carnival from the fair tradition. A fair today without a carnival midway is hardly a fair at all. Although lively fair entertainment dates very clearly from the medieval market fairs with their tumblers, fire-eaters, rope dancers, conjurors, and makeshift theater performances, the American practice of traveling carnivals is of more recent vintage. Traveling circuses were well established by the middle of the nineteenth century, but the circus tradition and that of the carnival are quite different (see chapter 3). The stimulus for the traveling carnival dates, as does the amusement park, from the Chicago World's Columbian Exposition in 1893. The decision to move the attractions to other localities led to the creation of the street fair or modern carnival. The traveling carnival was, in fact, realized the same year as the Chicago World's Fair when Frank C. Bostock presented a collection of attractions at Coney Island, the location later of the great amusement park. Bostock's entertainment has been called the first modern carnival in that his efforts mark the first attempt to make portable a group of attractions.

American fairs have largely depended on these traveling carnivals to provide midway attractions for the patrons. Initially, fairs attempted to provide their own forms of entertainment, in particular, horse races. As expenses became too great, smaller fairs began to rent concessions and midway space to individual traveling showmen. To many, the presence of these showmen cheapened the rural fair. Many county fairs, and certainly most state fairs, have since either created partially permanent midways or have leased ground to large commercial concerns. Certainly the fair midway has come along way since P. T. Barnum, America's greatest showman and president of his local Fairfield County Agricultural Society in Connecticut, loaned a tent to a group of Connecticut farmers and manufacturers in 1869 for the neighboring fair in Danbury. The carnivals that played virtually every fair began moving their attractions by horse-drawn wagon, but by 1914 the "Smith Greater Shows," a traveling midway formed by Chris "Pop" Smith, was moved by truck. The adaptation of the traveling carnival to the agricultural fair was a natural wedding of traditions.

By the 1920s the American economy was booming, and jazz-age Americans began to demand more exciting and spectacular entertainment at state and county fairs. The carnival business became a large industry, no doubt made possible by the large number of fairs in need of midway entertainment. Today, only the smaller traveling carnivals continue to set up their attractions in town streets and vacant lots without an affiliation with a fair or civic exhibition of some sort. Most of the larger carnivals travel throughout the United States and Canada each year from early summer until late fall playing fair dates. One of the largest of the traveling carnivals, the "Royal American Shows," has traveled on as many as 80 double-length railroad cars loaded with 145 massive pieces of equipment. Their midway features more than fifty rides and attractions and seven under-canvas shows, illustrating vividly the three distinctive features of the carnival—riding devices, shows or exhibits, and concessions. Like the "Royal American Shows," the James E. Strates show travels in railway cars and boasts of a "mile-long midway." Today it is estimated that as many as 580 carnivals are still on the road, most of them shabby suggestions of what they once were. The large carnivals, such as Amusements of America or Gooding's Million Dollar Midway, are clearly the exceptional operations in today's outdoor amusement industry.

The sideshow, an auxiliary or under-canvas show attached to a midway (or at a circus), was once a staple of the carnival, and a popular attraction at the fair. The most common sideshow exhibited freaks or human oddities, although the term also encompasses girlie shows, revues, or any other type of exhibition or entertainment. The first sideshow dates from circa 1904. By the 1930s and 1940s there were several hundred of the freak-show type of sideshow, considered by some as distasteful at best. Today, because of the difficulty involved in populating them, there are fewer than a dozen freak-shows traveling with carvivals or circuses. Other types of auxiliary entertainment, however, especially the girlie show, are still commonplace on most fair midways.

Concessions, selling trinkets and generally worthless goods, continue to be part of the midway, as do games of chance and skill. For years the presence of dishonest or rigged "joints" on a carnival midway was the norm. Such establishments are now under tight legal control in most areas, and thus a major offender of the carnival is less prevalent. Unscrupulous carnival owners and irresponsible fair operators are no longer able to fleece the marks or rubes as they once could do so easily. As carnivals struggle to survive, they simply cannot afford to have engagements cancelled because of unsavory practices. In some respects, the elimination of dishonest games and somewhat seedy sideshows has eliminated some of the old-time carnival's "charm." As P. T. Barnum observed many years ago, people love to be fooled or humbugged; it is questionable today, however, whether the kind of sucker born every minute in Barnum's day still exists.

Since the 1930s the future of the fair and the carnival have been questioned by doomsters. For decades the fair, with its carnival midway, provided the only chance of escape for many Americans; the fair truly provided "something for everyone." The modern fair perpetuates this basic credo but must be open to change if it is to survive in today's age of electronic marvels, home video centers, video discs, and large, home television screens. As will soon be seen with the evolution of the amusement park, the death of participatory, environmental entertainment is not likely to occur soon. Film and television can only offer us passive, spectator experiences. Outdoor amusement forms continue to provide unique, direct experience in a lively, often garish environment that for masses of the American populace is still irresistable. And, as Lila Perl illustrates, in *America Goes to the Fair,* the American fair remains one of the more enjoyable reflections "of the occupations and interests, achievements and aspirations of mankind." Americans appear to be returning to rural areas in large numbers. Perhaps Helen Augur was correct when she wrote over fifty years ago that if all the large county fairs vanished, "little neighborhood festivals would still spring out of the ground like trees sown by Johnny Appleseed."

EXPOSITIONS

The exposition is a truly international phenomenon, although the United States has also had its share of prominent examples of what might be considered an environmental entertainment form. From 1851 to the present there have been countless international expositions of varying sizes under various names: Expo, World's Fair, Exposition Universelle, Weltausstellung, Exposición Internacional, and International Exhibition. As John Allwood has indicated, in *The Great Exhibitions,* all exhibitions since the first International Exhibition held in London in 1851 at Joseph Paxton's famous "Crystal Palace" have had the same basic aims: "the exhibition of manufactured goods from various countries, in one place and in sorted categories, so that easy comparisons could be made." Allwood goes on to say that after the initial thrust of making each subsequent exhibition bigger and better than its immediate predecessor, a shift occurred from bolstering trade through the exposition to the use of the event as a means of fostering international public relations and the rivalry of whole life-styles.

The international exposition has been able, far more effectively than the ancient local village marketplace, the medieval fair, or even the modern-day county and state fair, to establish international status for the host country. And, it would certainly be a mistake, despite all the legitimate explanations for the survival of the international exhibition, to deny these occasions are opportunities for pure amusement. In time, as shall be seen, special areas designed to entertain were even added to the more purely exhibition sections. The Paris Exposition Universelle in 1867 took the first step toward altering the pattern of the first six international expositions by adding a theme to unify the exhibits and thus bring greater interest and stimulation to the whole. The 1867 exhibition was likewise the first to have individual buildings, paid for by participating countries, to house exhibits in national surroundings.

The first American attempt at an international exposition was the "World's Fair of the Works of Industry of all Nations" in New York in

1853-1854. Housed primarily in a version of London's Crystal Palace, the project failed financially from the very beginning; even P. T. Barnum, America's most successful impresario, failed to save the venture. When the exhibition closed on November 1, 1854, its debt totalled more than $300,000 and its attendance had been only 1.2 million.

The second international exposition in this country was the Philadelphia "Centennial Exposition" in 1876 and, although its financial loss was considerable, the ultimate success of the exposition overshadowed the fiscal loss. Indeed, this was the first truly international exposition built on a 236-acre plot in Fairmount Park; 5 main structures were augmented by 250 smaller pavilions and buildings. By the close of the exposition, almost 10 million patrons had attended.

Two additional international expositions preceded the next major landmark in the history of the American exposition, neither of which were of much note. The modest "American Exhibition of Products, Arts and Manufactures of Foreign Nations" in Boston during 1883 was followed by the more successful "World's Industrial and Cotton Centennial Exhibition" in New Orleans during 1884-1885.

In 1893 a number of traditions came together to create the prototype of all subsequent expositions and to establish an amusement area as an integral part of the exhibition grounds. Taking its place alongside pavilions and exhibition buildings was the midway. Although the first midway at an American exposition was at the Chicago World's Columbian Exposition, its beginnings can be traced to various European traditions—the medieval fair and carnival and the seventeenth-century pleasure garden of England and France. Indeed, although there is not room for further exploration here, it is possible to trace elements of the midway, and consequently the fair, carnival, and amusement park traditions, back to antiquity. Before the American Revolution, pleasure gardens, modeled on London's most famous gardens, Vauxhall and Ranelagh, appeared in major cities on the East Coast. Like Vauxhall, which was the first internationally famous pleasure garden when it opened in 1661, the American version offered visitors food, drink, music, and free variety acts. Jones's Wood, for example, a grove of some 150 acres along the East River, offered New Yorkers in the early nineteenth century a large variety of amusements. As in England and France, the simple pleasure of strolling, eating, and drinking at pleasure gardens became tiresome, as did the limited array of amusements at most international expositions. It was quite natural, then, that amusements of a more thrilling and exciting nature would be sought.

In addition to the Chicago World's Fair, to which we shall return, the end of the nineteenth century witnessed a new amusement phenomenon made possible as a result of improved transportation and technology. With the invention of the trolley came the institution of so-called trolley parks. Dozens of such parks were established by street railways at the end of the line all over the country as an economical method of encouraging weekend riders to use the cars. Initially, however, these parks offered little that had not been found at the earlier pleasure gardens. During the nineteenth century, however, and largely because of the impetus of the 1893 World's Fair, amusements offered at the gardens, at rural picnic groves, and at shore resorts began to increase in number and in sophistication. Also, by the 1880s, thanks to new technology, mechanical pleasure rides such as the carousel and a device called "the Ferris wheel" developed.

The most obvious stimulus for the growth spurt of the outdoor amusement industry, which was first adopted in Chicago, began when the Vienna World's Fair was held at "The Prater" in Vienna in 1873. A new concept of outdoor entertainment was presented with its large array of amusement machines or rides, fun houses, games of chance, and other activities, which created a new and exciting kind of park. It was this new phenomenon that led to the emergence of the American carnival and the exploitation of amusement rides and concessions. And, although the more traditional state fairs had been invaded by the amusement business as early as 1883, the presence of an area outside the exposition grounds proper, called the "Midway Plaisance" in Chicago in 1893, established the copestone of all subsequent midways, traveling carnivals, and amusement parks.

Many historians still consider the Columbian Exposition the greatest of all international expositions. Fifteenth in the line of international exhibits, the Chicago fair was established to celebrate the 400th anniversary of the discovery of America by Christopher Columbus; Chicago was selected because it was a centrally located railroad city. The scope of the fair was greater than any of its predecessors. Chicago took Philadelphia's gridlike layout of buildings and complex landscaping much further. A veritable new city, dubbed "The White City," was planned and executed to become, as David Burg explains in *Chicago's White City of 1893,* "a celebration of America's coming of age." Gross outlays for the exposition totalled over 28 million; over three years were needed to complete the buildings and grounds.

In order to enhance the international flavor of the exposition, the "Midway Plaisance" was constructed outside the grounds proper. It was a six-hundred-feet-wide and mile-long avenue connecting Jackson and Washington Parks. Its features were privately sponsored, although they did constitute a sanctioned part of the exposition. The midway offered the patrons a potpourri of international attractions: Persian, Japanese, and Indian bazaars; a Moorish palace; Chinese, Algerian, and Tunisian villages; a concert hall for musical, juggling, and dancing performances, and much more. Especially popular was "Cairo Street" and demonstrations by belly-dancers of the new Hoochy-cootch, although, despite popular tradition, "Little Egypt" most likely did not perform at the Chicago World's Fair. In all, seventy-two foreign nations exhibited at the fair, and many were represented on the "Midway Plaisance." One hundred native Africans demonstrated their domestic, religious, and marital customs in the Cohamony village; American Indian dances were displayed at Sitting Bull's Cabin, with its enticing sign, "War Dance Given Daily."

Although the international clientele represented on the midway could be considered to have had some instructional value, it was the pure entertainment that made the 1893 fair a true landmark in the history of outdoor amusements. A wide variety of entertainment was proffered the patrons, ranging from Carl Hagenbeck's Animal Show to demonstrations by the strongman Eugene Sandow (managed by the youthful Florenz Ziegfeld, Jr.) to an act from New York billed as the Houdini Brothers, Harry and Dash. And, near by, although not officially associated with the fair, William "Buffalo Bill" Cody presented his Wild West exhibition. Without doubt, the added attractions of the midway helped to attract many of the 27 million patrons who entered the Columbian Exposition under its motto of "Make Culture Hum!"

Behind all the so-called cultural attractions of the midway stood the professional showmen; the ultimate goal of these participants was to get all the money they could. An observer of the fair, Ben Truman, unequivocably stated:

> They have not come thousands of miles merely to add a picturesque feature to this wonderful exhibit. Almost all of them are professional travelling showmen, who pitch their tents in whatever portion of the globe offers the greatest inducements in hard cash. All the profuse explanations that they are here by the special permission of Sultan this and Emperor that is bosh. As a consequence, they do not propose to let any opportunity slip by which they may pocket a coin, be it small or large.

Of great importance, and to many the dominant attraction of the "Midway Plaisance," was not a live performance or exhibition but the Ferris wheel, envisioned several years before by George Washington Gale Ferris but never before demonstrated (similar devices had been built earlier at Atlantic City by Isaac Newton Forrester in 1872 and by William Somers in 1892). Modelled after the structural principles of the bicycle wheel and driven by two 1,000 horsepower reversible engines, Ferris's famous wheel was almost 300 feet tall and 30 feet wide. The wheel carried 36 pendulum cars, each able to hold 40 passengers with a total capacity of 1,400 people. Ferris's own puffery, quoted by David F. Burg, stated that "The Ferris Wheel stands alone, it is without precedent, and while it is doubtful if ever a greater wheel will be constructed, in such an event, Mr. Ferris's name will always be coupled with it." The continuing popularity of the Ferris wheel certainly attests to the truth of this statement.

The Chicago World's Columbian Exposition officially closed at sunset on October 30, 1893; it had shown a profit of $807,000, making it the first

United States international exposition to end with a profit. From the stand-point of the amusement industry, the success of the fair far exceeded its monetary profit. Although the attraction of the "Midway Plaisance" began slowly, its ultimate hyping by the professional showmen and the critical decision that the assembled attractions should be moved to various cities assured the success of the midway at this and all subsequent world expo-sitions. As Edo McCullough in *World's Fair Midway* has concluded: "Out of the American idea that there should be more to an exposition than beautiful gardens, imposing buildings, scientific displays, and exhibits meant to advertise everything from a state's industry to mother's pies came the Midway." No longer were amusement people relegated to the fringes of world fairs; indeed, as an integral part of the whole, they added a very important spontaneous form of amusement, providing a much needed escape from the harsh realities of daily life and, perhaps, providing the patron relief from the idealism of progress, science, and advanced technology so evident everywhere else on the exhibition grounds. And, as will soon be evident, enterprising showmen soon saw the profitable possibilities of exploiting outdoor amusements as an autonomous and unencumbered industry.

Since the Chicago's World Fair, the United States has witnessed fifteen more international expositions of varying sizes and success: the California Midwinter International Exposition in San Francisco (1894); the Pan-American Exposition in Buffalo (1901); the Louisiana Purchase Exposition in St. Louis (1904); the Jamestown Ter Centennial Exhibition at Hampton Roads (1907); the Alaska-Yukon Pacific Exposition in Seattle (1909); the Panama-Pacific Exposition in San Francisco (1915); the Panama-California (International) Exposition in San Diego (1915-1916); the Sesqui-Centennial Exposition in Philadelphia (1926); A Century of Progress International Exposition in Chicago (1933-1934); the New York World's Fair (1938-1940); the Golden Gate International Exposition in San Francisco (1939-1940); Century 21 Exposition in Seattle (1962); the New York World's Fair (1964-1965); HemisFair '68 in San Antonio; and Expo '74 World's Fair in Spokane.

The future of the international exposition is precarious. Most have lost money; few have accrued large profits. Despite efforts on the parts of various countries, notably the United States and Spain, attempts to organize world fairs in recent years have been unsuccessful because of a shortage of funds. Only Australia has projected an international exposition, and that is not scheduled to occur until her bicentennial year of 1988. A 1982 World's Fair has been announced recently to run for a limited period in Knoxville, Tennessee. In the meantime, the midway, in the form of traveling carnivals, amusement parks, and theme parks, continues to be an integral part of the American entertainment scene.

AMUSEMENT AND THEME PARKS

With the exception of the circus, and to a lesser extent the fair/carnival tradition, the traditional amusement park and its newest version, the theme park, have managed to survive changing times and tastes. After the stimulus of the Columbian Exposition in 1893, the modern concept of the amusement park developed at Coney Island, originally a beach resort in Brooklyn, New York, which contained a series of parks and independent entertainments. There, beginning in 1895, street railway companies and seaside entertainment entrepreneurs witnessed the evolution of the ultimate model on which to base their operations. Although other seaside resorts, most notably Atlantic City, New Jersey, created major entertainments, none succeeded so completely as did Coney Island. Piers, concert halls, dining rooms, zoos, and bandstands were installed to attract patrons at other resort areas, such as Jantzen Beach, Portland; Revere Beach outside Boston; and at Gravesend Beach on Long Island. Invariably, the only way to get to these resorts was by trolley, since the trolley companies were largely responsible for the development of such amusement areas. By the turn of the century some resorts, such as Ulmer Park By the Sea at Gravesend Beach, had created permanent and seemingly elaborate rides, which were certainly more appealing than the typical fair ride. On a summer's evening people would pack into trolley cars in order to spend a few pleasant hours at the pleasure beaches, escaping the hustle and bustle of urban centers.

These early parks, however, were prosaic compared to the imaginative amusements and the gigantic operations that evolved at Coney Island which set the pattern and example for the great twentieth-century version of the amusement park. And, as John F. Kasson has so vividly illustrated in his important study of Coney Island at the turn of the century, the changing economic and social conditions of that period helped to create the basis of a new mass culture that would emerge in the early years of this century. When Coney Island was developed this culture was still in the process of formation and had not been totally assimilated by the society as a whole. "Its purest expression at this time," writes Kasson, "lay in the realm of commercial amusements, which were creating symbols of the new cultural order, helping to knit a heterogeneous audience into a cohesive whole. Nowhere were these symbols and their relationship to the new mass audience more clearly revealed than at turn-of-the-century Coney Island."

Coney Island's greatest fame began when Billy Boynton built Sea Lion Park in 1895, although during the twenty years prior to the development of this park Coney Island was already established as a resort area. Some time after the 1876 Philadelphia Centennial Exposition, the Sawyer Observatory, a three-hundred-foot-tall observation tower with steam powered elevators, the hit of the fair, was moved to Coney Island, renamed the "Iron Tower," and became the first mechanical amusement device at Coney

Island (it stood until 1911). In 1884 LaMarcus Adna Thompson built the first primitive version of a roller coaster, called the "Switchback," at Coney Island. Thompson, however, was not a consummate showman but a religious man who saw such rides as healthy and moral alternatives to the drinking and gaming associated with the grove recreation halls. The earliest of these picnic groves, Lake Compounce Park in Bristol, Connecticut (1846), and Rocky Point in Warwick, Rhode Island (1847), incorporated primitive rides but failed to exploit these new mechanical devices as did Coney Island.

Boynton was unsuccessful in developing Sea Lion Park to its potential, and it remained for his successor to further the cause of the amusement industry. In 1897 George C. Tilyou built Steeplechase Park, adding one of the earliest and most famous rides of Coney Island: the Steeplechase, consisting of track-bound, gravity-powered, metal horses. Sea Lion Park added the "Shoot-the-Chutes," the predecessor of the modern-day mill chute or log flume. At the 1901 Buffalo Pan-American Exposition Elmer "Skip" Dundy and Frederic Thompson, the former a showman and the latter an engineer, owned most of the amusement concessions. After the Pan-American Exposition they moved their major attractions, including the "Aerio Cycle," an early double-Ferris wheel, and "A Trip to the Moon," a spectacular theatrical dark ride, to Steeplechase Park on a concession basis. In 1903 Dundy and Thompson bought Boynton's faltering Sea Lion Park and rebuilt it into a lavish version of Chicago's "Midway Plaisance"— Luna Park—at a cost of nearly $1 million. Many amusement park experts still consider Luna to have been the epitome of amusement enterprises. Luna offered, on a more or less permanent basis, a wildly eclectic environment of attractions, illuminated at night by more than 250,000 incandescent lights.

Within a year, across Surf Avenue from Luna, a real estate speculator and sometime politician named William H. Reynolds quickly countered, copied Luna's fanciful and elaborate style, and built Dreamland Park at a cost of $3.5 million. Dreamland, although it burned to the ground nine years later, was on an even more exuberant scale than Luna, including illumination by one million bulbs.

With the example of Coney Island's successful amusement parks and the showcase of new rides displayed at the 1904 St. Louis World's Fair, the amusement industry experienced a veritable building boom. By 1919 the estimated number of amusement parks hit the astronomical figure of 1,500. Without question, the great period of the traditional amusement park dates from Coney Island's spectacular growth at the turn of the century to about World War II, although its decline began around World War I, as did that of all outdoor entertainments. However, while it lasted, the Coney Island model inspired countless other Luna Parks and Dreamlands all over America, until by the early years of the new century, the amusement park had become a fixture of most large cities. While in the 1920s mechanical rides reached a zenith in their development, the 1930s and the depression brought new patrons seeking escape from dreary lives into the parks. From World War II to the present, the decline of the traditional amusement park has been slow but steady, with the announcement of the closing of major amusement parks a commonplace event. The lack of needed materials during the war, patrons' boredom with the aging attractions, natural disasters, vandalism, and other less tangible factors have all contributed to the traditional amusement park's demise. The postwar baby boom did bring a resurgence of interest in the amusement park during the 1950s. Today there are still at least seventy-five major traditional amusement parks, most in disrepair and varying states of deterioration. Many of the older (and smaller) urban traditional parks were unable to survive the 1960s and closed (including Palisades Park in New Jersey, Chicago's Riverview, and Cleveland's Euclid Beach).

In this age of nostalgia traditional parks that are financially able to rehabilitate themselves might survive. Sites and carousels of some of the more historic parks are being declared landmarks, and citizens of a number of local communities are battling land developers and local governments in order to save amusement areas—or at least to enshrine a number of the beautifully constructed older carousels still in existence. Even many modern theme parks are adding traditional amusement park areas for rides; the prominent theme parks are each trying to outdo the other in the size and apparent danger of their "ultimate" roller coaster. And, it might be added, as long as more patrons ride roller coasters than attend professional football and baseball games combined, as has been true in the late 1970s and early 1980s, such escapist amusement is far from dead.

To many entrepreneurs, the salvation of the amusement park is to be found in its new mutation, the "theme" park. The theme park is a vivid example of Madison Avenue advertising packaging at its most persuasive and an amazing example of organizational know-how (especially the Disney operations). Yet, it should be mentioned that these theme parks are no longer the products of professional showmen of the amusement park tradition but are the brainstorms of large corporations and businessmen. The entertainment value of these new amusement centers cannot be denied, and for a generation who never experienced the traditional amusement park in its heyday, they are wonders to behold.

The theme park, conceived first by Walt Disney, was a revolutionary concept in the 1950s. The notion of organizing amusement areas around a theme offered a wholly new gimmick for the amusement industry. Since the 1955 opening of Disneyland in Anaheim, California, built on a fifty-five-acre tract with a $17 million investment, the theme park idea has spread throughout the United States. Although the idea was initially scoffed at, and backers hesitated to invest, within a very few years modest imitations of Disneyland began to spring up. Even traditional amusement parks sensed the inevitable and many attempted to revamp themselves within the theme idea in order to remain competitive. By the 1970s there were numerous large and prosperous operations, including Astroworld, Cedar Point in Ohio; Hersheypark in Pennsylvania; Kings Island in Ohio; the revamped Knott's Berry Farm in Buena Park, California; Magic Mountain in Valencia, California; Opryland, U.S.A., in Nashville; the Six Flags circuit in Texas, Georgia, and Missouri; and the giant of them all, Walt Disney World in Orlando, Florida. Walt Disney World, built on a site of over 27,000 acres, continues to expand. Their latest attraction, "Big Thunder Mountain," built at a cost of $17 million, opened in November 1980.

It is significant to note that despite the success of the best-known theme parks, they have not all succeeded. Several "Biblelands" never managed to open; a few months after it opened Magic Mountain near Denver closed its doors; and Freedomland in the Bronx, New York, survived only a few years. Other theme parks, such as Busch Gardens in Tampa, Florida, or the several Lion Country Safaris, are actually animal preserves with the veneer of the theme park or a few added rides to embellish their appeal.

There are major differences other than the "theme" concept separating the traditional amusement park and the theme park. Indeed, the theme park is almost the antithesis of the old amusement park in its quality and atmosphere. As Tim Onosko points out in *Fun Land U.S.A.,* "first and foremost is cleanliness." The emphasis is on courtesy and family togetherness, a far cry from that of the typical traditional amusement park of the past. Whereas traditional parks moved closer and closer to urban centers, the theme park seeks isolation, though proximity to a major highway. Instead of seasoned showmen, the personnel of the typical theme park are youthful and clean-cut. Traditional showmanship, gaming operations, pitchmen, and somewhat seedy and worn attractions have been replaced by an atmosphere that is homogenized, hygienic, and to some, almost plastic. The traditional amusement park frequently expanded haphazardly around its midway; the theme park is a carefully planned and executed collection of attractions, with plenty of open spaces and landscaping provided to make it aesthetically pleasing.

The progression in the outdoor amusement industry has followed a natural course: the turn of the century trolley park and picnic grove was supplanted by the urban amusement park, which in turn has been overshadowed by the theme park. What is next? Perhaps the "West World" or "Future World" of the movies is not really so far off.

SURVEY OF SOURCES

Fairs, pleasure gardens, expositions, carnivals, amusement parks, theme parks, and other outdoor amusement forms are, in many respects, closely related to variety shows and the circus, with the major difference being an ambulatory audience in contrast to the stationary audience of most staged variety entertainment. Instead of conventional theatrical presentations, these forms depend more on entertainment environments. Despite the prominence of these environmental forms of entertainment, they have only recently been examined as entertainment vehicles with theatrical elements. Indeed, most of these forms have yet to receive truly serious treatment, although in recent years there have been notable exceptions. Those forms in greatest need of attention appear to be the American pleasure garden, the American fair (other than world fairs), and the theme park. The special issue of the *Journal of Popular Culture* on "Circuses, Carnivals and Fairs in America," edited by Marcello Truzzi, makes an excellent beginning place for a study of these forms. Patrick C. Easto and Truzzi's "Towards an Ethnography of the Carnival Social System" includes a useful review and evaluation of much of the available literature. Don B. Wilmeth's *American and English Popular Entertainment: A Guide to Information Sources* contains a section entitled "Outdoor Amusements and Environmental Entertainments" that should be consulted for sources not discussed here, although this present assessment supplements that listing appreciably.

Few surveys of the full range of the outdoor amusement industry have been undertaken. Certainly a starting point is William F. Mangels's *The Outdoor Entertainment Business,* the focus of which is the amusement park and Joe McKennon's *A Pictorial History of the American Carnival*, an excellent overview that includes essays on European roots and related topics in addition to its focus on the carnival. Less comprehensive but still recommended are Al Griffin's *"Step Right Up Folks!"* a survey of American amusement parks, and Gary Kyriazi's *The Great American Amusement Parks,* a useful pictorial history of the amusement park. The section of *American Popular Entertainment,* edited by Myron Matlaw, entitled "Environmental Entertainment (Amusement Parks and Theme Parks)" is also a useful basic source.

In order to examine the various specific forms of American outdoor amusements, background sources are essential. The following items provide an adequate starting place: Samuel McKechnie's *Popular Entertainment Through the Ages;* William Addison's *English Fairs and Markets;* David Braithwaite's *Fairground Architecture: The World of Amusement Parks, Carnivals, and Fairs* and brief little guide titled *Travelling Fairs;* Duncan Dallas's *The Travelling People;* Thomas Frost's *The Old Showman and the Old London Fairs* is a standard source; T.F.G. Dexter's *The Pagan Origins of Fairs;* Henry Morley's classic work, *Memoirs of Bartholomew Fair;* R. W. Muncey's *Our Old English Fairs;* Ian Starsmore's *English Fairs;* H. W. Waters's *History of Fairs and Expositions;* and Cornelius Walford's *Fairs, Past and Present.* The English pleasure garden is best covered in W. S. Scott's *Green Retreats, the Story of Vauxhall Gardens, 1661-1859;*

James Southworth's *Vauxhall Gardens: A Chapter in the Social History of England;* Mollie Sands's *Invitation to Ranelagh, 1742-1803;* Edmund Yates's *The Business of Pleasure* (volume 1 on Cremorne); and Warwick Wroth's *The London Pleasure Gardens in the Eighteenth Century* (with Edgar Arthur) and *Cremorne and the Later London Gardens.* The most reliable study of performances at London fairs is Sybil Rosenfeld's *The Theatre of the London Fairs in the Eighteenth Century.* The American version of the pleasure garden has received scant attention, although Thomas M. Garrett's "A History of Pleasure Gardens in New York City, 1700-1865" surveys forty-eight such places of amusement and suggests further research possibilities. Joseph Jackson, in "Vauxhall Garden," discusses a Pennsylvania garden (1814-1824), and David Ritchey, in "Columbia Garden: Baltimore's First Pleasure Garden," focuses on another early example. O. G. Sonneck, in *Early Concert Life in America (1731-1831),* devotes much of this study to concerts performed at early pleasure gardens, and Charles Hamm, in *Yesterdays: Popular Song in America,* also discusses songs written for pleasure gardens.

In recent years world expositions have received a number of judicious and serious studies. Edo McCullough's *World's Fair Midway: An Affectionate Account of American Amusement Areas from the Crystal Palace to the Crystal Ball* provides a fascinating history of major American fairs and indicates the strong influence that midways exert on the entire realm of public entertainment. A world survey is provided in John Allwood's *The Great Exhibitions,* which also contains several useful appendixes. Although devoted exclusively to English exhibitions, Richard D. Altick's *The Shows of London* is a superb scholarly investigation. A brief survey of major American world expositions can be found in George R. Leighton's "World's Fairs: From Little Egypt to Robert Moses" and "The Year St. Louis Enchanted the World." Suzanne Hilton's *Here Today and Gone Tomorrow: The Story of World's Fairs and Expositions,* although intended principally for older children, is a reasonably good introduction and survey. An older survey, including all types of fairs, is H. W. Waters's *History of Fairs and Expositions.* Of the specific United States world's expositions, the 1893 Columbian Exposition in Chicago has received the most and best attention. Two recent works are highly recommended: David F. Burg's *Chicago's White City of 1893* and Reid Badger's *The Great American Fair.* Burg's account is most thorough and contains perceptive commentary on the meaning of the exposition and a lengthy chapter on the exhibits and entertainment; Badger, who includes a superb bibliography, also provides good background and a useful chapter on the midway. John Kasson's *Amusing the Million,* though essentially an analysis of Coney Island, incorporates a perceptive overview of the Columbian Exposition, comparing it to New York's Central Park and Coney Island. For an account by the man hired to oversee the concessions on the midway, see Sol Bloom's

The Autobiography of Sol Bloom. Other recommended sources on specific expositions include: *The Artistic Guide to Chicago and the World's Columbian Exposition;* E. L. Austin and Odell Hauser's *The Sequi-Centennial International Exposition;* Patrick Beaver's *The Crystal Palace 1851-1936; A Portrait of a Victorian Enterprise* (in London); Anthony Bird's *Paxton's Palace* (also the London Crystal Palace); *Dawn of a New Day: The New York's World's Fair, 1939/40,* edited by Sara Blackburn; Justus D. Doenecke's "Myths, Machines and Markets: The Columbian Exposition of 1893" (an outline of the significant thematic elements in this exposition); Morton Eustis's analysis of the New York World's Fair as a form of theater, "Big Show in Flushing Meadows"; "Exhibition Architecture: 16 Designs for the New York World's Fair"; Yvonne ffrench's *The Great Exhibition: 1851* (London Crystal Palace); John Maass's *The Glorious Enterprise: The Centennial Exhibition of 1876;* John D. McCabe's *The Illustrated History of the Centennial Exhibition;* John Moses and Paul Selby's *The White City: The Historical, Biographical and Philanthropical Record of Illinois;* Octave Thanet's "The Trans-Mississippi Exposition" (in Omaha, Nebraska); Ben C. Truman's *History of the World's Fair Being a Complete and Authentic Description of the Columbian Exposition from Its Inception;* and Margaret Johanson Witherspoon's *Remembering the St. Louis World's Fair.*

Of the smaller United States fair tradition, little of significance has been written. The sources above on world fairs frequently contain relevant material. Helen Augur's *The Book of Fairs,* written in 1930, provides a broad and somewhat impressionistic history from primitive fairs to the world fairs of 1939 in San Francisco and New York. Olive Cook provides an interesting but limited study on the rides of the English fairground, also applicable to the American fair, in "Fairground Baroque"; Braithwaite's two sources on fairground architecture also serve the same purpose. Lila Perl's *America Goes to the Fair: All About State and County Fairs in the USA,* although written for younger readers, gives a serviceable overview of fair history and entertainment on the midway. Other juvenile books provide brief texts but vivid illustrations. These include Steve Lesberg and Naomi Goldberg's *County Fair;* Audree Distad's *Come to the Fair* (which includes a list of State Fairs, locations, and selected features); and Jack Pierce's *The State Fair Book.* A useful guide to fairs and expositions is the *Directory of North American Fairs and Expositions.*

Specific sources on the carnival are quite uneven and vary from excellent to mediocre, but even the latter are still informative or revelatory. Among the better sources are: Don Bole's *The Midway Showman,* an excellent, albeit brief, collection of tips for the carnival hopeful; Jack Dadswell's *Hey There Sucker*, a veteran carnival press agent's inside story of the carnival; Theodore M. Dembroski's "Hanky Panks and Group Games versus Alibis and Flats: The Legitimate and Illegitimate of the Carnival's

Front End''; Patrick C. Easto and Marcello Truzzi's ''Carnivals, Road-shows, and Freaks,'' ''Toward an Ethnography of the Carnival Social System,'' and ''The Carnival as a Marginally Legal Work Activity: The Typological Approach to Work Systems''; William Lindsay Gresham's *Monster Midway;* Wittold Krassowski's ''Social Structure and Profession-alization in the Occupation of the Carnival Worker''; Daniel P. Mannix's *Step Right Up* (also called *Memoirs of a Sword Swallower*); and Patricia A. Nathe's ''Carnivals, Also Fairs, Circuses, and Amusement Parks: A Historical Perspective.'' Again, Marcello Truzzi's specially edited number of the *Journal of Popular Culture* on carnivals is strongly recom-mended in its entirety.

The gaming aspect of the carnival, in addition to being treated in the Dembroski essay, is specifically covered in the following recommended sources: Walter Gibson's *The Bunco Book;* ''I'll Gyp You Every Time''; Will Irwin's *The Confessions of a Con Man;* Frederick C. Klein's ''Step Right Up: How 'Heels' Shapiro Makes a Tidy Living Off a Carnival Game''; and John Scarne's ''Carnival, Fair, Bazaar, Arcade and Amuse-ment Park Games.'' Essays on specific carnival operations can be found in the following: William Lindsay Gresham's ''The World of Mirth''; J. Kobler's ''World's Biggest Show: Royal American Shows''; Gilbert Millstein's ''Carnie Biz—Bigger Than Ever''; James Poling's ''Sawdust in Their Shoes''; and William K. Zincser's ''A Lot of Quarters'' (on the James E. Strates Show).

Although not always reliable, some of the most atmospheric and vivid pieces on the carnival have been written by journalists and writers of fiction. The writing of Daniel Mannix, a former carnie, provides insights into carnival performers. Especially useful are *Step Right Up* and ''Sex on Sawdust'' (a fictional account of sex shows on the carnival midway). Harry Crews's ''Carny'' is a journalist's look at the modern carnival in rather exploitative and pornographic terms. The seamy side of carnival life is also captured effectively in Susan Meiselas's *Carnival Strippers.* Arthur Lewis's *Carnival,* although its total reliability is questionable, makes entertaining reading; William Lindsay Gresham's *Nightmare Alley* is a well-known fictional story with a carnival background; David Mark's novel, *And Where It Stops Nobody Knows,* provides similar atmosphere.

Carnival sideshows are discussed in the section on dime museums and P. T. Barnum (chapter 5), and sources can be found there, although Andrew J. Bakner's ''Side Show Attractions'' provides a brief history useful to the study of the carnival. David Braithwaite's *Fairground Archi-tecture,* along with other sources on fairs and amusement parks listed elsewhere in this section, should be investigated for discussions of rides germane to the carnival. Hereward Carrington's *Sideshow and Animal Tricks* reveals gimmicks of the carnival performer; ''Hey Rube'' provides a brief analysis of the decline of traveling carnivals in the 1920s; the contemporary carnival is briefly discussed in Norton Mockridge's "Carnival"; "No More Rubes" records the diminishing number of marks on the lot; Sid Sidenberg's "Pitchdom Forty Years Ago and Today" provides a retrospective comparison as of 1969; and Robert Lewis Taylor's "Talker" records the memoirs of one of the last great carnival "talkers" or spielers. The distinctive slang of the carnival is given special treatment in Don B. Wilmeth's *The Language of American Popular Entertainment;* a brief glossary is David W. Maurer's "Carnival Cant: A Glossary of Circus and Carnival Slang"; and *The Language of Show Biz,* edited by Sherman Louis Sergel, includes a few select carnival terms.

In addition to the historical surveys of American outdoor entertainment mentioned above (Mangels, McKennon, Griffin, and Kyriazi), Brooks McNamara's "Come On Over: The Rise and Fall of the American Amusement Park" provides a succinct but useful summary of that development. Sylvester Baxter's "The Trolley in Rural Parks"; William D. Middleton's "Gems of Symmetry and Convenience"; and Day Allen Willey's "The Trolley-Park" provide an understanding of the recreation grounds run by street railway companies.

American seaside resorts and amusement areas are most fully discussed in Richmond Barrett's *Good Old Summer Days;* Charles F. Funnell's *By the Beautiful Sea: The Rise and High Times of That Great American Resort, Atlantic City;* Irvin R. Glazer's "The Atlantic City Story"; Maury Klein's "Summering at the Pier"; Sarah Howell's *The Seaside* (American and English resorts); Vicki Gold Levi and Lee Eisenberg's *Atlantic City: 125 Years of Ocean Madness;* William McMahon's *So Young . . . So Gay* (Atlantic City); Sean Manley and Robert Manley's *Beaches: Their Lives, Legends, and Lore;* and Frank Butler's *Book of the Boardwalk.*

From its inception through its decline, Coney Island has received more specific attention than any other amusement park (and seaside resort), with the possible exception of the Disney operations. The most useful overviews and histories of Coney Island are the following: Peter Lyon's "The Master Showman of Coney Island" (George Tilyou); Edo McCullough's *Good Old Coney Island;* Robert E. Snow and David E. Wright's "Coney Island: A Case Study in Popular Culture and Technical Change"; and Oliver Pilat and Jo Ranson's *Sodom by the Sea: An Affectionate History of Coney Island.* The study with the greatest perspective and the one that most effectively analyses the "meaning" of Coney Island is John F. Kasson's *Amusing the Million: Coney Island at the Turn of the Century.* This is a relatively brief but extremely perceptive study.

A number of early sources are worth investigation, including: Bruce Bliven's "Coney Island for Battered Souls" (1921); Guy Wetmore Carryl's "Marvelous Coney Island" (1901); Lindsay Denison's "The Biggest Playground in the World" (1905); Richard LeGallienne's "Human Need of Coney Island" (1905); Robert Wilson Neal's "New York's City of Play"

(1906); Albert Bigelow Paine's "The New Coney Island" (1904); Elmer Blaney Harris's "The Day of Rest at Coney Island" (1908); "The Mechanical Joys of Coney Island" (1908); Francis Metcalf's *Side Show Studies* (1906); Edwin E. Slosson's "The Amusement Business" (1904); Edward F. Tilyou's "Human Nature with the Brakes Off—Or: Why the Schoolma'am Walked into the Sea" (1922); and Frederic Thompson's "Amusing the Million" (1908), an examination of the psychology of the crowd by one of the builders of Luna Park.

Of the other miscellaneous essays on the traditional amusement park, including more up-to-date coverage of Coney Island, the following are of interest: an early twentieth-century prediction is discussed in Frank L. Albert's "The Future of the Amusement Park in America"; the poet e.e. cummings, a great appreciator of the "pleasure park," expresses his views in "Coney Island"; an interesting collection of Coney Island postcards can be found in "A Greeting from Coney Island"; Lucy P. Gillman's "Coney Island" provides a good overview of Coney Island's history and its changes from a mecca for the upper classes to the masses; although dated, Rollin Lynde Hartt's "The Amusement Park" is an interesting analysis of the amusement park as "an artificial distraction for an artificial life"; an early twentieth-century appraisal is James S. Hutton's "The Amusement Park: American Institution"; and Day Allen Willey's "The Open-Air Amusement Park" is a similar journalistic appraisal. John F. Cuber's "Patrons of Amusement Parks" is an interesting sociological study of amusement park patrons in the Cleveland area in the 1930s.

The amusement park was a popular subject for several prominent artists; foremost among them were Reginald Marsh and Joseph Stella. Marsh's bravura style recorded the popular pursuit of pleasure in a most revealing way. Lloyd Goodrich's *Reginald Marsh,* a gorgeous book with magnificent color reproductions, is a marvelous way to sense Coney Island's changes over the years. Less useful but still of value is Norman Sasowsky's *The Prints of Reginald Marsh.* Irma Jaffe's *Joseph Stella* is the definitive source on this modernist. Richard Cox's "Coney Island, Urban Symbol in American Art" includes discussions of Marsh, Stella, and other artists who saw Coney Island as a mirror that reflected key sociopolitical problems facing a fast changing America. A stimulating and often controversial modern investigation of Coney Island's unique architecture and its symbiotic relationship to the city (Coney Island as a fetal Manhattan) can be found in Rem Koolhaas's *Delirious New York: A Retroactive Manifesto for Manhattan* (in the chapter called "Coney Island: The Technology of the Fantastic"). Koolhaas's essay is also notable for its illustrations and descriptions of rides and attractions.

The carousel or merry-go-round, an essential ride at all amusement parks, is given broad coverage in Frederick A. Fried's *Pictorial History of the Carousel,* a well-researched and superbly illustrated book. Fred and Mary

Fried's *America's Forgotten Folk Arts* deals with aspects of the amusement park, fair, circus, and carnival that are now considered important pieces of folk art, in particular carousel figures, midway show fronts, banner paintings, and shooting galleries. Nina Fraley's *The American Carousel* is an excellent brief introduction to the carousel with good illustrations. Other essays and books of interest on the carousel include: Tina Gottdenker, *Carvers and Their Merry-Go-Rounds;* John Neary, "The First Lady of Merry-Go-Rounds"; T. H. Watkins, "And the History Goes 'Round and 'Round"; Gary K. Wolf, "The Merry-Go-Round at Tilden Park"; Roland Summit, *Flying Horses;* and Barbara F. Charles, "Mix antique charm and artistry, add children and spin."

The latest phase of the outdoor amusement industry—the theme park—has received scant serious attention other than coverage in the survey sources listed above. An excellent starting place, however, is the special issue of *Theatre Crafts,* "Theme Parks," which contains ten excellent essays on various aspects of the parks. Numerous articles in more popular magazines, nonetheless, have been written, mostly on Disneyland and Walt Disney World. The following are typical and among the better efforts: "America's Theme Parks"; Patricia MacKay, "Theme Parks: U.S.A."; Peter Blake, "Walt Disney World" (one of the better essays on the inner workings of the park); James H. Bierman, "Disneyland and the 'Los Angelization' of the Arts" (one of the more serious and speculative pieces); Alexander Moore, "Walt Disney World: Bounded Ritual Space and the Playful Pilgrimage Center"; "Disneyland and Disney World" (an illustrated tour through both); Robert DeRoos, "The Magic Worlds of Walt Disney" (a copiously illustrated essay); Paul Goldberger, "Mickey Mouse Teaches the Architects" (one of the more perceptive treatments of technological achievements); Karen Kreps, "The Magic Mountain"; A. Menen, "Dazzled in Disneyland"; "Tinker Bell, Mary Poppins, Cold Cash" (on Disneyland's fiscal status); Kevin Wallace, "Onward and Upward with the Arts: The Engineering of Ease" (on Disneyland); and H. Sutton, "Booked for Travel." Valerie Childs's *The Magic of Disneyland and Walt Disney World,* though containing only essential text, provides a wealth of color photographs of both theme parks. In *Theme Parks: A Partially Annotated Bibliography of Articles About Modern Amusement Parks,* James C. Starbuck lists almost 330 articles, few of a serious nature, on the theme park. Few scholarly efforts, other than Bierman's and Moore's essays, have appeared on the amusement or theme park. Two 1970 master's theses from Georgia Tech indicate possible directions, however. These are: J. D. Parks, "Minimizing the Detrimental Effects of Commercial Entertainment Park Development" and C. D. Dyer, Jr., "An Investigation of the Effect of Traveltime on Trips Attracted to a Major Recreational Area."

With the increasing popularity of theme parks, guides to amusement parks are becoming more common. *Fun Land U.S.A.* by Tim Onosko provides a reliable guidebook to one hundred major amusement and theme parks plus a brief history; Raymond Carlson, editor of the *National Directory of Theme Parks and Amusement Parks,* provides a geographical listing of over 530 locations with brief descriptions; James W. Reed, *The Top 100 Amusement Parks of the United States* ranks parks on the number and quality of their rides and park attendance; Jeff Ulmer, *Amusement Parks of America: A Comprehensive Guide* is a guide to 319 parks and is similar to Onosko in format; Michael Strauss's "We've Got a Ticket to Ride," though dated, evaluates major theme parks; G. G. Green's "Super Colossal Amusement Parks: America's Fifteen Best" provides a similar guide.

A study of any aspect of the outdoor amusement industry is incomplete without frequent use of *Amusement Business* (published in Nashville), the bible of the outdoor amusement business and a spin-off of *Billboard,* another major show business weekly paper. Of special interest is *Amusement Business*'s seventy-fifth anniversary issue (December 1969). *Funspot,* another industry house organ, is less useful. For other relevant periodicals, see the lists at the end of chapters 1, 3, and 8. There are no significant special collections that focus extensively on forms of outdoor entertainment, although several organizations, in particular the International Association of Amusement Parks and Attractions (in North Riverside, Illinois) and the Outdoor Amusement Business Association (in Minneapolis) promote the interest of the industry.

BIBLIOGRAPHY

For greater accessibility, this section has been subdivided into three sections: pleasure gardens, fairs, and expositions; carnivals; and amusement parks, theme parks, and seaside resorts.

PLEASURE GARDENS, FAIRS, EXPOSITIONS, AND GENERAL SOURCES

Addison, William. *English Fairs and Markets.* London: B. T. Batsford, 1953.

Allwood, John. *The Great Exhibitions.* London: Studio Vista, 1977.

Altick, Richard D. *The Shows of London: A Panoramic History of Exhibitions, 1600-1862.* Cambridge, Mass. and London: Belknap Press of Harvard University Press, 1978.

The Artistic Guide to Chicago and the World's Columbian Exposition. [Chicago]: Columbian Art Co., 1892.

Augur, Helen. *The Book of Fairs.* New York: Harcourt, Brace & Co., 1930.

Austin, E. L., and Hauser, Odell. *The Sequi-Centennial International Exposition.* 1929. Reprint. New York: Arno Press, 1976.

Badger, Reid. *The Great American Fair.* Chicago: Nelson-Hall, 1979.

Beaver, Patrick. *The Crystal Palace 1851-1936: A Portrait of Victorian Enterprise.* London: Hugh Evelyn, 1970.

Bird, Anthony. *Paxton's Palace.* London: Cassell, 1976.

Blackburn, Sara, ed. *Dawn of a New Day: The New York's World Fair, 1939/40*. New York and London: New York University Press, 1980.

Bloom, Sol. *The Autobiography of Sol Bloom*. New York: G. P. Putnam's Sons, 1948.

Braithwaite, David. *Fairground Architecture: The World of Amusement Parks, Carnivals, and Fairs*. New York: Frederick A. Praeger, 1968.

_____. *Travelling Fairs*. Aylesbury, England: Shire Publications, 1976.

Burg, David F. *Chicago's White City of 1893*. Lexington: University Press of Kentucky, 1976.

Cook, Olive. "Fairground Baroque." In *The Saturday Book 31,* edited by John Hadfield. New York: Clarkson N. Potter, 1971.

Dallas, Duncan. *The Travelling People*. London: Macmillan Co., 1971.

Dexter, T.F.G. *The Pagan Origin of Fairs*. Perranporth, Cornwall: New Knowledge Press, 1930.

Directory of North American Fairs and Expositions. 79th ed. Nashville: Amusement Business, 1978.

Distad, Audree. *Come to the Fair*. New York: Harper & Row, 1977.

Doenecke, Justus D. "Myths, Machines and Markets: The Columbian Exposition of 1893." *Journal of Popular Culture* 6 (Winter 1972):550-66.

Easto, Patrick C., and Truzzi, Marcello. "Towards an Ethnography of the Carnival Social System." *Journal of Popular Culture* 6 (Winter 1972):550–66.

"Environmental Entertainment (Amusement Parks and Theme Parks)." In *American Popular Entertainment*, edited by Myron Matlaw. Westport, Conn. and London: Greenwood Press, 1979.

Eustis, Morton. "Big Show in Flushing Meadows." *Theatre Arts Monthly* 23 (August 1939):566–77.

"Exhibition Architecture: 16 Designs for the New York World's Fair." *Architectural Forum* 119 (August 1963):33-41.

ffench, Yvonne. *The Great Exhibition: 1851*. London: Harvill Press, [1950].

Frost, Thomas. *The Old Showmen and the Old London Fairs*. 1881. Reprint. Ann Arbor, Mich.: Gryphon Books, 1971.

Garrett, Thomas M. "A History of Pleasure Gardens in New York City, 1700-1865." Ph.D. dissertation, New York University, 1978.

Hamm, Charles. *Yesterdays: Popular Song in America*. New York and London: W. W. Norton and Co., 1979.

Hilton, Suzanne. *Here Today and Gone Tomorrow: The Story of World's Fairs and Expositions*. Philadelphia: The Westminster Press, 1978.

Jackson, Joseph. "Vauxhall Garden." *Pennsylvania Magazine of History and Biography* 57, no. 4 (1933):289-98.

Kasson, John F. *Amusing the Million: Coney Island at the Turn of the Century*. New York: Hill and Wang, 1978.

Leighton, George R. "World's Fairs: From Little Egypt to Robert Moses." *Harper's Magazine* 221 (July 1960):27-37.

_____. "The Year St. Louis Enchanted the World." *Harper's Magazine* 221 (August 1960):38-47.

Lesberg, Steve, and Goldberg, Naomi. *County Fair*. New York and London: Peebles Press, 1978.

Maass, John. *The Glorious Enterprise: The Centennial Exhibition of 1876.* Watkins Glen, N.Y.: American Life Foundation, 1973.

McCabe, James D. *The Illustrated History of the Centennial Exhibition.* Philadelphia: The National Publishing Co., 1975.

McCullough, Edo. *World's Fair Midway: An Affectionate Account of American Amusement Areas from the Crystal Palace to the Crystal Ball.* 1966. Reprint. New York: Arno Press, 1976.

McKechnie, Samuel. *Popular Entertainment Through the Ages.* 1931. Reprint. New York: Benjamin Blom, 1969.

Morley, Henry. *Memoirs of Bartholomew Fair.* 1857. 2d ed. 1874. 3d ed. 1880. Reprint. Detroit: Singing Tree Press, 1969.

Moses, John, and Selby, Paul. *The White City: The Historical, Biographical and Philanthropical Record of Illinois.* Chicago: Chicago World Book Co., 1895.

Muncey, R. W. *Our Old English Fairs.* London: Sheldon Press, 1936.

Perl, Lila. *America Goes to the Fair: All About State and County Fairs in the USA.* New York: William Morrow & Co., 1974.

Pierce, Jack. *The State Fair Book.* Minneapolis: Carolrhoda Books, 1980.

Ritchey, David. "Columbia Garden: Baltimore's First Pleasure Garden." *Southern Speech Communication Journal* 39 (Spring 1974):241-47.

Rosenfeld, Sybil. *The Theatre of the London Fairs in the Eighteenth Century.* Cambridge: Cambridge University Press, 1960.

Sands, Mollie. *Invitation to Ranelagh, 1742-1803.* London: John Westhouse, 1946.

Scott, W. S. *Green Retreats, The Story of Vauxhall Gardens, 1661-1859.* London: Odhams Press, 1955.

Sonneck, O. G. *Early Concert Life in America (1731-1800).* Leipzig: Breitkopf and Hartel, 1907.

Southworth, James Granville. *Vauxhall Gardens: A Chapter in the Social History of England.* New York: Columbia University Press, 1944.

Starsmore, Ian. *English Fairs.* N. Village Green, Levittown, N.Y.: Transatlantic Arts, 1976.

Thanet, Octave. "The Trans-Mississippi Exposition." *Cosmopolitan* 25 (October 1898):598-614.

Truman, Ben C. *History of the World's Fair Being a Complete and Authentic Description of the Columbian Exposition from Its Inception.* 1893. Reprint. New York: Arno Press, 1976.

Truzzi, Marcello, ed. "Circuses, Carnivals and Fairs in America." *Journal of Popular Culture* 6 (Winter 1972):531-619.

Walford, Cornelius. *Fairs, Past and Present.* 1883. Reprint. New York: A. M. Kelly, 1968.

Waters, H. W. *History of Fairs and Expositions.* London, Ontario: Reid Bros. and Co., 1939.

Wilmeth, Don B. "Outdoor Amusements and Environmental Entertainments." In *American and English Popular Entertainment: A Guide to Information Sources,* edited by Don B. Wilmeth. Detroit: Gale Research Co., 1980.

Witherspoon, Margaret Johanson. *Remembering the St. Louis World's Fair.* St. Louis: Folkestone Press, 1973.

Wroth, Warwick. *Cremorne and the Later London Gardens.* London: Elliot Stock, 1907.

_____, and Wroth, Arthur Edgar. *The London Pleasure Gardens in the Eighteenth Century,* 1896. Reprint. Hamden, Conn.: Archon Books (The Shoe String Press), 1979.

Yates, Edmund. *The Business of Pleasure.* 2 vols. London: Chapman and Hall, 1865.

CARNIVALS

Bakner, Andrew J. "Side Show Attractions." *Bandwagon* 17 (November-December 1973):35-38.

Boles, Don. *The Midway Showman.* Atlanta: Pinchpenny Press, 1967.

Braithwaite, David. *Fairground Architecture: The World of Amusement Parks, Carnivals, and Fairs.* New York: Frederick A. Praeger, 1968.

Carrington, Hereward. *Sideshow and Animals Tricks.* 1913. Reprint. Atlanta: Pinchpenny Press, 1973.

Crews, Harry. "Carny." *Playboy* 23 (September 1976):96, 98, 195, 196, 200, 201-4. Reprinted in *Blood and Grits.* New York: Harper and Row, 1979.

Dadswell, Jack. *Hey There Sucker.* Boston: Bruce Humphries, 1946.

Dembroski, Theodore M. "Hanky Panks and Group Games versus Alibis and Flats: The Legitimate and Illegitimate of the Carnival's Front End." *Journal of Popular Culture* 6 (Winter 1972):567-82.

Easto, Patrick C., and Truzzi, Marcello. "Carnivals, Roadshows, and Freaks." *Society* 9 (March 1972):26-34.

_____. "Toward an Ethnography of the Carnival Social System." *Journal of Popular Culture* 6 (Winter 1972):550-66.

_____. "The Carnival as a Marginally Legal Work Activity: The Typologial Approach to Work System." In *Deviant Behavior: Occupational and Organizational Bases,* edited by Clifton D. Bryant. Chicago: Rand McNally, 1974.

Gibson, Walter. *The Bunco Book.* Holyoke, Mass.: Sidney H. Radner, 1946.

Gresham, William Lindsay. *Nightmare Alley.* New York and Toronto: Rinehart and Co., 1946.

_____. *"Monster Midway.* New York: Rinehart and Co., 1953.

_____. "The World of Mirth." *Life* 25 (13 September 1948):142-44, 146, 149-50, 152, 154, 156.

"Hey Rube." *Nation* 129 (6 November 1929):513.

"I'll Gyp You Every Time." *Saturday Evening Post,* 17 September 1949, p. 24.

Irwin, Will. *The Confessions of a Con Man.* New York: B. W. Huebsch, 1909.

Klein, Frederick C. "Step Right Up: How 'Heels' Shapiro Makes a Tidy Living Off a Carnival Game." *Wall Street Journal,* 30 September 1969, pp. 1, 21.

Kobler, J. "World's Biggest Show: Royal American Shows." *Cosmopolitan* 135 (November 1953):78-83.

Krassowski, Wittold. "Social Structure and Professionalization in the Occupation of the Carnival Worker." Master's thesis, Purdue University, 1954.

Lewis, Arthur H. *Carnival.* New York: Trident Press, 1970.

McKennon, Joe. *A Pictorial History of the American Carnival.* Vols. 1 and 2. Sarasota, Fla.: Carnival Publishers of Sarasota, 1972; vol. 3, same publisher, 1981.

Mannix, Daniel P. *Step Right Up.* New York: Harper and Bros., 1950.
_____. "Sex on Sawdust." *Playboy* 6 (June 1958):17-18, 28, 64-65.
Mark, David. *And Where It Stops Nobody Knows.* Garden City, N.Y.: Doubleday and Co., 1960.
Maurer, David W. "Carnival Cant: A Glossary of Circus and Carnival Slang." *American Speech* 6 (June 1931):327-37.
Meiselas, Susan. *Carnival Strippers.* New York: F., S., and G. Publishing Co. [Farrar, Straus, and Giroux], 1976.
Millstein, Gilbert. "Carnie Biz—Bigger Than Ever." *New York Times Magazine,* 18 May 1952, pp. 22-23, 58-59.
Mockridge, Norton. "Carnival." *American Way* [American Airlines magazine]. (May 1970):8-21.
Nathe, Patricia A. "Carnivals, Also Fairs, Circuses, and Amusement Parks: a Historical Perspective." Master's thesis, University of California, Berkeley, 1969.
"No More Rubes." *Time,* 29 September 1958, pp. 41-42.
Poling, James. "Sawdust in Their Shoes." *Saturday Evening Post,* 11 April 1953, pp. 32-33, 102-3, 105, 107.
Scarne, John. "Carnival, Fair, Bazaar, Arcade and Amusement Park Games." In his *Scarne's Complete Guide to Gambling.* rev. ed. New York: Simon and Schuster, 1974.
Sergel, Sherman Louis, ed. *The Language of Show Biz.* Chicago: Dramatic Publishing Co., 1973.
Sidenberg, Sid. "Pitchdom Forty Years Ago and Today." *Amusement Business,* 31 December 1969, p. 153.
Taylor, Robert Lewis. "Talker." *New Yorker,* 19 April 1958, p. 47; 26 April 1958, p. 39.
Truzzi, Marcello, ed. "Circuses, Carnivals and Fairs in America." *Journal of Popular Culture* 6 (Winter 1972):531-619.
Wilmeth, Don B. *The Language of American Popular Entertainment: A Glossary of Argot, Slang, and Terminology.* Westport, Conn. and London: Greenwood Press, 1981.
Zincser, William K. "A Lot of Quarters." *Look,* 5 September 1967, p. 18.

AMUSEMENT PARKS, THEME PARKS, AND SEASIDE RESORTS

Albert, Frank L. "The Future of the Amusement Park in America." *Billboard,* 19 March 1910, pp. 20, 21, 86.
"America's Theme Parks." *Newsweek,* 4 August 1980, pp. 56-58.
Barrett, Richmond. *Good Old Summer Days.* Introduction by Mary Lasswell. Boston: Houghton Mifflin, 1952.
Baxter, Sylvester. "The Trolley in Rural Parks." *Harper's Monthly* 97 (June 1898): 60-69.
Bierman, James H. "Disneyland and the 'Los Angelization' of the Arts." In *American Popular Entertainment,* edited by Myron Matlaw. Westport, Conn. and London: Greenwood Press, 1979.
Blake, Peter. "Walt Disney World." *Architectural Forum* 136 (June 1972):24-41.

Bliven, Bruce. "Coney Island for Battered Souls." *New Republic,* 23 November 1921, pp. 372-74.

Butler, Frank. *Book of the Boardwalk.* Atlantic City, N.J.: The 1954 Association, Inc., 1953.

Carlson, Raymond, ed. *National Directory of Theme Parks and Amusement Areas.* New York: Pilot Books, 1978.

Carryl, Guy Wetmore. "Marvelous Coney Island." *Munsey's Magazine* 25 (September 1901):809-17.

Charles, Barbara F. "Mix antique charm and artistry, add children and spin." *Smithsonian* 3 (July 1972):41-47.

Childs, Valerie. *The Magic of Disneyland and Walt Disney World.* New York: Mayflower Books, 1979.

Cox, Richard. "Coney Island, Urban Symbol in American Art." *New York History Society Quarterly* 60 (January-April 1976):35-52.

Cuber, John F. "Patrons of Amusement Parks." *Sociology and Social Research* 24 (September-October 1939):63-68.

cummings, e.e. "Coney Island." In *E.E. Cummings: A Miscellany Revised,* edited by George J. Firmage. New York: October House, 1965.

Denison, Lindsay. "The Biggest Playground in the World." *Munsey's Magazine,* 33 (August 1905):556-66.

DeRoos, Robert. "The Magic Worlds of Walt Disney." *National Geographic* 124 (August 1963):157-67, 173-207.

"Disneyland and Disney World." *Theatre Crafts* 11 (September 1977):23-31.

Dyer, C. D., Jr. "An Investigation of the Effect of Traveltime on Trips Attracted to a Major Recreational Area." Master's thesis, Georgia Tech, 1970.

"Environmental Entertainment (Amusement Parks and Theme Parks)." In *American Popular Entertainment,* edited by Myron Matlaw. Westport, Conn. and London: Greenwood Press, 1979.

Fraley, Nina. *The American Carousel.* Berkeley, Calif.: Redbug Workshop (2807 Cherry St.), 1979.

Fried, Frederick A. *Pictorial History of the Carousel.* New York: A.S. Barnes and Co., 1964.

Fried, Fred, and Fried, Mary. *America's Forgotten Folk Arts.* New York: Pantheon Books, 1978.

Funnell, Charles F. *By the Beautiful Sea: The Rise and High Times of That Great American Resort, Atlantic City.* New York: Alfred A. Knopf, 1975.

Gillman, Lucy P. "Coney Island." *New York History* 36 (July 1955):255-90.

Glazer, Irvin R. "The Atlantic City Story." *Marquee* 12 (January 1981-lst and 2d quarters, 1980):4-12.

Goldberger, Paul. "Mickey Mouse Teaches the Architects." *New York Times Magazine,* 22 October 1972, pp. 40-41, 92-98.

Goodrich, Lloyd. *Reginald Marsh.* New York: Harry N. Abrams, [1972].

Gottdenker, Tina Cristiani. *Carvers and Their Merry-Go-Rounds.* West Babylon, N.Y.: Second Annual Conference Committee, NCR, 1974.

Green, G. G. "Super Colossal Amusement Parks: America's Fifteen Best." *Better Homes and Gardens* 52 (August 1974):95-100.

"A Greeting from Coney Island." *American Hertiage* 26 (February 1975):49-55.

Griffin, Al. *"Step Right Up Folks!"* Chicago: Henry Regnery Co., 1974.

Harris, Elmer Blaney. "The Day of Rest at Coney Island." *Everybody's Magazine* 19 (July 1908):24-34.

Hartt, Rollin Lynde. "The Amusement Park." *Atlantic Monthly* 99 (May 1907): 667-77.

Howell, Sarah. *The Seaside.* London: Studio Vista, 1974.

Hutton, James S. "The Amusement Park: American Institution." *Billboard,* 19 March 1910, pp. 25, 84.

Jaffe, Irma. *Joseph Stella.* Cambridge, Mass.: Harvard University Press, 1970.

Kasson, John F. *Amusing the Million: Coney Island at the Turn of the Century.* New York: Hill and Wang, 1978.

Klein, Maury, "Summering at the Pier." *American History Illustrated* 13 (May 1978):32-36, 38-43.

Koolhaas, Rem. *Delirious New York: A Retroactive Manifesto for Manhattan.* New York: Oxford University Press, 1978.

Kreps, Karen. "The Magic Mountain." *Eastern Review* (November 1980):93.

Kyriazi, Gary. *The Great American Amusement Parks.* Secaucus, N.J.: Citadel Press, 1976.

LeGallienne, Richard. "Human Need of Coney Island." *Cosmopolitan* 39 (July 1905):239-46.

Levi, Vicki Gold, and Eisenberg, Lee. *Atlantic City: 125 Years of Ocean Madness.* New York: Clarkson N. Potter, 1979.

Lyon, Peter. "The Master Showman of Coney Island." *American Heritage* 9 (June 1958):14-20, 92-95.

McCullough, Edo. *Good Old Coney Island.* New York: Charles Scribner's Sons, 1957.

MacKay, Patricia. "Theme Parks: U.S.A." *Theatre Crafts* 11 (September 1977): 27, 56, 65-69.

McKennon, Joe. *A Pictorial History of the American Carnival.* Sarasota, Fla.: Carnival Publishers of Sarasota, 1972.

McMahon, William. *So Young . . . So Gay.* Atlantic City, N.J.: Atlantic City Press, 1970.

McNamara, Brooks. "Come on Over: The Rise and Fall of the American Amusement Park." *Theatre Crafts* 11 (September 1977):33, 84-86.

Mangels, William F. *The Outdoor Entertainment Business.* New York: Vantage Press, 1952.

Manley, Sean and Robert. *Beaches: Their Lives, Legends, and Lore.* Philadelphia, New York, and London: Chilton Book Co., 1968.

"The Mechanical Joys of Coney Island." *Scientific American,* 15 August 1908, pp. 101, 108-10.

Menen, A. "Dazzled in Disneyland." *Holiday* 34 (July 1963):68.

Metcalf, Francis. *Side Show Studies.* Illustrated by Oliver Herford. New York: Outing Publishing Co., 1906.

Middleton, William D. "Gems of Symmetry and Convenience." *American Heritage* 24 (February 1973):23-37, 99.

Moore, Alexander. "Walt Disney World: Bounded Ritual Space and the Playful Pilgrimage Center." *Anthropological Quarterly* 53 (October 1980):207-18.

Neal, Robert Wilson. "New York's City of Play." *World To-Day* 11 (August 1906):818-26.

Neary, John. "The First Lady of Merry-Go-Rounds." *Americana* 2 (January 1975):12-16.

Onosko, Tim. *Fun Land U.S.A.* New York: Ballantine Books, 1978.

Paine, Albert Bigelow. "The New Coney Island." *Century Magazine* 68 (August 1904):528-38.

Parks, J. D. "Minimizing the Detrimental Effects of Commercial Entertainment Park Development." Master's thesis, Georgia Tech, 1970.

Pilat, Oliver, and Ranson, Jo. *Sodom by the Sea: An Affectionate History of Coney Island.* Garden City, N.Y.: Doubleday, Doran and Co., 1941.

Reed, James W. *The Top 100 Amusement Parks of the United States: The 1978 Guidebook to Amusement Parks.* Quarryville, Pa.: Reed Publishing Co., 1978.

Sasowsky, Norman. *The Prints of Reginald Marsh.* New York: Clarkson N. Potter, 1976.

Slosson, Edwin E. "The Amusement Business." *Independent,* 21 July 1904, pp. 134-39.

Snow, Robert E., and Wright, David E. "Coney Island: A Case Study in Popular Culture and Technical Change." *Journal of Popular Culture* 9 (Spring 1976): 960-75.

Starbuck, James C. *Theme Parks.* Monticello, Ill.: Council of Planning Libraries, 1976.

Strauss, Michael. "We've Got a Ticket to Ride." *Holiday* 55 (June/July/August 1974):4, 10, 12, 14, 73-75.

Summit, Roland. *Flying Horses.* Rolling Hills: Flying Horses, 1970.

Sutton, H. "Booked for Travel." *Saturday Review,* 10 June 1967, pp. 80-82.

"Theme Parks." *Theatre Crafts* 11 (September 1977), Entire issue.

Thompson, Frederic. "Amusing the Million." *Everybody's Magazine* 19 (September 1908):378-87.

Tilyou, Edward F. "Human Nature with the Brakes Off—Or: Why the Schoolma'am Walked into the Sea." *American Magazine* 94 (July 1922):19-21, 86, 91-92, 94.

"Tinker Bell, Mary Poppins, Cold Cash." *Newsweek,* 12 July 1965, pp. 74-76.

Ulmer, Jeff. *Amusement Parks of America: A Comprehensive Guide.* New York: The Dial Press, 1980.

Wallace, Kevin. "Onward and Upward with the Arts: The Engineering of Ease." *New Yorker,* 7 September 1963, pp. 104, 106, 108, 110, 114, 116, 118, 120, 122, 124-29.

Watkins, T. H. "And the History Goes 'Round and 'Round . . ." *American Heritage* 31 (December 1979):74-75.

Willey, Day Allen. "The Trolley-Park." *Cosmopolitan* 33 (July 1902):265-72.
_____. "The Open-Air Amusement Park." *Theatre Magazine* 10 (July 1909):18-19.

Wolf, Gary K. "The Merry-Go-Round at Tilden Park." *Americana* 7 (September-October 1979):44-51.

CHAPTER 3

The American Circus

HISTORICAL SUMMARY

George Speaight, the author of the most recent history of the circus and a notable English historian of popular entertainment, devotes almost half of his *History of the Circus* to the circus in America. He is quite correct in stating that the circus is an international art, with a steady flow of "artistes" criss-crossing the Atlantic and the Pacific. In a very unselfish comment, Speaight, who gives great detail to the birth of the modern circus in England, states unequivocally that it was the United States that was ultimately preeminent in "the quantity and quality of the performers it supplied to English circuses." Although Englishmen had brought the circus to these shores, "the debt was repaid with interest." Indeed, despite the rich and fascinating history of European circuses, the United State's traditions and contributions to the circus are unique and notable.

Before an overview is possible, however, some explanation is in order. In 1968 Marcello Truzzi, in "The Decline of the American Circus," defined the circus as "a traveling and organized display of animals and skilled performances within one or more circular stages known as 'rings' before an audience encircling these activities." This definition, which provides a workable framework for a study of the circus, includes the traditional circus and the Wild West exhibition under the general category of a circus. It clearly excludes, as it should, the carnival, which is socially a very distinct organization and depends, as does the amusement park, on its audience's active participation. On the other hand, the circus demands and, if it is successful, receives a high degree of emotional empathy and passive involvement. The circus, therefore, is more closely related to traditional theater, whereas the carnival and its kin, discussed in chapter 2, have evolved from the medieval fair tradition. Despite Truzzi's inclusion of the Wild West show as a form of circus, during its heyday its evolution and form were quite distinctive and thus will be dealt with as a separate and distinctive entertainment.

In its various forms, the circus is one of the oldest and richest of popular entertainments and thus a thorough historical survey is impossible in this brief overview. Only highlights can be touched upon here, providing a sense of the circus's evolution, with the focus on America's own circus tradition.

Historians have rather unsuccessfully attempted to trace individual circus acts to antiquity, but the modern circus's connection with Rome's Circus Maximus or the Flavian Amphitheatre or even earlier traditions is tenuous at best and misleading at worse. Certainly the origins of the American circus must be found elsewhere. Historians of the circus have been altogether too easily misled by the ancient use of the word "circus," which comes from the Latin word for circle (but then there is no requirement that a circus must be presented in a ring, despite its practicality for equestrian acts, which are a rather modern innovation).

The American circus as we know it today dates, in fact, from the equestrian training circle of the eighteenth century. By the middle of that century English riding masters offered exhibitions combining skills of horsemanship with other acrobatic skills. Although a number of these equestrians might be given credit for being the father of the modern circus, it is Philip Astley who emerges as the most obvious progenitor. Between 1768 and 1773, Astley developed what amounted to a one-ring circus in London, featuring horsemanship acts, and ultimately developed not only the modern circus, but also a form of theatre called "hippodrama" or "equestrian drama." European circuses stayed close to Astley's original form, often in fixed locations, although adding in time clowns, acrobats, jugglers, trapeze artists, trained animals, and other common circus acts. In contrast, the American circus's early trend was toward size and movement. In the course of the circus's history, there have been in America, Mexico, and Canada since 1771 over 1,100 circuses and menageries (an even earlier tradition and one of the definite predecessors of the circus in England and America). The peak period of the American circus was in 1903, with approximately ninety-eight circuses and menageries in existence. Since 1903 the number of circuses has steadily declined.

The early American circus, then, was virtually transported from England, although elements of the circus were present in the form of itinerant entertainments some years prior to the establishment of a "circus" proper.

A troupe of rope dancers was performing in Philadelphia in 1724; a performer was juggling and balancing on the slack wire and the tightrope in New York in 1753; tumblers and rope dancers were in Boston in 1792; and animals were being exhibited in the Colonies as early as 1716. And, in the English tradition, trick riding might have been seen as early as 1770. Certainly a Mr. Faulks was performing feats of horsemanship in Philadelphia in 1771, and others followed. Shows and exhibitions of all varieties were formally forbidden by an Act of Congress in 1774, so the evolution of the circus had to wait until the conclusion of the Revolutionary War and the repeal of the ban in 1780. One of the first circus amusements to be offered after the war was a large menagerie of birds, reptiles, and quadrupeds.

The man who finally brought the previously disparate elements together in Philadelphia in 1793 was John Bill Ricketts, a Scotsman who arrived in America in 1792. In his permanent building in Philadelphia, Ricketts presented trick riding, a tightrope walker, and a clown. Ricketts had been a pupil of Charles Hughes, whose Royal Circus at Blackfriar's Bridge in London had been rival to Astley's since 1782 (Hughes also claimed that he had visited America in 1770). Subsequently, between 1792 and 1799, Ricketts's circus made appearances in New York, Boston, and Albany, as well as other cities in the United States and Canada, and was even seen by George Washington.

The American circus, then, began with single acts. The amalgamation of elements developed slowly. The opening of the Erie Canal in 1825 afforded the increasing number of American circuses greater freedom in travel. At the same time, the number of traveling animal menageries continued to parallel the growing number of circuses. By the end of the first quarter of the nineteenth century, efforts were made to merge the menagerie and the circus. The elephant, which was to have a key role in the American circus, was first exhibited in 1796 by a Mr. Owen, and his elephant continued to be seen for fifteen years up and down the eastern seaboard. The second and the most famous early elephant in the new country, Old Bet, was shown by Hackaliah Bailey with great success until 1816, although the first elephant that was part of any circus was seen in New York in 1812. Hackaliah Bailey, however, was so fond of Old Bet that he built the Elephant Hotel in his hometown of Somers, New York, and erected a monument to Old Bet. The area around Somers is still called the "Cradle of the American Circus." Most early pioneers of the American circus came from this area, where animals were bred and trained, acts were rehearsed, and tents and wagons were constructed. Somers remained the center of the American circus until 1927, when the Ringlings moved their winter quarters from Bridgeport, Connecticut, to Sarasota, Florida. Unfortunately, Old Bet has mistakenly been associated by historians with Nathan Howe's circus. Howe and his partner Aaron Turner also have been incorrectly credited with the introduction of the circus tent around 1824. Recent research indicates, however, that the tent was probably not introduced in the American circus until 1825 or 1826 by J. Purdy Brown in Wilmington, Delaware.

During the first half of the nineteenth century, distinctive characteristics of the American circus began to evolve. Although menageries on display began to be associated with the circus, the horses remained the top performers; they also provided the means for moving the show from one location to another. Beginning in 1837, when a short-lived circus marched through the streets of Albany, the horse made possible one of the American circus's most unique features, the circus parade. The circus and its horse-drawn wagons most frequently traveled by night, pausing on the outskirts of the next show town in order to make a triumphal entry for the early morning citizens. As the circus parade developed, elaborately decorated specially made wagons with magnificent wood carvings were added. A beautiful band wagon led the procession, while a calliope or steam fiddle (invented in 1856), the most popular of circus musical instruments, provided a loud and raucous conclusion to the spectacle.

By the early nineteenth century, land as far west as Illinois had been incorporated into the union. With poor or nonexistent roads or trails available, other means of transportation were necessary, so enterprising showmen turned to water travel via the Ohio and Mississippi Rivers (see chapter 12). Competition between the various circuses became more intense; the Somer's group created a merger of several animal companies and in 1835 formed the first circus trust, which was to become the Zoological Institute. In quick succession, many circus firsts occurred: in 1838 the circus first used rail travel as transportation (from Forsythe to Macon, Georgia); the first recorded boat circus (under Gilbert Spalding and Charles Rogers), an early example of the showboat, appeared in 1852; Richard Sands, who developed his own circus in 1842 and took the first American circus to England in 1843, invented a new kind of poster—the first printed in color from wood-blocks on rag paper and intended for reuse.

The migration of the Mormons to Utah beginning in 1847 established the Mormon Trail, and the California Trail expanded travel westward from Salt Lake City to San Francisco. With the 1849 gold rush, the circus, like other forms of popular entertainment, almost immediately moved west. Indeed, Joseph Andrew Rowe established the Olympic Circus in San Francisco in 1849.

Although circuses continued to travel over land during the last half of the nineteenth century, and many wagon shows continued well into the twentieth century, the trend was toward greater use of the railroad. With useful trackage available that allowed for longer trips to major cities and more profit, circuses took to the rails. Den Stone was an early pioneer on the rails in 1854; Dan Castello's Circus and Menagerie was far enough west when the transcontinental railroad was completed in 1869 to complete the season on the Pacific Coast. By 1885 fifty or more circuses were on the road; the 1890s and early years of this century saw many small railroad circuses traveling across the country. In time, motorized transportation and the railroad displaced mule power and horse power. The circus of Tom Mix made the first motorized transcontinental tour of the United States in 1936.

Among the major changes in the pattern of the American circus, in addition to mobility, was the introduction of multiple rings, in contrast to the typical European one-ring arrangement. Around 1873 Andrew Haight's Great Eastern Circus and Menagerie announced that it would present its show in two rings; at the same time William Cameron Coup added a second ring to the circus utilizing the name of P. T. Barnum; in 1881, James A. Bailey negotiated the merger of several great circus operations, including Barnum's circus, and opened with a three-ring show. By 1885, in fact, when Barnum was briefly merged with Adam Forepaugh, their circus had four rings plus two stages placed between them for acrobats. By the 1890s, however, virtually all American circuses had adopted the three rings. An important philosophy of the American circus was to give the spectator more than he could possibly see at one time, on the basis of bigger is better. The circus now incorporated the menagerie, the concert, the sideshow (a term for any auxiliary show), and the street parade as integral ingredients.

The period between 1830 and 1870 saw the emergence of numerous prominent circuses in the history of the American circus, each with colorful and important histories: the George F. Bailey Circus; circuses utilizing the name of the "Lion King" (Isaac Van Amburgh); the several circuses of Seth B. Howes; the Mabie Brothers Circus; the Yankee (Fayette Ludovic) Robinson Circus; the John Robinson Circus (a name used longer than any other in circus titles); the Spalding and Rogers Circus; the Dan Castello Circus; the Dan Rice Circus (capitalizing on the name of the early American clown); and the W. W. Cole Circus.

The so-called golden age of the American circus—which lasted until about 1917—began in 1871, when W. C. Coup persuaded P. T. Barnum, the showman and museum entrepreneur, to become a partner in a circus enterprise. The circus with Barnum's name attached to it opened in Brooklyn with the largest tent and the greatest number of men and horses in the history of the circus. Barnum, always the master publicist, billed the 1873 three-ring circus "P. T. Barnum's Great Traveling World's Fair Consisting of Museum, Menagerie, Caravan, Hippodrome, Gallery of Statuary and Fine Arts, Polytechnic Institute, Zoological Garden and 100,000 Curiosities, combined with Dan Castello's, Sig. Sebastian's and Mr. D'Atelie's Grand Triple Equestrian and Hippodramatic Exposition." Barnum, it should be noted, lent his name to other shows in addition to Coup's, which ultimately caused a split with Coup in 1875. In 1880 Barnum joined James A. Bailey and James L. Hutchinson in a new opearation. This lucrative partnership lasted until 1885 when Barnum refused to deal further with Bailey, and Bailey sold his interest to James Cooper and W. W. Cole. In 1887, after Barnum had experienced a number of setbacks, including the loss of a Madison Square Garden contract to the rival Adam Forepaugh Circus, Barnum gave Bailey full control of the circus and added his name to the new "Barnum & Bailey Greatest Show on Earth." During this golden age, a number of the older circuses continued to compete or operate in their own regional circuits; and other new prominent circuses came into their own, including the Sells Brothers Circus, the Great Wallace Circus, and the Lemen Brothers Circus.

The Ringlings, the name most frequently associated with the circus today, were late arrivals on the circus scene. None of the five brothers was involved until 1882. After seeing a traveling circus in their hometown of Baraboo, Wisconsin, they began to do a variety show around Wisconsin. In 1895, after adding more circus acts and animals to their menageries, they made their first tour outside the Midwest and entered Barnum and Bailey's territory in New England. A year after Bailey's death in 1907, the Ringlings bought the Barnum and Bailey Circus; they finally merged as one in 1918, becoming "Ringling Brothers and Barnum & Bailey Combined Shows." Various competitors tried to shut out the Ringlings, but the circus had become big business, and their efforts were fruitless.

After 1910, circuses declined in number and in extravagance. In 1905 Barnum & Bailey eliminated their free parade, a victim of an unsustainable cost escalation that had begun to steal their profits. Many circus parades had become such good shows in themselves that patrons stayed away from the tent shows. In many ways the parade had been the epitome of the circus, demonstrating to the public the gigantic scale of the circus. The costs of the ever more spectacular wagons sky-rocketed. In 1896 Barnum & Bailey's "Two Hemisphere" wagon cost $40,000 to build and required a team of forty horses to pull the vehicle. The elimination of the menagerie was not far behind the demise of the parade; and even the big top would practically disappear (Ringling Brothers last performed under canvas in 1956). Mechanization deprived the circus of much of its uniqueness and flair; individual initiative became dampened as well.

Today only a dozen or so circuses travel in the United States, and they are only a faint reminder of the glories of the traveling tent circus of the turn of the century. During the 1940s and 1950s, the larger circuses—the Clyde Beatty, the King Brothers, and the Ringling shows—experienced a series of disasters and setbacks. When "The Greatest Show on Earth" was forced to put away its big top and perform only in permanent facilities, the major circus in the United States was deprived of one of its greatest attractions. But the circus is far from being a totally endangered species. In 1967 Ringling Brothers and Barnum & Bailey was purchased by Irvin Feld for $8 million. Two years later it was placed on the New York Stock Exchange; in 1971 it was purchased by Mattel Toy for $47 million. Feld, as David Hammarstrom in *Behind the Big Top* so aptly puts it, is "an incurable ballyhoo man who would like to carve his initials next to those of P. T. Barnum" and he has been amazingly successful in selling his circus. With two large units on the road each season, Feld has found a formula that makes it possible to convince the patrons that the circus is bigger and better than ever, which is clearly not so. Hammarstrom explains Feld's very slick and carefully rehearsed approach as "a big splash of color with less heads, more feathers, and a strong solo star around which to build each show." And, ironically, despite the diminution of the number of circuses, the total audience continues to grow (thanks in part to television and film) and the revenue to swell. Feld clearly represents the "big business" thrust of the modern circus; fortunately, a few showmen of the old tradition are still trying to return the circus to the way it once was, most notably Cliff Vargas and his Circus Vargas. Regardless of the best way to do it, the modern circus must make adjustments to modern demands while at the same time retaining its age-old appeal. The circus has survived because it touches something central in its audience, something without an age barrier; there is a closeness to nature beneath its showy facade and an ability to transcend natural laws. But Robert C. Toll perhaps is correct when he concludes in *On with the Show* that the circus is largely a relic, "a nostalgic re-creation of the nature-based rituals of an earlier day."

SURVEY OF SOURCES

The literature on the circus is vast. Of all forms of American popular amusement it has received the greatest attention. On an international level, no form of entertainment has been written about as frequently or on such a continuing basis with the possible exception of magic. Still, a great deal of primary material remains in private collections, and many of the published sources are by amateur historians and devoted circus fans whose materials, until recently, have avoided careful documentation. As a result, a comprehensive, reliably researched and documented history of the American circus has yet to be written, although a number of notable efforts in that direction have recently appeared. In the meantime, students of the circus must refer to those published sources that are most reliable and search for information in circus collections and in the pages of various periodicals and serials. These will be discussed at the conclusion of this section.

The most comprehensive guide to circus sources and an indispensable reference for anyone researching the circus is Raymond Toole-Stott's four-volume *Circus and Allied Arts, A World Bibliography* and his more

selective list in *A Bibliography of the Books on the Circus in England.*
Toole-Stott's major bibliographical volumes contain over fifteen thousand
entries drawn from works in thirteen languages. It should be noted, however, that this guide is far more useful on foreign antecedents than it is on
the American circus. A fifth volume is currently in preparation and promises
to fill much of the void. Volume 1, which includes sections on William
Cody, Adah Menken, P. T. Barnum, and Philip Astley, has a foreword
by M. Willson Disher; Volume 2 is especially strong on pantomime and
equestrian drama (foreword by D. L. Murray); Volume 3, with a section on
periodicals and a list of compiler's one hundred best circus books, has
a foreword by Antony D. Hippisley Coxe; Volume 4's foreword is by
A. H. Saxon. Robert Sokan's *A Descriptive and Bibliographic Catalog of
the Circus and Related Arts Collection at Illinois State University, Normal,
Illinois,* contains details on 1,373 items and is a useful guide as well. Don B.
Wilmeth's *American and English Popular Entertainment* annotates 254
sources on the circus and 120 items on the Wild West exhibition and
William Cody. For the American circus, one would be well served to review
Richard Flint's "A Selected Guide to Source Material on the American
Circus" for his discussion of types of circusiana.

There are numerous general histories and surveys of the circus. George
L. Chindahl's *History of the Circus in America* is especially good on the
nineteenth century (it also covers the circus in Canada and Mexico and the
Wild West exhibition); John and Alice Durant's *Pictorial History of the
American Circus* is sumptuously illustrated and contains a useful list of
American circuses; C. P. Fox and Tom Parkinson's *Circus in America* is
one of the better overviews of the circus in its heyday. Isaac. J. Greenwood's
The Circus: Its Origin and Growth Prior to 1835 remains a useful early
history, as do R.W.G. Vail's "The Early Circus in America" and "This
Way to the Big Top," and John J. Jennings's *Theatrical and Circus Life;
or, Secrets of the Stage, Greenroom and Sawdust Arena.* Of all the available
surveys, Earl Chapin May's *The Circus from Rome to Ringling* (not to be
confused with the less definitive *Circus! From Rome to Ringling* by Marian
Murray) remains a good starting place and is considered by many circus
authorities the best single-volume history of the earlier efforts. For the
uninitiated, Mildred S. and Wolcott Fenners's *The Circus: Lure and Legend*
covers the entire gamut of circus literature. Joe McKennon's *Horse Dung
Trail: Saga of American Circus,* although a partially fictionalized history
of American circus from Yankee Robinson (1856) to the end of the horse
drawn circus (1940), is essentially factual and generally reliable. A good
historical summary is Marcello Truzzi's "Circus and Side Shows." Among
the more recent world histories, Rupert Croft-Cooke and Peter Cotes's
Circus: A World History and Peter Verney's *Here Comes the Circus* offer
generally reliable but undocumented accounts that place the American

circus in international perspective, as does Rolf Lehmann's *Circus* (in German), most notable for its 205 color photographs. *Le Grand Livre Du Cirque* (two volumes), although in French, contains essays on all aspects of world circus, including a section on the American circus by A. H. Saxon. Dominique Jando's *Histoire Mondiale Du Cirque,* also in French, is generally trustworthy although undocumented (it is based largely on essays in the journal *Le Cirque dans l'Univers*). It does, however, cover all aspects of the circus on an international scale. Henry Thetard's *La Marveilleuse Histoire du Cirque* (two volumes) remains an authoritative French text. George Speaight's recent *A History of the Circus,* unlike most circus histories, does contain some documentation and gives excellent coverage to the American circus. Felix Sutton's *The Big Show: A History of the Circus* is adequate but not notable, and Charles Bayly, Jr.'s "The Circus" provides a brief historical survey.

The English prototype and antecedents of the early American circus is covered with scholarly exactitude in A. H. Saxon's *Enter Foot and Horse* and *The Life and Art of Andrew Ducrow & The Romantic Age of the English Circus.* Indeed, Saxon's work in general is indicative of the type of scholarship possible in the field of circus history. Less reliable and less thorough but still recommended are: Thomas Frost's *Circus Life and Circus Celebrities,* a classic study of the early English circus; and M. Willson Disher's *Greatest Show on Earth,* which provides an informative and amusing history of Astley's amphitheatre. Two suggested doctoral dissertations are Paul Alexander Daum's "The Royal Circus 1782-1809: An Analysis of Equestrian Entertainments" and George Palliser Tuttle's "The History of the Royal Circus, Equestrian and Philharmonic Academy, 1782-1816, St. George's Fields, Surrey, England." Also useful are Antony D. Hippisley Coxe's "The Lesser-Known Circuses of London" and "Historical Research and the Circus," and Jacob Decastro's *The Memoirs of the Life of J. Decastro, Comedian* (fifty pages deal with "The History of the Royal Circus").

The early period of the American circus has recently begun to receive more serious attention. Stuart Thayer's *Annals of the American Circus 1793-1829* is a careful and documented account; a second volume is in preparation, which will bring his account to mid-nineteenth century. Also useful are: James S. Moy's "Entertainment at John B. Rickett's Circus, 1793-1800," "A Checklist of Circus Buildings Constructed by John B. Ricketts," and "The Greenwich Street Theatre 1797-1799" (each based in part on his doctoral dissertation, "John B. Ricketts's Circus 1793-1800"); C. H. Amidon's "Inside Ricketts' Circus with John Durang"; William W. Clapp, Jr.'s *A Record of the Boston Stage;* Joseph Cowell's *Thirty Years Passed Among the Players in England and America;* John Durang's *The Memoirs of John Durang,* edited by Alan S. Downer; and Chang Reynolds's *Pioneer Circuses of the West.*

Other studies, some historical in nature and others of a more anecdotal complex, deal with specific circuses, periods, or regions. Of the plethora of sources, the following selective list offers informative and sometimes insightful accounts: Bob Barton's *Old Covered Wagon Show Days* (the traveling Cole Brothers circus in the 1890s); E. J. Bateman's "The Origin of the Barnum and Bailey Circus"; Elbert R. Bowen's "The Circus in Early Rural Missouri"; Sverre O. and Faye O. Braathen's "Circus Monarchs" (on Wm. Cameron Coup, P. T. Barnum, James A. Bailey, the Ringling Brothers, and other circus pioneers); Joseph T. Bradbury's "The Coop & Lent Circus," "Tom Mix Circus 1936 Coast to Coast Tour," "Campbell-Bailey-Hutchinson Circus," "The Rhoda Royal Circus, 1919-1922," and "A History of the Cole Bros. Circus 1935-40"; Fred Bradna and Hartzell Spence's *The Big Top: My 40 Years with the Greatest Show on Earth;* Gordon M. Carver's history of the Sells-Floto Circus, 1906-1918; Bert J. Chipman's *Hey Rube,* which includes routes of major circuses and a roster of the staffs of major circuses (1900-1915); John S. Clark's *Circus Parade* (based on thirty-five years with the circus); Herb Clement's *The Circus, Bigger and Better Than Ever?,* an account of smaller, more contemporary circuses; George Conklin's *The Ways of the Circus, Being the Memories and Adventures of George Conklin, Tamer of Lions* (circus life during the forty years after the Civil War); Richard E. Conover's *The Affairs of James A. Bailey, The Great Forepaugh Show, Give 'Em a John Robinson,* and *The Circus, Wisconsin's Unique Heritage;* Courtney Ryley Cooper's "The Big Show" and *Under the Big Top* (the circus in the 1920s); W. C. Coup's *Sawdust and Spangles: Stories and Secrets of the Circus* (Coup died in 1895 and the actual author or editor is not given); Charles Phelps Cushing's "Behind the Scenes at the Circus" (a typical week with a traveling circus); Ayres Davies's "Wisconsin, Incubator of the American Circus"; Will Delavoye's *Show Life in America,* a not very reliable but an unusual source on the illegal methods used by some traveling circuses; William G. Dodd's "Theatrical Entertainment in Early Florida"; *California's Pioneer Circus, Joseph Rowe, Founder. Memoirs and Personal Correspondence Relative to the Circus Business Through the Gold Country in the 50's,* edited by Albert Dressler; William L. Elbirn's "Austin Bros. 3 Ring Circus and Real Wild West" (1945 show); James Waldo Fawcett's "The Circus in Washington [D.C.]"; *This Way to the Big Show: The Life of Dexter Fellows,* the life story of the press agent for Ringling Brothers and Barnum & Bailey, by Dexter W. Fellows and Andrew A. Freeman; Al G. Field's *Watch Yourself Go By,* circus life in the nineteenth century; Richard W. Flint's "Refus Welch: America's Pioneer Circus Showman" and "The Evolution of the Circus in Nineteenth-Century America"; Gene Fowler's *Timber Line* (on the Sells-Floto circus); Robert H. Gollmar's *My Father Owned a Circus* (on the Gollmar Brothers Circus, a major competitor of the Ringling Brothers early in the century); E. S. Hallock's

"The American Circus" (outlines history of the American circus for the period 1875 to 1905); George A. Hamid's *Circus* (life of a circus family and proprietor); Alvin F. Harlow's *The Ringlings—Wizards of the Circus;* Charles T. Hunt, Sr.'s *The Story of Mr. Circus;* Dean Jensen's beautifully produced *The Biggest, The Smallest, The Longest, The Shortest,* on the history of Wisconsin's circus tradition; F. Beverly Kelley's "The Land of Sawdust and Spangles—A World in Miniature," "The Wonder City That Moves by Night," and *Denver Brown and the Traveling Town* (fictional but accurate account); John C. Kunzog's "Dan Rice Ledger Reveals Circus Conditions in 1870" and *Tanbark and Tinsel;* Albert Lee's "The Moving of a Modern Caravan"; Isaac F. Marcosson's "Sawdust and the Gold Dust, the Earnings of the Circus People"; Copeland MacAllister's "The First Successful Railroad Circus was in 1866"; Penelope Marguerite Leavitt's dissertation, "Spalding and Rogers' Floating Palace, 1852-1860"; George Middleton's *Circus Memories* (turn-of-the-century circus); Charles Theodore Murray's "On the Road with the Big Show"; Henry Ringling North's *The Circus King,* on the Ringling family; Esse F. O'Brien's *Circus: Cinders to Sawdust,* a hodge-podge of circus lore and history but useful on nineteenth-century circus; Bob Parkinson's "John Robinson Circus" (1836-1938); Fred D. Pfening, Jr.'s "The Big Show of the World—Sells Brothers Enormous United Shows," "Buck Jones Wild West and Round Up Days," and "The Frontier and the Circus"; Gene Plowden's *Those Amazing Ringlings and Their Circus,* the best source on the Ringlings; John F. Polacsek's "The Development of the Circus and Menagerie, 1825-1860" and "The Circus in New Orleans 1861-1865"; Alf T. Ringling's *Life Story of the Ringling Bros.* (published for promotional purposes); Dave Robeson's *Al G. Barnes, Master Showman, As Told By Al G. Barnes;* Gil Robinson's "The Circus Life in the Early Days" and *Old Wagon Show Days* (includes a list of traveling shows from 1865-1889 and a list of crews, 1857-1893); A. H. Saxon's "A Franconi in America: The New York Hippodrome of 1853"; J. J. Schlicher's "On the Trail of the Ringlings"; Charles Stow's "The Pioneers of 'The American Circus' "; C. G. Sturtevant's "The Circus in Philadelphia" (1700s to late nineteenth century); Bob Taber's "Ringling and Sells-Floto Battles" (rivalry from 1909); Harold C. Tedford's "Circuses in Northwest Arkansas Before the Civil War"; Stuart Thayer's *Mudshows and Railers: The American Circus in 1879,* "The Anti-Circus Laws in Connecticut 1773-1840," "The Geography of Early Show Movements," and "P. T. Barnum's Great Travelling Museum Menagerie, Caravan and Hippodrome"; Richard Thomas's undistinguished biography, *John Ringling;* William C. Thompson's *On the Road with a Circus* (by press agent with the Forepaugh Circus); Marcello and Massimiliano Truzzi's "Notes Toward a History of Juggling"; and Marian Hannah Winter's "The Prices—An Anglo-Continental Theatrical Dynasty" (from the eighteenth century to the present).

A large number of sources deal with various general aspects of the circus, including the parade and circus life. In addition to the historical sources listed above, the following are suggested, a large number of which are primarily pictorial in content: Boris Aronson's "The Circus"; the August 1931 issue of *Theatre Arts Monthly* devoted to the circus; *Circus!* with an introduction by Charles Fox; Maxwell Frederick Coplan and F. Beverly Kelley's *Pink Lemonade;* Claire H. Fawcett's *We Fell in Love with the Circus;* Charles Philip Fox's *A Ticket to the Circus* and *A Pictorial History of Performing Horses*; Fox and Tom Parkinson's *The Circus Moves by Rail*; Jill Freedman's *Circus Days* (photographic essay on the Beatty-Cole Circus); *Great Days of the Circus;* and Tom Maloney's *Circus Days and What Goes on Back of the Big Top.* The circus poster and the use of the press have received special attention; among the numerous sources the following are recommended: William Koford's "Old Time Billing Wars" (the John Robinson Circus versus the Sells-Floto Circus in 1920); Bob Parkinson's "The Circus and the Press"; Fred D. Pfening, Jr.'s "Circus Couriers of the Late 1800s"; Jack Rennert's superb collection of posters, many in color, *100 Years of Circus Posters,* a number of which have been reproduced in "When the Circus Comes to Town"; C. G. Sturtevant's "Opposition in Circus Press Writing"; and Charles Philip Fox's *American Circus Posters in Full Color* and *Old-Time Circus Cuts: A Pictorial Archive of 202 Illustrations.*

The special nature of the circus parade is covered by the following: Richard E. Conover's *Telescoping Tableaux* and "The European Influence on the American Circus Parade"; Charles Philip Fox's *Circus Parades: A Pictorial History of America's Pageant* and Fox's and F. Beverly Kelley's recent *The Great Circus Street Parade in Pictures;* Gene Plowden's *Singing Wheels and Circus Wagons* (largely pictorial); Bob Parkinson's "Circus Balloon Ascensions" (competition to the free parade); George Speaight's "The Origin of the Circus Parade Wagon"; and R. E. Conover's *The Fielding Band Chariots.*

Music of the circus has been treated in the following: Fred Dahlinger, Jr.'s "A Short Analysis of Steam Calliope History Before 1900"; Fred D. Pfening, Jr.'s "Circus Songsters"; Gene Plowden's *Merle Evans, Maestro of the Circus;* and Marcello Truzzi's "Folksongs of the American Circus." The American circus has frequently been the subject of fiction (such as James Otis's *Toby Tyler; or, Ten Weeks with a Circus,* Walter D. Edmonds's *Chad Hanna,* and West Lathrop's *River Circus*). Guides and studies of the circus in fiction include: Donald L. Hensey's "The Circus and the American Short Story"; Fred D. Pfening III's "The Circus in Fiction: An Interpretation"; Marcello Truzzi's "The American Circus as a Source of Folklore: An Introduction" (which includes discussions of the language and the music and songs of the circus); and Leonidas Westervelt's *The Circus in Literature: An Outline of Its Development and a Bibliography with Notes.*

A number of important or impressionistic sources do not fall easily into any general category but are worthy of serious consideration. Among the more impressionistic sources are: George Brinton Beal's *Through the Back Door of the Circus;* Charles Bernard's *Half Century Reviews and Red Wagon Stories;* Harry P. Bowman's *As Told on a Sunday Run;* Courtney Ryley Cooper's *Circus Day;* Rupert Croft-Cooke's *The Circus Book* and *The Circus Has No Home;* Croft-Cooke's and W. S. Meadmore's *The Sawdust Ring;* Tony Denier's *How to Join a Circus;* David Jamieson and Sandy Davidson's handsome new book *The Colorful World of the Circus*; Fred Powledge's *Mud Show: A Circus Season,* a fascinating account of a third-rate circus (the Hoxie Bros.) during the 1974 season; Alan Wykes's *Circus! An Investigation Into What Makes the Sawdust Fly;* David Lewis Hammarstrom's recent *Behind the Big Top,* which contains intriguing behind-the-scenes stories about circus performers, owners, and so forth, over the last fifty years; and Joseph Durso's *Madison Square Garden: 100 Years of History,* which includes the circus and Wild West show in the arena. Similar to Hammarstrom but less effective is Rhina Kirk's *Circus Heroes and Heroines.* Antony D. Hippisley Coxe's *A Seat at the Circus,* recently reissued in a revised edition, is one of the better books in English on the circus, including descriptions of typical circus acts, their history, and appeal.

A few scholarly treatments of the circus other than those by circus historians have begun to appear in recent years. A number of these are important sociological investigations, including Walter M. Gerson's "The Circus: A Mobile Total Institution"; Robert C. Sweet's "The Circus: An Institution in Continuity and Change"; Sweet's and Robert W. Habenstein's "Some Perspective on the Circus in Transition"; and Marcello Truzzi's "The Decline of the American Circus: The Shrinkage of an Institution" (see also his other essays discussed above). Paul Bouissac's *Circus & Culture: A Semiotic Approach,* although using European circuses as examples, suggests a unique semiotic method of analyzing the phenomenon of the circus as "a complex medium of mass communication."

The unique language of the circus is included in Sherman Louis Sergel's *The Language of Show Biz,* Don B. Wilmeth's *The Language of American Popular Entertainment,* and is dealt with explicitly in Bill Ballantine's "Circus Talk," Joe McKennon's *Horse Dung Trail* and *Circus Lingo,* George Milburn's "Circus Words," and David W. Maurer's "Carnival Cant: A Glossary of Circus and Carnival Slang." Other sources of circus terminology can be found in Wilmeth's glossary.

A few essays have dealt with various aspects of the circus operation that are not included above or concern the circus today. David Black's "Circus" considers the contemporary circus as a triumph over conditions as much as a spectacle and thus a metaphor for life; James Wilde's "The Circus: Escaping into the Past" reviews the contemporary Circus Vargas and its attempt to return to the traveling circus under canvas; Peter Angelo Simon's *Big Apple Circus* details the creation of a permanent one-ring circus in New York City and the country's first full-fledged circus school. Other miscellaneous essays of interest include Hartley Davis's "The Business Side of the Circus" (as of 1910); Karl Edwin Harriman's "Social Side of the Circus"; James A. Inciardi and David M. Pettersen's "Gaff Joints and Shell Games: A Century of Circus Grift"; "How the Circus Dodges the Railroad Blockage" (in 1918); H. E. Miller's "The Sanitation of a Large Circus" (1934 survey); and "Old Days of Sawdust and Spangles" (pre-1900 methods of training animals, the early clown, and accidents in the ring).

Of the many animal acts and individual or group acts of the circus, a great deal has been written. It should be added that many of these sources are chatty autobiographies or biographies and include little that cannot be found in the more reliable general histories and surveys. Specific sources on animal acts include the following: Edward Allen and F. Beverly Kelley, *Fun By the Ton* (one hundred and fifty years of elephants in the American circus); Joanne Joys, "The Wild Animal Trainer in America," a useful scholarly overview; Bill Ballantine, *Wild Tigers and Tame Fleas,* a good study and history of animals in the circus; Charly Baumann, *Tiger Tiger— My 25 Years with the Big Cats;* Clyde Beatty, *The Big Cage;* Frank Bostock, *The Training of Wild Animals,* on early methods of animal training; Paul A. Bouissac, "Myths vs. Rites: A Study of 'Wild' Animal Displays in Circuses and Zoos"; Courtney Ryley Cooper, *Lions 'n' Tigers 'n' Everything* and *With the Circus;* Alfred Court, *Wild Circus Animals* (life of a wild cat tamer) and *My Life With the Big Cats;* Damoo G. Dhotre, *Wild Animal Man;* John H. Glenroy, *Ins & Outs of Circus Life* (forty-two year career as a bareback rider); Lorenz Hagenbeck, *Animals Are My Life;* James L. Haley, "The Colossus of His Kind," on Jumbo, the elephant owned by Barnum; Heinrich Hediger, *Studies of the Psychology and Behavior of Captive Animals in Zoos and Circuses,* an important study of animal psychology; J. Y. Henderson, *Circus Doctor* (career of the chief veterinarian of the Ringling Brothers and Barnum & Bailey Circus); George Keller, *Here, Keller—Train This!;* Alex Kerr, *No Bar Between. Lion Tamer to Bertram Mills Circus* (an English lion tamer; little on the American circus); George "Slim" Lewis and Byron Fish, *I Loved Rogues: The Life of an Elephant Tramp;* Edwin P. Norwood, *The Other Side of the Circus* (good, accurate source) and *The Circus Menagerie,* Fred D. Pfening III, "William P. Hall" (career of a major supplier of circus and Wild West animals and equipment); Gene Plowden, *Gargantua, Circus Star of the Century* (life of the famous gorilla who died in 1949); Jake Posey, *Last of the Forty Horse Drivers,* a horse driver's career from the 1880s to 1937; Roman Proske, *Lions, Tigers and Me;* Ben Riker, *Pony Wagon Town, Along U.S. 1890;* Dave Robeson, *Louis Roth; Forty Years with Jungle*

Killers; J. A. Rowe's *California's Pioneer Circus* (memoirs of a nineteenth-century equestrian and horse trainer); Josephine DeMott Robinson, *The Circus Lady,* the autobiography of an equestrienne; Matthew Scott, *Autobiography of Jumbo's Keeper and Jumbo's Biography;* Henry Thetard, *Les Domteurs, ou La Menagerie des Origines a Nos Jours,* a history of animal trainers by the French circus performer-historian (international in scope); and Lucia Zora, *Sawdust and Solitude,* the life of an elephant trainer and performer.

The techniques of the circus performer are analyzed expertly by Hovey Burgess in "The Classification of Circus Technique" and *Circus Techniques* (juggling, equilibrium, and vaulting). Also useful, though dated, are Irving K. Pond's *A Day Under the Big Top: A Study in Life and Art* and *Big Top Rhythms,* and C. G. Sturtevant's "The Flying Act and Its Technique."

Of the numerous biographies, autobiographies, and essays on specific performers or classifications of circus acts, the following are recommended: Olga Bailey, *Mollie Bailey, The Circus Queen of the Southwest;* G. L. Banks, *Blondin, His Life and Performances* (life of the famous tightrope walker); E. J. Bateman, "Trouping in the Early Days" (on the career of John H. Glenroy, an early-nineteenth-century equestrian); Connie Clausen, *I Love You Honey, But the Season Is Over;* "Fall! Fall! Fall!" (a vivid description of Elvin Bale's "Giant Gyrating Gyro-Wheel" act); Richard Hubler, *The Cristianis;* Jill Krementz, *A Very Young Circus Flyer* and Fred Powledge, *Born on the Circus,* both juvenile books on young circus performers; David Lano, *A Wandering Showman, I* (life of a marionette impresario with the circus, 1887 to 1935); Herschel C. Logan, *Buckskin and Satin* (life of Texas Jack, or J. B. Omohundro, and his wife Mlle. Morlacchi); Ernest Schlee Millette, *The Circus That Was* (life of an acrobat); Cleveland Moffett, *Careers of Danger and Daring*; Charles R. Sherlock, "Risking Life for Entertainment," a wide ranging survey of death-defying circus turns; "Sit Down, Poppy, Sit Down" (life and death of Karl Wallenda); Robert Lewis Taylor, *Center Ring* (essays on circus people, most previously published in *The New Yorker*); Lowell Thomas, *Men of Daring;* and William R. Watson, *My Desire* (life of an armless circus performer).

Sources on or about circus clowns are legion; the term itself is quite ambiguous, thus the sources discussed below must be limited to those comic performers and performances associated with the world of the circus and not clowns in the broadest sense. A few of the sources included deal with European or internationally known clowns, although the focus here is on the American clown.

In the last decade a large number of surveys and histories of the clown have appeared, thus forming a major nucleus on the topic. The one most highly recommended source is John H. Towsen's *Clowns,* an important, documented study of the clown in its many forms. In addition, the following, though not consistently excellent, can be recommended: George Speaight, *The Book of Clowns,* superbly illustrated with a serviceable introduction to the history of circus clowns; Beryl Hugill, *Bring on the Clowns,* another recent survey with good illustrations but an inadequate survey when compared to Speaight or Towsen; and Lowell Swortzell, *Here Comes the Clowns: A Cavalcade of Comedy from Antiquity to the Present,* adequate but less useful than the other three. Other surveys, less inclusive, include: George Bishop, *The World of Clowns* (most impressive because of its illustrations); Douglas Newton, *Clowns;* Laurence Senelick and Bill Venne, *A Cavalcade of Clowns* (a succinct account of major clowns); and Felix Sutton, *The Book of Clowns,* a small book for juvenile readers. A recent scholarly study, Phyllis A. Rogers's "The American Circus Clown," provides a good discussion of the process by which one becomes a clown and gives an ethnographic description of the world and process from the clowns' point of view.

Various aspects of clowning can be found in the following: Paul A. R. Bouissac, "Clown Performances as Metasemiotic Texts," a linquistic analysis of clown performances; Lucille Horner Charles, "The Clown's Function," with a focus on the "primitive" clown; Brander Matthews, "The Clown in History, Romance and Drama"; George Speaight's "Some Comic Circus Entrees" and "A Note on Shakespearean Clowns"; and M. Willson Disher's standard work *Clowns and Pantomimes.*

The lives of famous clowns, especially early American clowns, are chronicled in the following: the life of America's first great clown, Dan Rice, is treated in Maria Ward Brown's *The Life of Dan Rice,* Don Carle Gillette's *He Made Lincoln Laugh: The Story of Dan Rice,* and John C. Kunzog's *The One-Horse Show. The Life and Times of Dan Rice.* Other early circus clowns are discussed in Robert J. Loeffler's "Biographies of Some of the Early Singing Clowns" and "The Clowns of Yesteryear"; F. P. Pitzer's "Gay Carusos of the Circus"; John Tyron's *The Old Clowns History;* and William F. Wallett's *The Public Life of W. F. Wallett, The Queen's Jester,* autobiography of the famous nineteenth-century talking clown.

The most worthwhile of the many clown biographies and autobiographies, including a number of international stars, are: *Behind the Greasepaint* by Coco the Clown or Nicholai Poliakoff; *Life's a Lark* by Grock or Adrian Wettach; *Clown* by Emmett Kelly, known as "Willie"; *Autobiography of a Clown,* the life of Jules Turnour, edited by Isaac F. Marcosson; and *Here We Are Again: Recollections of an Old Circus Clown* and *Hold Yer Hosses! The Elephants Are Coming* by Robert Edmund Sherwood.

Finally, although intended for children, Gladys Emerson Cook's *Circus Clowns on Parade* provides an introduction to twenty-three American clowns; Christopher Morley's *Pipefuls* provides an impressionistic view of

Ringling clowns at Madison Square Garden; Arnold Rattenbury, *The Story of English Clowning,* records some rare illustrations and commentary on English origins; Tristan Remy, in *Les Clowns* and *Entrees Clownesque,* has written what are considered classic works on clowns, although the focus is not the American clown. For a look at the decline of circus clowning in America, Earl Shipley's "Old Hand Looks at Clown Alley. Sees Decline of Clowning Art. Few Newcomers Fill Ranks" is enlightening.

Of prime significance in the study and research of the American circus are articles from circus periodicals. Among the sources discussed in this section, only a few of the many specialized essays have been included as representative. No attempt has been made to be exhaustive, and a number of superb sources have not been tapped here at all. For example, the *New York Clipper* for the latter half of the nineteenth century and *Billboard* for this century remain two major sources on the circus. Although quality and depth of contributions vary, essays in *Bandwagon,* the journal of the Circus Historical Society, provide useful glimpses at specific circuses and at limited time spans in circus history. Of less value are essays in *White Tops,* the journal of the Circus Fans Association of America, and in *Little Circus Wagon,* the journal of the Circus Model Builders Association. A superb international journal, and the most reliable of them all, is *Le Cirque dans l'Univers,* published for the Club du Cirque in France. Also useful on occasion is *Calliope,* published by the Clowns of America.

The major circus collections are: The Circus World Museum Library in Baraboo, Wisconsin, which has a collection especially rich in advertising materials (a helpful and colorful brochure, titled *Circus World Museum,* which includes a special sixteen-page section of colored reproductions, is available upon request); the Hertzberg Circus Collection in the San Antonio, Texas, Public Library (Main Annex), with extensive holdings of late nineteenth-century material; the Joe E. Ward Collection of circus memorabilia in the Hoblitzelle Theatre Arts Library at the University of Texas in Austin; the Illinois State University Circus and Related Arts Collection in Normal, Illinois, one of the better balanced collections in the United States (the guide by Robert Sokan was discussed at the beginning of this section); the McCaddon Collection in the Princeton University Library, which houses the working papers of the Barnum and Bailey Circus, circa 1890 to 1910; the New York Historical Society, which holds the Westervelt Collection of Barnum material, plus some items on the circus; the Ringling Museum of the Circus in Sarasota, Florida, a relatively minor but attractively displayed collection (for a guide and essay on the circus, see Mel Miller, *Ringling Museum of the Circus: The Circus and Its Relation to the History of the Circus);* and the Somers, New York, Historical Society, with materials on the early American circus from the area called the "cradle of the American circus." A brief guide to museums and collections can be found in John Papp's *Those Golden Years—The Circus*. Until recently the Circus Hall of Fame in Sarasota, Florida, included a well-displayed museum of the American circus, including a sideshow museum and a number of famous circus wagons, including the famed "Two Hemispheres." In 1980 the Hall of Fame was sold with plans of making it part of an entertainment hall of fame somewhere in the Orlando, Florida, area. As of this writing, I am unaware if these plans have been completed. Of related interest is the Barnum Institute of Science and History and the Tom Thumb Collection, included in the section on Barnum and the dime museum (chapter 5).

BIBLIOGRAPHY

BOOKS AND ARTICLES

Allen, Edward, and Kelley, F. Beverly. *Fun By the Ton*. New York: Hastings House, 1941.

Amidon, C. H. "Inside Ricketts' Circus with John Durang." *Bandwagon* 19 (May-June 1975):15-17.

_____. "A History of Circus Parades in America." *White Tops* 49, no. 3 (1976).

Aronson, Boris. "The Circus." *Theatre Arts Monthly* 21 (March 1937):216-26.

Bailey, Olga. *Mollie Bailey, The Circus Queen of the Southwest*. Dallas: Harben-Spotts, 1943.

Ballantine, Bill. "Circus Talk." *American Mercury* 76 (June 1953):21-25.

_____. *Wild Tigers and Tame Fleas*. New York and Toronto: Holt, Rinehart and Winston, 1958.

Banks, G. L. *Blondin, His Life and Performances*. London and New York: Routledge, Warne and Routledge, 1862.

Barton, Bob, as told to G. Ernest Thomas. *Old Covered Wagon Show Days*. New York: E. P. Dutton and Co., 1939.

Bateman, Dr. E. J. "The Origin of the Barnum and Bailey Circus." *Bandwagon* 6 (September 1956):7-9.

_____. "Trouping in the Early Days." *Bandwagon* 4 (March-April 1960):1-2, 14.

Baumann, Charly, with Leonard A. Stevens. *Tiger Tiger—My 25 Years With the Big Cats*. Chicago: Playboy Press, 1975.

Bayly, Charles, Jr. "The Circus: Say, Pa, Which Cage Is Barnum In?" *Theatre Arts Monthly* 15 (August 1931):655-58, 671-86, 691-99.

Beal, George Brinton. *Through the Back Door of the Circus*. Springfield, Mass.: McLoughlin and Reilly Co., 1938.

Beatty, Clyde, with Edward Anthony. *The Big Cage*. New York: Century Co., 1933.

Bernard, Charles. *Half Century Reviews and Red Wagon Stories*. N.p.: By the author, 1930.

Bishop, George. *The World of Clowns*. Los Angeles: Brooke House Publishers, 1976.

Black, David. "Circus." *Gallery* 7 (March 1979):23-24.

Bostock, E. H. *Menageries, Circuses and Theatres*. 1927. Reprint. New York: Benjamin Blom, 1972.

Bostock, Frank. *The Training of Wild Animals*. New York: Century Co., 1933.

Bouissac, Paul A. "Myths vs. Rites: A Study of 'Wild' Animal Displays in Circuses and Zoos." *Journal of Popular Culture* 6 (Winter 1972):607-14.

_____. "Clown Performances as Metasemiotic Texts." *Language Sciences,* no. 19 (February 1972), pp. 1-7.

_____. *Circus & Culture: A Semiotic Approach.* Bloomington and London: Indiana University Press, 1976.

Bowen, Elbert R. "The Circus in Early Rural Missouri." *Missouri Historical Review* 47 (October 1952):1-17.

_____. "The Circus in Early Rural Missouri." *Bandwagon* 9 (September-October 1965):12-17.

Bowman, Harry P. *As Told On a Sunday Run.* Flint, Mich.: Circus Research Foundation, 1942.

Braathen, Sverre O., and Braathen, Faye O. "Circus Monarchs." *Bandwagon* 14 (March-April 1970):4-17; 14 (May-June 1970):11-24; 16 (November-December 1972):4-8.

Bradbury, Joseph T. "Tom Mix Circus 1936 Coast to Coast Tour." *Bandwagon* 7 (April-May 1952):5-8.

_____. "The Coop & Lent Circus." *Bandwagon* 3 (May-June 1959):3-14.

_____. "Campbell-Bailey-Hutchinson Circus." *Bandwagon* 4 (May-June 1960): 3-9, 12-17.

_____. "The Rhoda Royal Circus, 1919-1922." *Bandwagon* 5 (May-June 1961):3-19.

_____. "A History of the Cole Bros. Circus 1935-40." *Bandwagon* 9 (May-June 1965):4-19; (July-August 1965):9-19; (September-October 1965):4-11; (November-December 1965):30-35; 10 (January-February 1966):15-25; 11 (March-April 1967):17-29; (July-August 1967):20-22; (September-October 1967:16-30; (November-December 1967):9-11.

Bradna, Fred, as told to Hartzell Spence. *The Big Top: My 40 Years with the Greatest Show on Earth.* New York: Simon and Schuster, 1952.

Brown, Maria Ward. *The Life of Dan Rice.* London Branch, N.Y.: By the author, 1901.

Burgess, Hovey. "The Classification of Circus Technique." *The Drama Review* 18 (March 1974):65-70.

_____. *Circus Techniques.* New York: Drama Book Specialists, 1976.

Carver, Gordon M. "Sells-Floto Circus 1906-1910." *Bandwagon* 18 (July-August 1974):4-13; "Sells-Floto Circus 1910 to 1913." 19 (July-August 1975):4-12; "Sells-Floto Circus 1914-1915." 19 (November-December):22-29; "Sells-Floto Circus 1916-1918." 20 (May-June 1976):4-12.

Charles, Lucille Horner. "The Clown's Function." *Journal of American Folklore* 58 (January-March 1945):25-34.

Chindahl, George L. *History of the Circus in America.* Caldwell, Idaho: Caxton Printers, 1959.

Chipman, Bert J. *Hey Rube.* Hollywood: Hollywood Print Shop, 1933.

Circus! Introduction by Charles Fox. New York: Hawthorn Books, 1964.

Circus World Museum. Baraboo, Wis.: Circus World Museum and Library, n.d.

Clapp, William W., Jr. *A Record of the Boston Stage.* 1853. Reprint. New York: Benjamin Blom, 1968.

Clarke, John S. *Circus Parade.* New York: Charles Scribner's Sons, 1936.

Clausen, Connie. *I Love You Honey, But the Season Is Over.* New York: Holt, Rinehart and Winston, 1961.

Clement, Herb. *The Circus, Bigger and Better Than Ever?* South Brunswick, N.J.: A. S. Barnes, 1974.

Coco the Clown [Nicholai Poliakoff]. *Behind My Greasepaint.* London and New York: Hutchinson and Co., 1950.

Conklin, George. *The Ways of the Circus, Being the Memories and Adventures of George Conklin, Tamer of Lions.* New York: Harper and Bros., 1921.

Conover, Richard E. *Telescoping Tableaux.* Xenia, Ohio: By the author, 1956.

_____. *The Affairs of James A. Bailey.* Xenia, Ohio: By the author, 1957.

_____. *The Great Forepaugh Show.* Xenia, Ohio: By the author, 1959.

_____. "The European Influence on the American Circus." *Bandwagon* 5 (July-August 1961):3-9.

_____. *Give 'Em a John Robinson.* Xenia, Ohio: By the author, 1965.

_____. *The Circus, Wisconsin's Unique Heritage.* Baraboo, Wis.: Circus World Museum, 1967.

_____. *The Fielding Band Chariots.* Xenia, Ohio: By the author, 1969.

Cook, Gladys Emerson. *Circus Clowns on Parade.* New York: Franklin Watts, 1956.

Cooper, Courtney Ryley. "The Big Show." *Century Magazine* 107 (December 1923):182-94.

_____. *Lions 'n' Tigers 'n' Everything.* Boston: Little, Brown and Co., 1924.

_____. *Under the Big Top.* Boston: Little, Brown and Co., 1929.

_____. *With the Circus.* Boston: Little, Brown and Co., 1930.

_____. *Circus Day.* New York: Farrar and Rinehart, 1931.

Coplan, Maxwell Frederick, and Kelley, F. Beverly. *Pink Lemonade.* New York: McGraw-Hill, 1945.

Coup, W. C. *Sawdust and Spangles: Stories and Secrets of the Circus.* Chicago: H. S. Stone and Co., 1901.

Court, Alfred. *Wild Circus Animals.* London: Burke, 1954.

_____. *My Life With the Big Cats.* New York: Simon and Schuster, 1955.

Cowell, Joseph. *Thirty Years Passed Among the Players in England and America.* 1844. Reprint. Hamden, Conn.: Archon Books (The Shoe String Press), 1979.

Coxe, Antony D. Hippisley. *A Seat at the Circus.* 1951. Revised edition. Hamden, Conn.: Archon Books (The Shoe String Press), 1980.

_____. "The Lesser-Known Circuses of London." *Theatre Notebook* 13 (Spring 1959):89-100.

_____. "Historical Research and the Circus." *Theatre Notebook* 21 (Autumn 1966):40-42.

Croft-Cooke, Rupert. *The Circus Book.* London: S. Low, Marston, [1948].

_____. *The Circus Has No Home.* Rev. ed. London: Falcon Press, 1950.

_____, and Cotes, Peter. *Circus: A World History.* New York: Macmillan Co., 1976.

_____, and Meadmore, W. S. *The Sawdust Ring.* London: Odhams Press, 1951.

Cushing, Charles Phelps. "Behind the Scenes at the Circus." *Independent,* 2 August 1919, pp. 156-58, 164-65.

Dahlinger, Fred, Jr. "A Short Analysis of Steam Calliope History Before 1900." *Bandwagon* 16 (November-December 1972):25-27.

Daum, Paul Alexander. "The Royal Circus 1782-1809: An Analysis of Equestrian Entertainments." Ph.D. dissertation, Ohio State University, 1973.

Davies, Ayres. "Wisconsin, Incubator of the American Circus." *Wisconsin Magazine of History,* 25 (March 1942):283-96.

Davis, Hartley. "The Business Side of the Circus." *Everybody's* 23 (June 1910): 118-28.

Decastro, Jacob. *The Memoirs of the Life of J. Decastro, Comedian.* Edited by R. Humphreys. London: Sherwood, Jones and Co., 1824.

Delavoye, Will. *Show Life in America.* East Point, Ga.: By the author, 1925.

Denier, Tony. *How to Join a Circus.* New York: Dick and Fitzgerald, 1877.

Dhotre, Damoo G., as told to Richard Taplinger. *Wild Animal Man.* Boston: Little, Brown and Co., 1961.

Disher, M. Willson. *Clowns and Pantomimes.* 1925. Reprint. New York and London: Benjamin Blom, 1968.

_____. *Greatest Show on Earth. Astley's—Afterwards Sanger's—Royal Amphitheatre of Arts, Westminster Bridge Road.* 1937. Reprint. New York: Benjamin Blom, 1969.

Dodd, William G. "Theatrical Entertainment in Early Florida." *Florida Historical Quarterly* 25 (October 1946):121-74.

Dressler, Albert, ed. *California's Pioneer Circus, Joseph Rowe, Founder. Memoirs and Personal Correspondence Relative to the Circus Business Through the Gold Country in the 50's.* San Francisco: H. S. Crocker Co., 1926.

Durang, John. *The Memoir of John Durang. (American Actor, 1795-1816).* Edited by Alan S. Downer. Pittsburgh: University of Pittsburgh Press, 1966.

Durant, John, and Durant, Alice. *Pictorial History of the American Circus.* New York: A. S. Barnes and Co., 1957.

Durso, Joseph. *Madison Square Garden: 100 Years of History.* New York: Simon and Schuster, 1979.

Edmonds, Walter D. *Chad Hanna.* Boston: Little, Brown and Co., 1940.

Elbirn, William L. "Austin Bros. 3 Ring Circus and Real Wild West." *Bandwagon* 6 (January-February 1962):12-17.

"Fall! Fall! Fall!" *Time,* 26 April 1979, pp. 85-86.

Fawcett, Claire H. *We Fell in Love with the Circus.* New York: H. L. Lindquist, 1949.

Fawcett, James Waldo. "The Circus in Washington [D.C.]." *Records of the Columbia Society* 50 (1948-1050):265-72.

Fellows, Dexter W. and Freeman, Andrew A. *This Way to the Big Show: The Life of Dexter Fellows.* New York: Viking Press, 1936.

Fenner, Mildred S. and Fenner, Wolcott, eds. and comps. *The Circus: Lure and Legend.* Englewood Cliffs, N.J.: Prentice-Hall, 1970.

Field, A. G. *Watch Yourself Go By.* Columbus, Ohio: Spaar and Glenn, 1912.

Flint, Richard W. "Rufus Welch: America's Pioneer Circus Showman." *Bandwagon* 14 (September-October 1970):4-11.

_____. "A Selected Guide to Source Material on the American Circus." *Journal of Popular Culture* 6 (Winter 1972):615-19.

_____. "The Evolution of the Circus in Nineteenth-Century America." In *American Popular Entertainment,* edited by Myron Matlaw. Westport, Conn. and London: Greenwood Press, 1979.

Fowler, Gene. *Timber Line.* New York: Covici Friede Publishers, 1933.

Fox, Charles Philip. *Circus Parades: A Pictorial History of America's Pageant.* Watkins Glen, N.Y.: Century House, 1953.

_____. *A Ticket to the Circus.* New York: Bramhall House, 1959.

_____. *A Pictorial History of Performing Horses.* New York: Bramhall House, 1960.

_____, ed. *American Circus Posters in Full Color.* New York: Dover Publications, 1978.

_____, ed. *Old-Time Circus Cuts: A Pictorial Archive of 202 Illustrations.* New York: Dover Publications, 1979.

_____, and Kelley, F. Beverly. *The Great Circus Street Parade in Pictures.* New York: Dover Publications, 1978.

_____, and Parkinson, Tom. *Circus in America.* Waukesha, Wis.: Country Beautiful, 1969.

_____. *The Circus Moves by Rail.* Boulder, Colo.: Pruett, 1978.

Freedman, Jill. *Circus Days.* New York: Crown Publishers (Harmony Books), 1975.

Frost, Thomas. *Circus Life and Circus Celebrities.* 1875. Reprint. Detroit: Singing Tree Press, 1970.

Gerson, Walter M. "The Circus: A Mobile Total Institution." In *Social Problems in a Changing World: A Comparative Reader,* edited by Walter M. Gerson. New York: Thomas Y. Crowell Co., 1969.

Gillette, Don Carle. *He Made Lincoln Laugh: The Story of Dan Rice.* New York: Exposition Press, 1967.

Glenroy, John H. *Ins & Outs of Circul Life.* Compiled by Stephen S. Stanford. Boston: M. M. Wing, 1885.

Gollmar, Robert H. *My Father Owned a Circus.* Caldwell, Idaho: Caxton Printers, 1965.

Le Grand Livre Du Cirque. Edited by Monica J. Renevey. 2 vols. Geneva: Edito-Servize, 1977.

Great Days of the Circus. New York: American Heritage Publishing Co., 1962.

Greenwood, Isaac J. *The Circus: Its Origins and Growth Prior to 1835.* 2d ed. with additions. New York: William Abbatt, 1909.

Grock. [Adrian Wettach]. *Life's A Lark.* Edited by E. Behrens. Translated by Madge Pemberton. London: W. Heinemann, 1931.

Hagenbeck, Lorenz. *Animals Are My Life.* Translated by Alec Brown, London: Bodley Head, 1956.

Haley, James L. "The Colossus of His Kind." *American Heritage* 24 (August 1973): 62-68, 82-85.

Hallock, E. S. "The American Circus." *Century Magazine* 70 (August 1905):568-85.

Hamid, George A., as told to his son George A. Hamid, Jr. *Circus.* New York: Sterling Publishing Co., 1950.

Hammarstrom, David Lewis. *Behind the Big Top*. South Brunswick, N.J. and New York: A.S. Barnes and Co., 1980.

Harlow, Alvin F. *The Ringlings—Wizards of the Circus*. New York: Julian Messner, 1951.

Harriman, Karl Edwin. "Social Side of the Circus." *Cosmopolitan* 41 (July 1906): 209-18.

Hediger, H. *Studies of the Psychology and Behavior of Captive Animals in Zoos and Circuses*. New York: Criterion Books, 1955.

Henderson, J. Y., as told to Richard Taplinger. *Circus Doctor*. Boston: Little, Brown and Co., 1952.

Hensey, Donald L. "The Circus and the American Short Story." *Bandwagon* 18 (July-August 1974):14-15.

"How the Circus Dodges the Railroad Blockade." *Literary Digest,* 16 March 1918, pp. 87-88.

Hubler, Richard. *The Cristianis*. Boston: Little, Brown and Co., 1966.

Hugill, Beryl. *Bring on the Clowns*. Seacaucus, N.J.: Chartwell Books, 1980.

Hunt, Charles T., Sr. as told to John C. Cloutman. *The Story of Mr. Circus*. Rochester, N.H.: Record Press, 1954.

Inciardi, James A., and Petersen, David M. "Gaff Joints and Shell Games: A Century of Circus Grift." *Journal of Popular Culture* 6 (Winter 1972): 591-606.

Jamieson, David, and Davidson, Sandy. *The Colorful World of the Circus*. London: Octopus Books, 1980.

Jando, Dominique. *Histoire Modiale Du Cirque*. Paris: Jean-Pierre Delange, 1977.

Jennings, John J. *Theatrical and Circus Life; or, Secrets of the Stage, Greenroom and Sawdust Arena*. St. Louis: Herbert and Cole, 1882.

Jensen, Dean. *The Biggest, The Smallest, The Longest, The Shortest*. Madison: Wisconsin House Book Publishers, 1975.

Joys, Joanne. "The Wild Animal Trainer in America." Master's thesis, University of Toledo, 1980.

Keller, George. *Here, Keller—Train This*. New York: Random House, 1961.

Kelley, Francis Beverly. "The Land of Sawdust and Spangles—A World in Miniature." *National Geographic* 60 (October 1931):463-516.

_____. "The Wonder City That Moves by Night." *National Geographic* 93 (March 1948):289-305.

_____. *Denver Brown and the Traveling Town*. New York: Exposition Press, 1966.

Kelly, Emmett, with F. Beverly Kelley. *Clown*. New York: Prentice-Hall, 1954.

Kerr, Alex. *No Bar Between. Lion Tamer to Bertram Mills Circus*. New York: Appleton-Century-Crofts, 1957.

Kirk, Rhina. *Circus Heroes and Heroines*. [Maplewood, N.J.]: Hammond, 1972.

Koford, William. "Old Time Billing Wars." *Bandwagon* 2 (May-June 1958):7.

Krementz, Jill. *A Very Young Circus Flyer*. New York: Alfred A. Knopf, 1979.

Kunzog, John C. "Dan Rice Ledger Reveals Circus Conditions in 1870." *Bandwagon* 5 (June 1954):6-9.

_____. *The One-Horse Show. The Life and Times of Dan Rice*. Jamestown, N.Y.: By the author, 1962.

_____. *Tanbark and Tinsel.* Jamestown, N.Y.: By the author, 1970.

Lano, David. *A Wandering Showman, I.* East Lansing: Michigan State University Press. 1957.

Lathrop, West. *River Circus.* New York: Random House, 1953.

Leavitt, Penelope Marguerite. "Spalding and Rogers' Floating Palace, 1852-1860." Ph.D. dissertation, Washington State University, 1979.

Lee, Albert, "The Moving of a Modern Caravan." *Harper's Weekly* 39 (25 May 1895):493-95.

Lehman, Rolf. *Circus: Magie der Manege.* Hamburg: Hoffmann und Campe, 1979.

Lewis, George "Slim," and Fish, Byron. *I Loved Rogues: The Life of an Elephant Tramp.* Seattle: Superior Publishing Co., 1978.

Loeffler, Dr. Robert J. "Biographies of Some of the Early Singing Clowns." *Bandwagon* 13 (September-October 1969):16-23.

_____. "The Clowns of Yesteryear." *Bandwagon* 18 (September-October 1974): 19-22.

Logan, Herschel C. *Buckskin and Satin.* Harrisburg, Pa.: Stackpole Co., 1954.

MacAllister, Copeland. "The First Successful Railroad Circus was in 1866." *Bandwagon* 19 (July-August 1975):14-16.

McKennon, Joe. *Horse Dung Trail: Saga of American Circus.* Sarasota, Fla.: Carnival Publishers of Sarasota, 1975.

_____. *Circus Lingo.* Sarasota, Fla.: Carnival Publishers of Sarasota, 1980.

Maloney, Tom. *Circus Days and What Goes on Back of the Big Top.* Philadelphia: Edward Stern, 1934.

Marcosson, Isaac F. "Sawdust and the Gold Dust, the Earnings of the Circus People." *Bookman* 31 (June 1910):402-10.

_____. ed. *Autobiography of a Clown.* Foreword by Alfred T. Ringling. New York: Moffatt, Yard and Co., 1910.

Matthews, Brander. "The Clown in History, Romance and Drama." *Mentor* 12 (December 1924):3-17.

Maurer, David W. "Carnival Cant: Glossary of Circus and Carnival Slang." *American Speech* 6 (June 1931):327-37.

May, Earl Chapin. *The Circus From Rome to Ringling.* 1932. Reprint. New York: Dover Publications, 1963.

Middleton, George. "Circus Words." *American Mercury* 24 (November 1931): 351-54.

_____, as told to and written by his wife. *Circus Memories.* Los Angeles: Geo. Rice and Sons, 1913.

Milhurn, George "Circus Words." *American Mercury* 24 (November 1931):351-54.

Miller, H. E. "The Sanitation of a Large Circus." *American Journal of Public Health* 26 (November 1936): 1106-12.

Miller, Mel. *Ringling Museum of the Circus: The Circus and Its Relation to the History of the Circus.* Sarasota, Fla.: John and Mable Ringling Museum of Art, 1963.

Millette, Ernest Schlee, as told to Robert Wyndham. *The Circus That Was.* Philadelphia: Dorrance and Co., 1971.

Moffett, Cleveland. *Careers of Danger and Daring.* New York: Century Co., 1906.

Morley, Christopher. *Pipefuls.* New York: Doubleday and Co., 1924.

Moy, James S. "John B. Ricketts' Circus 1793-1800." Ph.D. dissertation, University of Illinois, 1977.

_____. "Entertainments at John B. Ricketts's Circus, 1793-1800." *Educational Theatre Journal* 30 (May 1978):186-202.

_____. "A Checklist of Circus Buildings Constructed by John B. Ricketts." *Bandwagon* 22, no. 5 (1978).

_____. "The Greenwich Street Theatre 1797-1799." *Theatre Survey* 20 (November 1979):15-26.

Murray, Charles Theodore. "In Advance of the Circus." *McClure's* 3 (August 1894):252-60.

_____. "On the Road with the Big Show." *Cosmopolitan* 29 (June 1900):115-28.

Murray, Marian. *Circus! From Rome to Ringling.* New York: Appleton, Century, Crofts, 1956.

Newton, Douglas. *Clowns.* New York: Franklin Watts, 1957.

North, Henry Ringling, and Hatch, Alden. *The Circus Kings.* Garden City, N.Y.: Doubleday and Co., 1960.

Norwood, Edwin P. *The Other Side of the Circus.* Garden City, N.Y.: Doubleday and Co., 1926.

_____. *The Circus Menagerie.* Garden City, N.Y.: Doubleday and Co., 1929.

O'Brien, Esse F. *Circus: Cinders to Sawdust.* San Antonio: Naylor, 1959.

"Old Days of Sawdust and Spangles." *Literary Digest* 55 (18 August 1917):50, 53.

Otis, James. *Toby Tyler: Or, Ten Weeks with a Circus.* New York: Harper Brothers. 1881.

Papp, John. *Those Golden Years—The Circus.* Schenectady, N.Y.: John Papp, 1971.

Parkinson, Bob. "Circus Balloon Ascensions." *Bandwagon* 5 (March-April 1961): 3-6.

_____. "John Robinson Circus." *Bandwagon* 6 (March-April 1962):4-8.

_____. "The Circus and the Press." *Bandwagon* 7 (March-April 1963):3-9.

Pfening, Fred D., Jr. "Circus Couriers of the Late 1800s." *Bandwagon* 3 (January-February 1959):3-4.

_____. "Circus Songsters." *Bandwagon* 7 (November-December 1963):10-12.

_____. "The Big Show of the World—Sells Brothers Enormous United Shows." *Bandwagon* 8 (January-February 1964):4-15.

_____. "Buck Jones Wild West and Round Up Days." *Bandwagon* 9 (November-December 1965):25-28.

_____. "The Frontier and the Circus." *Bandwagon* 15 (September-October 1971): 16-20.

Pfening, Fred D. III. "William P. Hall." *Missouri Historical Review* 42 (April 1968):286-313.

_____. "The Circus in Fiction: An Interpretation." *Bandwagon* 16 (March-April 1972):14-19.

Pitzer, F. P. "Gay Carusos of the Circus." *Etude* (October 1942):676, 707.

Plowden, Gene. *Those Amazing Ringlings and Their Circus.* New York: Bonanza Books, 1967.

_____. *Merle Evans, Maestro of the Circus*. Miami, Fla.: E. A. Seemann Publishing, 1971.

_____. *Gargantua, Circus Star of the Century*. New York: Bonanza, 1972.

_____. *Singing Wheels and Circus Wagons*. Caldwell, Idaho: Caxton Printers, 1977.

Polacsek, John F. "The Development of the Circus and Menagerie, 1825-1860." Thesis, Bowling Green State University, 1974.

_____. "The Circus in New Orleans 1861-1865." *Bandwagon* 20 (September-October 1976):4-7.

Pond, Irving K. *A Day Under the Big Top: A Study in Life and Art*. Chicago: Chicago Literary Club, 1934.

_____. *Big Top Rhythms*. New York: Willet, Clark and Co., 1937.

Posey, Jake. *Last of the Forty Horse Drivers*. New York: Vantage Press, 1959.

Powledge, Fred. *Mud Show: A Circus Season*. New York and London: Harcourt Brace Jovanovich, 1975.

_____. *Born on the Circus*. New York and London: Harcourt Brace Jovanovich, 1976.

Proske, Roman. *Lions, Tigers and Me*. New York: Henry Holt and Co., 1956.

Rattenbury, Arnold. *The Story of English Clowning*. Nottingham, England: Nottingham Castle Museum, 1977.

Remy, Tristan. *Les Clowns*. Paris: Bernard Grasset, 1945.

_____. *Entrees Clownesque*. Paris: L'Archie, 1962.

Rennert, Jack. *100 Years of Circus Posters*. New York: Darien House, 1974.

Reynolds, Chang. *Pioneer Circuses of the West*. Los Angeles: Westernlore Press, 1966.

Riker, Ben. *Pony Wagon Town, Along U.S. 1890*. Indianapolis: Bobbs-Merrill Co., 1948.

Ringling, Alf T. *Life Story of the Ringling Bros*. Chicago: R. R. Donnelley and Sons, 1900.

Robeson, Dave. *Al G. Barnes, Master Showman, As Told by Al G. Barnes*. Caldwell, Idaho: Caxton Printers, 1935.

_____. *Louis Roth; Forty Years with Jungle Killers*. Caldwell, Idaho: Caxton Printers, 1941.

Robinson, Gil. "The Circus Life in the Early Days." *Billboard,* 9 December 1911, pp. 22, 72.

_____. *Old Wagon Show Days*. Cincinnati: Brockwell Publishers, 1925.

Robinson, Josephine DeMott. *The Circus Lady*. New York: Thomas Y. Crowell Co., 1925.

Rogers, Phyllis A. "The American Circus Clown." Ph.D. dissertation, Princeton University, 1979.

Rowe, J. A. *California's Pioneer Circus*. Edited by Albert Dressler. San Francisco: H. S. Crocker and Co., 1926.

Saxon, A. H. *Enter Foot and Horse: A History of Hippodrama in England and France*. New Haven: Yale University Press, 1968.

_____. "A Franconi in America: The New York Hippodrome of 1853." *Bandwagon* 19 (September-October 1975):13-17.

_____. *The Life and Art of Andrew Ducrow & The Romantic Age of the English*

Circus. Hamden, Conn.: Archon Books (The Shoe String Press), 1978.

Schlicher, J. J. "On the Trail of the Ringlings." *Wisconsin Magazine of History* 26 (September 1942):8-22.

Scott, Matthew. *Autobiography of Jumbo's Keeper and Jumbo's Biography.* Bridgeport, Conn.: Matthew Scott and Thomas E. Lowe, 1885.

Senelick, Laurence, and Venne, Bill. *A Cavalcade of Clowns.* San Francisco: Bellerophon Books, 1977.

Sergel, Sherman Louis, ed. *The Language of Show Biz.* Chicago: Dramatic Publishing Co., 1973.

Sherlock, Charles R. "Risking Life for Entertainment." *Cosmopolitan* 35 (October 1903):613-26.

Sherwood, Robert Edmund. *Here We Are Again: Recollections of an Old Circus Clown.* Indianapolis: Bobbs-Merrill Co., 1926.

_____. *Hold Yer Hosses! The Elephants Are Coming.* New York: Macmillan Co., 1932.

Shipley, Earl. "Old Hand Looks at Clown Alley. Sees Decline of Clowning Art. Few Newcomers Fill Ranks." *Billboard,* 29 November 1952, pp. 79, 111.

Simon, Peter Angelo. *Big Apple Circus.* New York: Penguin Books. 1978.

Soken, Robert *A Descriptive and Bibliographic Catalog of the Circus and Related Arts Collection at Illinois State University, Normal, Illinois.* Bloomington, Ill.: Scarlet Ibis Press, 1975.

"Sit Down, Poppy, Sit Down." *Time,* 3 April 1978, p. 27.

Speaight, George. "Some Comic Circus Entrees." *Theatre Notebook* 32, no. 1 (1978):24-27.

_____. "The Origin of the Circus Parade Wagon." In *American Popular Entertainment,* edited by Myron Matlaw. Westport, Conn. and London: Greenwood Press, 1979.

_____. "A Note on Shakespeare and Clowns." *Nineteenth-Century Theatre Research* 7 (Autumn 1979):93-98.

_____. *The Book of Clowns.* New York: Macmillan Co., 1980.

_____. *A History of the Circus.* San Diego and New York: A. S. Barnes and Co., 1980.

Stow, Charles. "The Pioneers of 'The American Circus.' " *Theatre Magazine* 5 (August 1905):192-94.

Sturtevant, Col. C. G. "The Flying Act and Its Technique." *White Tops* 6 (May 1932):4, 6.

_____. "Opposition in Circus Press Writing." *White Tops* 18 (November-December 1945):5-9.

_____. "The Circus in Philadelphia." *White Tops* 22 (November-December 1949): 3-9.

Sutton, Felix. *The Book of Clowns.* New York: Grosset and Dunlap, [1966].

_____. *The Big Show: A History of the Circus.* Garden City, N.Y.: Doubleday and Co., 1971.

Sweet, Robert C. "The Circus: An Institution in Continuity and Change." Ph.D. dissertation, University of Missouri, 1970.

_____, and Habenstein, Robert W. "Some Perspective on the Circus in Transition." *Journal of Popular Culture* 6 (Winter 1972):583-90.

Swortzell, Lowell. *Here Comes the Clowns: A Cavalcade of Comedy from Antiquity to the Present.* Illustrated by C. Walter Hodges. New York: Viking Press, 1978.

Taber, Bob. "Ringling and Sells-Floto Battles." *Bandwagon* 3 (March-April 1959):13.

Taylor, Robert Lewis. *Center Ring.* Garden City, N.Y.: Doubleday and Co., 1956.

_____. "Talker." *New Yorker,* 19 April 1958, p. 47; 26 April 1958, p. 39.

Tedford, Harold C. "Circuses in Northwest Arkansas Before the Civil War." *Arkansas Historical Quarterly* 26 (Autumn 1967):244-56.

Thayer, Stuart. *Mudshows and Railers: The American Circus in 1879.* Ann Arbor, Mich.: Privately printed, 1971.

_____. "The Geography of Early Show Movements." *Bandwagon* 17 (January-February 1973):12-13.

_____. "The Anti-Circus Laws in Connecticut 1773-1840." *Bandwagon* 20 (January-February 1976):18-20.

_____. "P. T. Barnum's Great Travelling Museum, Menagerie, Caravan and Hippodrome." *Bandwagon* 20 (July-August 1976):4-9.

_____. *Annals of the American Circus 1793-1829.* Manchester, Mich.: Rymack Printing Co., 1976.

Theatre Arts Monthly 15 (August 1931): Entire issue.

Thetard, Henry. *Les Domteurs, ou La Menagerie des Origines a Nos Jours.* Paris: Librairie Gallimard, 1928.

_____. *La Marveilleuse Histoire du Cirque.* 2 vols. Paris: Prisma, 1947.

Thomas, Lowell. *Men of Daring.* New York: Grosset and Dunlap Publishers, 1936.

Thomas, Richard. *John Ringling.* New York: Pageant Press, 1960.

Thompson, William C. *On the Road with a Circus.* N.p.: Goldmann, 1903.

Toole-Stott, Raymond. *Circus and Allied Arts, A World Bibliography.* 4 vols. Derby, England: Harpur, 1958-71.

_____. *A Bibliography of the Books on the Circus in English From 1773 to 1964.* Derby, England: Harpur, 1964.

Towsen, John H. *Clowns.* New York: Hawthorn Books, 1976.

Truzzi, Marcello. "The American Circus as a Source of Folklore: An Introduction." *Southern Folklore Quarterly* 30 (December 1966):289-300.

_____. "Folksongs of the American Circus." *New York Folklore Quarterly* 24 (September 1968):163-75.

_____. "The Decline of the American Circus: The Shrinkage of an Institution." In *Sociology and Everyday Life,* edited by Marcello Truzzi. Englewood Cliffs, N.J.: Prentice-Hall, 1968.

_____, ed. "Circuses, Carnivals and Fairs in America." *Journal of Popular Culture* 6 (Winter 1972):531-619.

_____. "Circus and Side Shows." In *American Popular Entertainment,* edited by Myron Matlaw. Westport, Conn. and London: Greenwood Press, 1979.

_____, with Truzzi, Massimiliano. "Notes Toward a History of Juggling." *Bandwagon* 18 (March-April 1974):4-7.

Tuttle, George Palliser. "The History of the Royal Circus, Equestrian and Phil-harmonic Academy, 1782-1816, St. George's Fields, Surrey, England." Ph.D. dissertation, Tufts University, 1972.

Tyron, John. *The Old Clown's History.* New York: Torrey Bros., 1872.

Vail, R.W.G. "The Early Circus in America." *Proceedings of the American Antiquarian Society,* N.S., 43 (April 1933):116-85. Reprint. Barre, Mass.: Barre *Gazette,* 1956.

————. "This Way to the Big Top." *New York Historical Society Bulletin* 29 (July 1945):137-59. Reprint. New York: New York Historical Society, 1953.

Verney, Peter, *Here Comes the Circus.* New York and London: Paddington Press (distributed by Grosset and Dunlap), 1978.

Wallett, William F. *The Public Life of W. F. Wallett, The Queen's Jester.* Edited by John Luntley. London: Bemrose and Sons, 1870.

Watson, William R. *My Desire.* Toronto: Macmillan Co. of Canada, 1936.

Westervelt, Leonidas. *The Circus in Literature: An Outline of its Development and a Bibliography with Notes.* New York: Privately printed, 1931.

"When the Circus Comes to Town." *Reader's Digest* 116 (July 1980):148-56.

Wilde, James "The Circus: Escaping into the Past." *Time,* 24 May 1976, p. 18.

Wilmeth, Don B., ed. *American and English Popular Entertainment: A Guide to Information Sources.* Detroit: Gale Research Co., 1980.

————. *The Language of American Popular Entertainment: A Glossary of Argot, Slang, and Terminology.* Westport, Conn. and London: Greenwood Press, 1981.

Winter, Marian Hannah. "The Prices—An Anglo-Continental Theatrical Dynasty." *Theatre Notebook* 28, no. 3 (1974):117-23.

Wykes, Alan. *Circus! An Investigation Into What Makes the Sawdust Fly.* London: Jupiter Books, 1977.

Zora, Lucia. *Sawdust and Solitude.* Edited by Courtney Ryley Cooper. Boston: Little, Brown and Co., 1928.

SELECT PERIODICALS AND SERIALS

Bandwagon. Columbus, Ohio. 1951- .

Billboard. Cincinnati, Ohio. 1894-1960.

Calliope. Baltimore, Maryland. Frequency varies.

Le Cirque dans l'Univers. Vincennes, France. 1950- .

Little Circus Wagon. Portland, Maine.

New York Clipper. New York. 1853-1924.

White Tops. Indianapolis, Indiana. 1928- .

CHAPTER 4

The Wild West Exhibition

HISTORICAL SUMMARY

The so-called Wild West show is invariably and undeniably associated with William Frederick "Buffalo Bill" Cody, who found the association of his enterprise with that of the circus or the use of the word "show" anathema. His billing was most frequently "Buffalo Bill's Wild West," without the "show," and, if pressed, his flamboyant press agent, John M. Burke, would insist that it was an exhibition. In its most ideal form, then, a Wild West show may be defined as an exhibition illustrating scenes and events characteristic of the American Far West frontier. The myth of Cody and his Wild West exhibition continues to the present day, despite efforts to demythologize the legend in Arthur Kopit's play *Indians* and Robert Altman's film adaptation, as well as in recent essays by William Brasmer.

The exact origin of the Wild West show is difficult to pinpoint. Cody, his early manager, Nate Salsbury, and his early partner, Dr. William F. Carver, who billed himself as the "Champion Shot of the World," each claimed to have originated the idea for such an entertainment. In actuality, the Wild West show was an amalgamation and culmination of several early traditions, beginning with the nineteenth-century tradition of exhibiting Indian activities and artifacts. As early as 1827 a group of Iroquois Indians were presented at Peale's Museum in New York, and Barnum got on the Indian bandwagon by 1841. Philadelphia had seen an Indian gallery operated by George Catlin even earlier. Other assorted exhibitions of cowboy skills and Indians date from the 1820s. In 1843 a herd of yearling buffalo was exhibited in New York, via Boston, where the same herd had been exhibited at the celebration dedicating the Bunker Hill monument. Tyler's Indian Exhibition toured in 1855 with Van Amburgh's Menagerie and Den Stone's Circus and in 1856 with Mabie Bros. Menagerie and Den Stone. James Capen Adams, better known as Grizzly Adams, assembled a menagerie of western animals in 1860.

As early as 1869, bronco-busting and various cowboy activities had been featured at exhibitions in Colorado and Wyoming. In 1872 Wild Bill Hickok appeared in a staged Buffalo hunt at Niagara Falls, his only foray into a Wild West show.

The Wild West show, then, owed a great deal to these early exhibitions of western activities and animals. It also evolved in part from the "specs" (or spectacular pageants) of the early American circus and the old traveling menageries. Certainly the numerous plays, novels, and cheap popular literature of the nineteenth century contributed to this entertainment tradition. The rodeo, which can be traced to the byplay and show-off of early cattle roundups, is related in part to the Wild West exhibition, insofar as a traveling rodeo with hired contestants would fit a common definition; yet the rodeo is normally a competitive sport in which the contestants pay an entrance fee and receive no pay except prize money. The kinship between the rodeo and the Wild West show, although they share a common beginning in terms of popularity, should not be stressed.

P. T. Barnum, who bought the herd of buffalo displayed in New York in 1843, deserves credit for the first organized Wild West exhibition. In 1874, as the concluding "spec" of the circus performance at the new Hippodrome in New York, Barnum presented an extravaganza billed as a "thrilling arenic contest" and titled *Indian Life or a Chance for a Wife.* During the same season William Cody was performing at the Bowery Theatre in *Scouts of the Prairie,* one of several mediocre border melodramas in which he appeared on and off for ten seasons, dramatizing the escapades of his career in the border states while serving as Indian scout, buffalo hunter, and frontiersman. If Cody did not see Barnum's presentation, he was certainly aware of it.

Despite Barnum's pioneer effort, most historians of the Wild West show still credit Cody with the consolidation and popularization of this form of outdoor entertainment. In the summer of 1882 Cody returned to his home of North Platte, Nebraska, where he was conjoled into planning the "Old Glory Blow-Out," a Fourth of July celebration of cowboy skill acts climaxed by a buffalo hunt in which Cody demonstrated with blank ammunition his methods of killing buffalo. The exhibition was staged in an open arena, actually a race track, with a fence surrounding it; 1,000 cowboy entrants competed for prizes in roping, shooting, riding, and bronco breaking. This date in 1882, then, marks the upsurge of both the

Wild West show and the rodeo, although it does not mark the first performances of either, as has been demonstrated. What was new in Cody's
Wild West exhibition was the combination that spelled success. In its
ultimate form, Cody's Wild West became a dominant form of outdoor
amusement, reaching its peak of popularity around 1893.

Cody's Wild West was on the upswing in 1883. Initially his operation was
not very successful, although it spawned a host of imitators. With the aid
of Nate Salsbury, who joined Cody in 1884, and Dr. William F. Carver
(the dentist/sharpshooter), whom he met in 1882-1883, Cody, who was not
a consummate showman, began to experience phenomenal success. With
the puffed releases of his colorful press agent-manager, "Arizona" or
"Major" John M. Burke, Cody's show became the epitome of the romanticized and glamourized American West, particularly in Europe, where
Cody made several successful tours. To Europeans, the Wild West show
represented a faraway land of romance and adventure. Audiences in
Europe and America flocked to see a dime novel hero whose record as
an Indian scout and Western pioneer was actually more impressive than his
press agent ever bothered to discover. Apparently this never bothered Cody,
who, according to most evidence, did not take himself very seriously
either.

In its ultimate form, Cody's show offered as many as eighteen events:
displays of horsemanship, "cowboy fun," shooting, buffalo hunts, capture
of the Deadwood Mail Coach by Indians, races, and other types of pageantry,
all culminating in a staged finale similar to the circus "spec," usually
depicting some historical or legendary event such as Custer's Last Stand or
the Battle of the Little Big Horn. Cody, who functioned in part in the
exhibition as a kind of master of ceremonies, surrounded himself with
talented performers or personages of notoriety. At various times Cody
featured notable personalities including Captain Adam H. Bogardus,
billed as the "Champion Pigeon Shot of America"; Gordon William Lillie,
later known as Major Lillie, Pawnee Bill, and "the White Chief of the
Pawnees"; Johnny Baker, the "Cowboy Kid"; Buck Taylor, soon known
as "King of the Cowboys"; Annie Oakley, dubbed by Sitting Bull "Little
Sure Shot"; and Chief Sitting Bull himself, who, despite Kopit's and
Altman's implications otherwise, got along well with Cody during his brief
stay with Cody's show.

For a brief time, roughly from 1886 to 1893, Cody's entertainment
attempted to give the exhibition some semblance of dramatic coherence,
although in reality the basic format did not vary much for almost thirty
years. Cody clearly had made the big time by 1886 when he appeared at
Madison Square Garden in New York with a scenario entitled *Drama of Civilization* written by the visionary, playwright, and inventor Steele MacKaye.
Seven episodes or "epochs" were designed to display the settlement of the

western frontier (this production is detailed in William Brasmer's "The Wild West Exhibition: A Fraudulent Reality"). In 1887 Cody's show was invited to be a part of the American Exhibition planned for Queen Victoria's Golden Jubilee in London, where it dominated the American Exhibition.

At the beginning of its history, the Wild West appeared to be a representation of the contemporary western scene, but as the old West vanished and the show added attractions foreign to the true West in order to remain competitive, it soon transcended the reality and created a legendary West based largely on illusion. It is not surprising that Cody's success spawned many imitators. In 1888 Adam Forepaugh, a major name in the American circus, developed a show called "The Forepaugh and Wild West Combination" (also called on occasion "The Combined Wild West and Forepaugh Exhibition"). Also in 1888 Gordon William Lillie organized "Pawnee Bill's Historical Wild West Exhibition and Indian Encampment." Other lesser operations followed.

By the turn of the century the Wild West show began to lose its contemporary interest. The format, which originally had been new and unique, lacked variety, and showmen fell victim to the temptation to combine it with a circus or to add circus acts to its own pageantry. Apparently if William Brasmer is correct, the perpetuation of the Wild West was made easier by the nature of its primary audience. He states in "The Wild West Exhibition: A Fraudulent Reality" that "essentially, the wild west exhibition was a show for urban cultures, primarily for recent immigrants who had never known the Indian or the West but relished stories and legends about frontier life and frightfulness of Indian captivity."

But even an urban or immigrant audience could not have helped but notice the incongruities and dichotomies of the evolving show. Gordon William Lillie thought the solution to the survival of the Wild West exhibition was to restyle his show as "Pawnee Bill's Historic Wild West and Great Far East." The latter included "every type of male and female inhabitant"— Hindu magicians, Singhalese dancers, Madagascar oxen cavalry, Australian bushmen, and others. Other shows featured notoriety almost exclusively. "Cummins's Wild West and Indian Congress" featured Red Cloud, Chief Joseph, Geronimo, and Calamity Jane. In 1903 the most notorious show must have been "The Cole Younger and Frank James Wild West."

Despite the changing nature of the Wild West show after the 1890s, the largest number of such entertainments flourished in the early years of the twentieth century. In the course of its history, according to Don Russell, the foremost historian of this phenomenon, there were over one hundred Wild West shows. With the great proliferation of such organizations at the turn of the century, it is not surprising that most of these shows became quite shabby and patronage diminished. Cody's last European tour began in 1902, and by 1909 he had to merge his operation with that of Pawnee Bill.

Cody was never able to adequately recoup financial losses that began to plague him from the turn of the century; a drinking problem compounded his professional problems. By 1908 the "101 Ranch Wild West Show," which began in 1892 as a byproduct of an Oklahoma ranch empire founded by George W. Miller, became a permanent institution and major competitor for the Cody-Pawnee Bill show. Cody died in Denver in 1917; ironically, no major Wild West show was extant by the following year. World War I, which marked the end of the golden era of outdoor show business, also was the death knell for the Wild West show. The rising popularity of the motion picture and the rising cost of touring live entertainment soon eliminated most Wild West shows, although a few stragglers continued into the 1930s and 1940s. Although films created their own myth of the American cowboy, to a gullible public the motion picture version seemed far more "believable" than the illusion depicted in the Wild West arena.

As Don Russell makes abundantly clear, the Wild West show, and William Cody in particular, left an indelible impression on the American consciousness. Its influence can still be found in Europe, where western clubs and dude ranches are still quite popular. Cody helped to change our image of the cowboy from that of a desperado to a hero; he changed the concept of the Indian from that of the James Fenimore Cooper romantic depiction of unhorsed Indians east of the Mississippi to wild-riding Indians of the West. Even though the myth he helped create might have been ultimately detrimental, presenting, as Brasmer says in his essay, "an incorrect picture of western life" and giving an unknowing public an image of the Indian as a "freak to be exhibited or as a silent combatant in a shoot-out in which the Indian always lost," there is no question about its impact and appeal as an entertainment that created heroes when they were needed and a glamour that offered an exciting and a seemingly carefree respite in many a dull and dreary existence.

SURVEY OF SOURCES

Most general histories of the circus, as well as collections and periodicals discussed in the last chapter, contain some mention of Wild West shows. There is, however, a growing literature devoted exclusively to this form of entertainment. Sources on William F. Cody are plentiful, and these usually contain some coverage of his exhibition. The most comprehensive study of the Wild West show to date is Don Russell's *The Wild West or, A History of the Wild West Shows.* This thorough study is likely to stand for sometime as the definitive history. Also useful are Russell's essays "Cody, Kings, and Coronets," covering the first ten years of Buffalo Bill's Wild West, and "The Golden Age of Wild West Shows," a good summary of the Wild West show's history based on a speech given in 1970. William W. Savage, Jr.'s *The Cowboy Hero: His Image in American History and Culture* relates the salesmanship of the cowboy and Cody and his image through the Wild West show, providing a useful context and perspective for this phenomenon.

Other studies of the form provide varying points of view. William Brasmer in "The Wild West Exhibition and the Drama of Civilization" and "The Wild West Exhibition: A Fraudulent Reality" presents a deprecating view of the phenomenon. Other less extreme points of view are found in the following: Ellsworth Collings and Alma Miller England's *The 101 Ranch,* the definitive documented source on the Miller brothers' ranch and its Wild West show; Carolyn Thomas Foreman's *Indians Abroad,* a history of the foreign travel of Indians, including their associations with Wild West shows; the many essays by former cowboy Milt Hinkle offer valuable tidbits on various shows (for example: "The Dusky Demon," on Bill Pickett, a black Wild West performer; "Cowboy!" on the origin and evolution of the term; "Kit Carson's Buffalo Ranch Wild West Big Three Ring Wild West Circus" and "The Kit Carson Wild West Show"; "A Texan Hits the Pampas," an account of the 101 Ranch show in South America; "Circuses and Contests"; "Milt Blew His Show in Chicago," on the Star Ten Ranch Wild West Show; "Winning or Losing," on the rodeo circuit; "Memoirs of My Rodeo Days," including his stint with Cody's Wild West; and "The Way a Wild West Show Operated"); also of interest is Milt Hinkle and Mildred Elder's "Suicide Ted Elder," on the career of a horseman with the 101 show and Ringling Brothers. Madelon B. Katigan's "The Fabulous 101," provides one of the better brief accounts of this important organization. Other sources on the same topic include: Fred Gipson's *Fabulous Empire. Colonel Jack Miller's Story;* Ruel McDaniel's "Requiem for the Wild West Shows"; Chang Reynolds's "101 Ranch Wild West Show, 1907-1916" and "Miller Brothers 101 Ranch Wild West Shows" (1925-1931). Other sources of interest include: Paul E. Mix's *The Life and Legend of Tom Mix* and the less useful *The Fabulous Tom Mix* by Olive Stokes Mix; Fred D. Pfening, Jr.'s *Col. Tim McCoy's Real Wild West and Rough Riders of the World,* the story of a late Wild West enterprise, as well as Pfening's "Buck Jones Wild West and Round Up Day," on Western motion picture personalities who have been featured with or owned circuses and Wild West shows; C. O. Robinson's "Tom Mix Was My Boss"; Stuart Thayer's "Tom Mix Circus and Wild West"; Joseph Schwartz's "The Wild West Show; 'Everything Genuine'," a good analysis of the show's appeal; and Glenn Shirley's *Pawnee Bill: A Biography of Major Gordon W. Lillie,* which contains an informative history of the Wild West show in general and valuable data on the association between the shows of Cody and Lillie; a more romanticized biography of Lillie is J. H. De Wolff's *Pawnee Bill (Major Gordon W. Lillie): His Experience and Adventure on the Western Plains*; Joseph T. Bradbury's "Tompkins Wild West Show 1913-17" and "Buck Jones Wild West Shows and Round Up Days"; Louise Cheney's

"Lucile Mulhall, Fabulous Cowgirl," one of the first to use the title; also her "Mr. Rodeo Himself: Milt Hinkle"; William L. Elbirn's "Austin Bros. 3 Ring Circus and Real Wild West"; Charles H. Tompkins's "Gabriel Brothers Wild West Show"; and Frank J. Pouska's "Young Buffalo Wild West Show" (1908-1914).

As might be expected, most published material on the Wild West concerns William "Buffalo Bill" Cody and his exhibition. Among the dozens of biographies and essays on Cody, a few deal not only with Cody's life before the Wild West show but also with the show itself and individuals associated with it. Cody's career as an actor is given adequate coverage in the following: William S. E. Coleman, "Buffalo Bill on Stage"; Jay Monaghan, "The Stage Career of Buffalo Bill"; and Paul T. Nolan, "When Curtains Rise, Scouts Fall Out," "J. W. Crawford: Poet Scout of the Black Hills," and "The Western Hero on Stage." The most recent full-length biography of Cody is Nellie Snyder Yost's *Buffalo Bill: His Family, Friends, Fame, Failures, and Fortunes,* although still equally informative and frequently more readable are Rupert Croft-Cooke and W. S. Meadmore's *Buffalo Bill: The Legend, The Man of Action, The Showman* and Don Russell's *The Lives and Legends of Buffalo Bill.* Also recommended is Henry Blackman Sell and Victor Weybright's *Buffalo Bill and the Wild West,* which deals knowledgeably with both the man and the legend. A good illustrated overview of Cody the man and showman is the recent essay "Buffalo Bill and the Enduring West" by Alice J. Hall. William E. Deahl, Jr.'s "Nebraska's Unique Contribution to the Entertainment World" covers the beginnings of the Wild West show in 1883, and his "Buffalo Bill's Wild West Show in New Orleans" examines Cody's appearances at the 1884 World's Industrial and Cotton Exposition. John Burke's *Buffalo Bill, The Noblest Whiteskin,* though not definitive, is a readable and essentially correct popularized biography. Sources by Cody and members of his family are plentiful and frequently not very reliable. Among the numerous autobiographies by Cody, *Life and Adventures of Buffalo Bill* (1917) incorporates the original 1879 autobiography and additions from the 1888 edition, plus a final chapter on Cody's death by Col. William Lightfoot Visscher. Cody's wife, Louisa Frederici Cody, left us *Memories of Buffalo Bill,* the record of an unhappy marriage; a reasonably accurate picture of Cody was written by his sister, Julia Cody Goodman (with Elizabeth Jane Leonard), entitled *Buffalo Bill, King of the Old West;* another sister, Helen Cody Wetmore, wrote *Last of the Great Scouts,* which apparently prompted Cody's elder sister Julia to write a correction (see Don Russell's edition, "Julia Cody Goodman's Memoirs of Buffalo Bill"). Other recommended sources on Cody's life and career include: Stella Adelyne Foote's *Letters From Buffalo Bill;* James M. Bentley's "William F. Cody, Buffalo Bill, An Iowa-Born Folk Hero"; J. W. Buel's

Heroes of the Plains (which also includes coverage of Wild Bill Hickok, California Joe, and Kit Carson); Edmund Collier's *The Story of Buffalo Bill,* a biography for younger readers; Frank C. Cooper's *Stirring Lives of Buffalo Bill and Pawnee Bill* (a superficial treatment); Tex Cooper's "I Knew Buffalo Bill," written by a member of his show beginning in 1892; W. B. Courtney's "The Prairie Prince"; Don Holm's "Were There Two Buffalo Bills?"; Henry Inman and William F. Cody's *The Great Salt Lake Trail;* Harold McCracken and Richard I. Frost's *The Buffalo Bill Story—A Brief Account;* M. I. McCreight's "Buffalo Bill as I Knew Him," by a gentleman who knew Cody off and on from 1887 to 1916; Dan Muller's *My Life With Buffalo Bill;* Richard J. Walsh's *The Making of Buffalo Bill,* a study of the process by which Cody became a semilegendary figure largely through publicity; *The Westerners Brand Book 1945-46,* which includes a useful symposium on "The Truth About Buffalo Bill"; John Wilstach's "Buffalo Bill's Last Stands"; Frank Winch's sentimental treatment of Cody's life but useful coverage of the show and Pawnee Bill as Cody's only legitimate successor, *Thrilling Lives of Buffalo Bill and Pawnee Bill;* and Walter Havighurst's *Buffalo Bill's Great Wild West Show,* written for younger readers.

The following sources deal with specific associates of Cody or aspects of his show. Annie Oakley has received a good deal of attention, although there is not one definitive biography. A good picture of her life and contributions to the Wild West can be gleaned from the following: Edmund Collier, *The Story of Annie Oakley* (for younger readers); Courtney Ryley Cooper, *Annie Oakley, Woman at Arms*; Walter Havighurst, *Annie Oakley of the Wild West,* a good popular account; Stewart H. Holbrook, *Little Annie Oakley and Other Rugged People;* Bonnie Kreps, "Annie Oakley's Untold Love Story" (her relationship with Frank Butler); E. B. Mann, "Little Sure Shot"; and finally, *Missie,* written by her niece, Annie Fern Swartwout. Other sources on associates of Cody, with insight on the Wild West exhibition, include: Captain Jack Crawford's *The Poet Scout;* William E. Deahl, Jr.'s "Buffalo Bill's Rival Dr. Carver"; Roy Sylvan Dunn's "Buffalo Bill's Bronc Fighter"; Gladys Shaw Erskine's *Broncho Charlie, A Saga of the Saddle;* H. Roger Grant's "An Iowan with Buffalo Bill: Charles Eldridge Griffin in Europe, 1903-1906" and Griffin's *Four Years in Europe with Buffalo Bill;* R. M. Harvey's "Some Inside Facts About Buffalo Bill's Wild West"; Mary Hardgrove Hebberd's "Notes on Dr. David Franklin Powell, Known as 'White Beaver' "; Jay Monaghan's *The Great Rascal: The Life and Adventures of Ned Buntline,* the best biography of Edward Zane Carroll Judson (Buntline) with an adequate coverage of his varied associations with Cody; Charles R. Nordin's "Dr. W. F. Carver"; Jake Posey's "With Buffalo Bill in Europe"; William B. Secrest's " 'Indian' John Nelson"; Agnes Wright Spring's *Buffalo Bill*

and His Horses; Raymond W. Thorp's *Spirit Gun of the West. The Story
of Doc W. F. Carver,* the best treatment of Carver's career and association
with Cody; Charles Wayland Towne's "Preacher's Son on the Loose with
Buffalo Bill Cody"; and Harry E. Webb's "My Years with Buffalo Bill's
Wild West Show."

The Indian in the Wild West show, in addition to being handled in
Foreman's *Indians Abroad,* mentioned above, is also treated in the follow-
ing: Stanley Vestal's *Sitting Bull: Champion of the Sioux* discusses Sitting
Bull's stint with Cody in 1885 (and subsequent associations); Ed Holm's
"Gertrude Kasabier's Indian Portraits" offers photographic portraits of
Indians that appeared with Cody; a checklist of photographs of Sitting
Bull, including a number made while with Cody, can be found in Elmo
Scott Watson's "The Photographs of Sitting Bull"; and Chauncey Yellow
Rob's "The Menace of the Wild West Show" deals with the effects of
Wild West shows on the American Indian.

In addition to the sources listed above on Indian portraits, the following
provide good illustrative material or text on illustrations of Wild West
exhibitions: *The West of Buffalo Bill* includes an illustrated life of Cody
and his Wild West with some superb reproductions; Jack Rennert's *100
Posters of Buffalo Bill's Wild West* is an excellent collection, with a useful
text; "Behind the 'Wild West' Scenes" with illustrations by Frederick
Remington includes a full page of drawings of Buffalo Bill's camp in
Brooklyn in 1894; Frederick A. Mark's "Last of the Old West Artists—
R. Farrington Elwell" includes Elwell's drawings and painting of Cody;
and Leigh Jerrard's "Rosa Bonheur Revealed as a Painter of Westerns"
discusses the French artist's visual depictions of Cody's Wild West show.

Other sources that are less explicitly relevant to Cody or Wild West
shows but still are useful for details or background include the following:
Lester U. Beitz, "The Original Deadwood Stage"; souvenir programs for
Buffalo Bill's Wild West, which can prove to be treasure houses of infor-
mation; Foghorn Clancy, *My Fifty Years in Rodeo* (on small Wild West
shows after the turn of the century); Samuel Clemens (Mark Twain),
"A Horse's Tale," a fictional pre-Wild West Story about Cody from his
horse's point of view; Walt Coburn, "The Inimitable Breeze Cox," a
rodeo performer, and "Tom Mix's Last Sundown"; Homer Croy, "Texas
Jack," on three western characters of this name; Dexter W. Fellows and
Andrew A. Freeman, *This Way to the Big Show,* with excerpts from
M. B. Bailey's Wild West diary of 1896; Mildred Fielder, *Wild Bill and
Deadwood,* including coverage of Hickok's foray into show biz, and Joseph
G. Rosa, *They Called Him Wild Bill,* with similar coverage; Albert Johannsen, *The House of Beadle and Adams,* the most complete reference source
on the major publisher of dime novels that provides extensive coverage
of Cody and stories about him; Jerrold J. Mundis, "He Took the Bull

by the Horns" and Esse Forrester O'Brien, *The First Bulldogger* (on Bill Pickett who performed with the 101 Wild West Show); William B. Secrest, "Bill Hickok's Girl on the Flying Trapeze," on Agnes Lake and her career with circuses and Wild West shows, including Cody's; Glenn Shirley, editor, *Buckskin Joe* (on Edward Jonathan Hoyt, who ran his own show in 1892); William C. Thompson, *On the Road with a Circus,* on Pawnee Bill's Wild West show; N. Howard Thorp and Neil M. Clark, *Pardner of the Wind,* an excellent first-hand account of the West at the turn of the century; and Gene Fowler, *Timber Line* and *A Solo in Tom-Toms,* both concerned primarily with journalists and journalism, although the former, on Harry Hege Tammen and Frederick Gilmer Bonfils, publishers and owners of the Denver *Evening Post,* provides an interesting portrait of Cody in the 1880s to 1913 and his problems late in his career, and the latter includes Fowler's encounter with Cody in 1899. Finally, for a useful and perceptive analysis of Arthur Kopit's play *Indians* (also the basis for the Altman film by Alan Rudolph and Altman) inspired by Cody and his Wild West show, see John Bush Jones's "Impersonation and Authenticity: The Theatre as Metaphor in Kopit's *Indians.*"

Virtually all the circus collections and periodicals enumerated in the last chapter contain a great deal on the Wild West show. From time to time, dozens of journals and magazines on the West include essays of interest on the subject of the Wild West show. I have found the most useful to be *American West, True West, Frontier Times, Old West, Real West,* and the circus journal *Bandwagon.* In addition to those collections already mentioned under the circus, the researcher should be familiar with the collections held in the Western History Department of the Denver Public Library, the Nebraska State Historical Society, and the Arizona Pioneers Historical Society. The best-known Buffalo Bill collections can be found at the Buffalo Bill Historical Center in Cody, Wyoming, which includes the Plains Indian Museum, the Buffalo Museum, and the Whitney Gallery of Western Art.

BIBLIOGRAPHY

Beitz, Lester U. "The Original Deadwood Stage." *Frontier Times* 40 (January 1966):41, 58.
Bentley, James M. "William F. Cody, Buffalo Bill, An Iowa-Born Folk Hero." *Annals of Iowa,* 39 (Winter 1968):161-68.
Bradbury, Joseph T. "Tompkins Wild West Show 1913-17." *Bandwagon* 15 (March-April 1971):4-14; 15 (May-June):30-31; 15 (November-December): 26-28.
———. "Buck Jones Wild West Shows and Round Up Days." *Bandwagon* 16 (March-April 1972):20-23; 16 (July-August):11-16.

Brasmer, William. "The Wild West Exhibition and the Drama of Civilization." In *Western Popular Theatre,* edited by David Mayer and Kenneth Richards. London: Methuen and Co., 1977.

_____. "The Wild West Exhibition: A Fraudulent Reality." In *American Popular Entertainment,* edited by Myron Matlaw. Westport, Conn. and London: Greenwood Press, 1979.

Buel, J. W. *Heroes of the Plains.* Philadelphia: West Philadelphia Publishing Co., 1891.

Buffalo Bill's Wild West. Hartford, Conn.: Calhoun Printing Co., 1884.

Buffalo Bill's Wild West and Congress of Rough Riders of the World: Historical Sketches and Programme, Greater New York. New York: Fless and Ridge Printing Co., 1897.

Burke, John. *Buffalo Bill, The Noblest Whiteskin.* New York: G. P. Putnam's Sons, 1973.

Cheney, Louise. "Lucile Mulhall, Fabulous Cowgirl." *Real West* 12 (March 1969): 13-15, 58-59, 73.

_____. "Mr. Rodeo Himself: Milt Hinkle." *Real West* 12 (June 1969):22-24, 58-59, 64, 74.

Clancy, Foghorn. *My Fifty Years in Rodeo.* San Antonio: Naylor Co., 1952.

Clemens, Samuel L. [Mark Twain]. "A Horse's Tale." *Harper's Monthly* 113 (August 1906):328-42; (September):539-49.

Coburn, Walt. "The Inimitable Breeze Cox." *True West* 15 (September 1967): 14-17, 54-57.

_____. "Tom Mix's Last Sundown." *Frontier Times* 42 (August-September 1968): 6-11, 48.

Cody, Louisa Frederici, in collaboration with Courtney Ryley Cooper. *Memories of Buffalo Bill.* New York: Appleton, 1919.

Cody, William Frederick. *Life and Adventures of Buffalo Bill.* Chicago: John R. Stanton Co., 1917.

Coleman, William S.E. "Buffalo Bill on Stage." *Players, Magazine of American Theatre* 47 (December-January 1972):80-91.

Collier, Edmund. *The Story of Buffalo Bill.* New York: Grosset and Dunlap, 1952.

_____. *The Story of Annie Oakley.* New York: Grosset and Dunlap, 1956.

Collings, Ellsworth, and England, Alma Miller. *The 101 Ranch.* Foreword by Glenn Shirley. Norman: University of Oklahoma Press, 1971.

Cooper, Courtney Ryley. *Annie Oakley, Woman at Arms.* New York: Duffield and Co., 1927.

Cooper, Frank C. *Stirring Lives of Buffalo Bill and Pawnee Bill.* New York: S. L. Parsons and Co., 1912.

Cooper, Tex. "I Knew Buffalo Bill." *Frontier Times* 33 (Spring 1959):19.

Courtney, W. B. "The Prairie Prince." *Collier's Weekly* 81 (14 April 1928):12-13, 50-52; 81 (21 April):16-17; 47; 81 (28 April):24-26, 44; 81 (5 May):13-14, 26, 28; 81 (12 May):18-20, 59, 60-61; 81 (19 May):22-24, 44-45.

Crawford, Captain Jack. *The Poet Scout.* New York: Funk and Wagnalls, 1886.

Croft-Cooke, Rupert, and Meadmore, W. S. *Buffalo Bill: The Legend, The Man of Action, The Showman.* London: Sidgwick and Jackson, 1952.

Croy, Homer. "Texas Jack." *The Westerners New York Posse Brand Book* 2, no. 2 (1955):29.

Deahl, William E., Jr. "Nebraska's Unique Contribution to the Entertainment World." *Nebraska History* 49 (Autumn 1968):283-97.

———. "Buffalo Bill's Rival Dr. Carver." *Bandwagon* 17 (November-December 1973):40, 42-43.

———. "Buffalo Bill's Wild West Show in New Orleans." *Louisiana History* 16 (Summer 1975):289-98.

De Wolff, J. H. *Pawnee Bill (Major Gordon W. Lillie): His Experience And Adventure on the Western Plains.* N.p.: Pawnee Bill's Historic Wild West Co., 1902.

Dunn, Roy Sylvan. "Buffalo Bill's Bronc Fighter." *Montana* 7 (April 1957):2-11.

Elbirn, William L. "Austin Bros. 3 Ring Circus and Real Wild West." *Bandwagon* 6 (January-February 1962):12-17.

Erskine, Gladys Shaw. *Broncho Charlie, A Saga of the Saddle.* New York: Thomas Y. Crowell Co., 1934.

Fellows, Dexter W., and Freeman, Andrew A. *This Way to the Big Show: The Life of Dexter Fellows.* New York: Viking Press, 1936.

Fielder, Mildred. *Wild Bill and Deadwood.* Seattle: Superior Publishing Co., 1965.

Foote, Stella Adelyne. *Letters From Buffalo Bill.* Billings, Mont.: Foote Publishing Co., 1954.

Foreman, Carolyn Thomas. *Indians Abroad.* Norman: University of Oklahoma Press, 1943.

Fowler, Gene. *Timber Line.* New York: Covici Friede Publishers, 1933.

———. *A Solo in Tom-Toms.* New York: Viking Press, 1946.

Gipson, Fred. *Fabulous Empire. Colonel Jack Miller's Story.* Boston: Houghton Mifflin Co., 1946.

Grant, H. Roger. "An Iowan with Buffalo Bill: Charles Eldridge Griffin in Europe, 1903-1906." *Palimpset* 54 (January-February 1973):2-15.

Griffin, Charles Eldridge. *Four Years in Europe with Buffalo Bill.* Albia, Iowa: Stage Publishing Co., 1908.

Hall, Alice J. "Buffalo Bill and the Enduring West." *National Geographic* 160 (July 1981):76-103.

Harvey, R. M. "Some Inside Facts About Buffalo Bill's Wild West." *Bandwagon* 3 (January-February 1959):13-14.

Havighurst, Walter. *Annie Oakley of the Wild West.* New York: Macmillan Co., 1954.

———. *Buffalo Bill's Great Wild West Show.* New York: Random House, 1957.

Hebberd, Mary Hardgrove. "Notes on Dr. David Franklin Powell, Known as 'White Beaver'." *Wisconsin Magazine of History* 35 (Summer 1952):36-39.

Hinkle, Milt "The Dusky Demon." *True West* 8 (July-August 1961):30-31, 55-57.

———. "Cowboy!" *True West* 8 (September-October 1961):38-39.

———. "Kit Carson's Buffalo Ranch Wild West Big Three Ring Wild West Circus." *Bandwagon* 7 (September-October 1963):4-9; 7 (November-December):17-21.

———. "The Kit Carson Wild West Show." *Frontier Times* 38 (May 1964):6-11, 57-58.

_____. "A Texan Hits the Pampas." *Old West* 2 (Fall 1965):2-11.

_____. "Circuses and Contests." *Old West* 3 (Fall 1966):24-28.

_____. "Milt Blew His Show in Chicago." *Frontier Times* 42 (February-March 1968):30-31, 52-54.

_____. "Winning or Losing." *Frontier Times* 42 (August-September 1968):26-28, 48.

_____. "Memoirs of My Rodeo Days." *Real West* 11 (September 1968):35-37, 65.

_____. "The Way a Wild West Show Operated." *Frontier Times* 43 (March 1969): 20-23, 50-52.

_____, and Elder, Mildred. "Suicide Ted Elder." *True West* 41 (June1969):40-42, 72.

Holbrook, Stewart H. *Little Annie Oakley and Other Rugged People.* New York: Macmillan Co., 1948.

Holm, Don. "Were There Two Buffalo Bills?" *Frontier Times* 39 (August-September 1965):35, 61.

Holm, Ed. "Gertrude Kasabier's Indian Portraits." *American West* 10 (July 1973): 38-41.

Inman, Henry, and Cody, William F. *The Great Salt Lake Trail.* Minneapolis: Ross and Haines, 1966.

Jerrard, Leigh. "Rosa Bonheur Revealed as a Painter of Westerns." *Westerners Brand Book* 10 (August 1953):41-42.

Johannsen, Albert. *The House of Beadle and Adams.* 3 vols. Norman: University of Oklahoma Press, 1950, 1962.

Jones, John Bush. "Impersonation and Authenticity: The Theatre as Metaphor in Kopit's *Indians.*" *Quarterly Journal of Speech* 59 (December 1973):443-51.

Katigan, Madelon B. "The Fabulous 101." *True West* 8 (September-October 1960):6-12, 50-51.

Kopit, Arthur. *Indians.* New York: Bantam Books, 1971.

Kreps, Bonnie. "Annie Oakley's Untold Love Story." *MS* 5 (January 1977):8, 12-13.

Leonard, Elizabeth Jane, and Goodman, Julian Cody. *Buffalo Bill, King of the Old West.* Edited by James William Hoffman. New York: Library Publishers, 1955.

McCracken, Harold, and Frost, Richard I. *The Buffalo Bill Story—A Brief Account.* Cody, Wyo.: Buffalo Bill Historical Center, n.d.

McCreight, M. I. "Buffalo Bill as I Knew Him." *True West* 4 (July-August 1957): 25, 41-42.

McDaniel, Ruel. "Requiem for the Wild West Show." *Frontier Times* 36 (Winter 1961):22-23.

Mann, E. B. "Little Sure Shot." *American Rifleman* 96 (April 1948):41-44.

Mark, Frederick A. "Last of the Old West Artists—R. Farrington Elwell." *Montana* 7 (January 1957):58-63.

Mix, Olive Stokes, with Eric Heath. *The Fabulous Tom Mix.* Englewood Cliffs, N.J.: Prentice-Hall, 1957.

Mix, Paul E. *The Life and Legend of Tom Mix.* New York and South Brunswick, N.J.: A. S. Barnes and Co., 1972.

Monaghan, Jay. "The Stage Career of Buffalo Bill." *Journal of the Illinois Historical Society* 31 (December 1938):411-23.

_____. *The Great Rascal: The Life and Adventures of Ned Buntline.* New York: Bonanza Books, 1951.

Muller, Dan. *My Life with Buffalo Bill.* Chicago: Reilly and Lee Co., 1948.

Mundis, Jerrold J. "He Took the Bull by the Horns." *American Heritage* 19 (December 1967):50-55.

Nolan, Paul T. "When Curtains Rise, Scouts Fall Out." *Southern Speech Journal* 29 (Spring 1964):175-86.

_____. "J. W. Crawford: Poet Scout of the Black Hills." *South Dakota Review* 2 (Spring 1965):40-47.

_____. "The Western Hero on Stage." *Real West* 11 (October 1968):37-38, 56-57, 66, 74-75.

Nordin, Charles R. "Dr. W. F. Carver." *Nebraska History* 10 (October-December 1927):244-51.

O'Brien, Esse Forrester. *The First Bulldogger.* San Antonio: Naylor Co., 1961.

Pfening, Fred D., Jr. *Col. Tim McCoy's Real Wild West and Rough Riders of the World.* Columbus, Ohio: Pfening and Snyder, 1955.

_____. "Buck Jones Wild West and Round Up Day." *Bandwagon* 9 (November-December 1965):25-28.

Posey, Jake. "With Buffalo Bill in Europe." *Bandwagon* (October 1953):4-6.

Pouska, Frank J. "Young Buffalo Wild West Show." *Bandwagon* 3 (May-June 1959):15-16, 18.

Remington, Frederick, illus. "Behind the 'Wild West' Scenes." Text by Julian Ralph. *Harper's Weekly,* 18 August 1894, pp. 775-76.

Rennert, Jack. *100 Posters of Buffalo Bill's Wild West.* New York: Darien House (Poster Art Library), 1976.

Reynolds, Chang. "101 Ranch Wild West Show, 1907-1916." *Bandwagon* 13 (January-February 1969):4-21.

_____. "Miller Brothers 101 Ranch Wild West Shows." *Bandwagon* 19 (March-April 1975):3-13; 19 (May-June):3-14.

Robinson, C. O. "Tom Mix Was My Boss." *Frontier Times* 43 (June-July 1969): 18-20, 42-43.

Rosa, Joseph G. *They Called Him Wild Bill.* Norman: University of Oklahoma Press, 1964.

Rudolph, Alan, and Altman, Robert. *Buffalo Bill and the Indians or Sitting Bull's History Lesson.* New York: Bantam Books, 1976.

Russell, Don. *The Lives and Legends of Buffalo Bill.* Norman: University of Oklahoma Press, 1960.

_____. ed. "Julia Goodman's Memoirs of Buffalo Bill." *Kansas State Historical Quarterly* 28 (Winter 1962):442-96.

_____. *The Wild West or, A History of the Wild West Show.* Fort Worth: Amon Carter Museum of Western Art, 1970.

_____. "Cody, Kings, and Cornets." *American West* 7 (July 1970):4-10, 62.

_____. "The Golden Age of Wild West Shows." *Bandwagon* 15 (September-October 1971):21-27.

Savage, William W., Jr. *The Cowboy Hero: His Image in American History and Culture.* Norman: University of Oklahoma Press, 1979.

Sayers, Isabelle. *Rifle Queen, Annie Oakley.* Ostrander, Ohio: By the author, 1973.

Schwartz, Joseph. "The Wild West Show; 'Everything Genuine'." *Journal of Popular Culture* 3 (Spring 1970):656-66.

Secrest, William B. "Bill Hickok's Girl on the Flying Trapeze," *Old West* 4 (Winter 1967):26-30, 68.

———. " 'Indian' John Nelson." *Old West* 5 (Spring 1969):24-27, 60-63.

Sell, Henry Blackman, and Weybright, Victor. *Buffalo Bill and The Wild West.* New York: Oxford University Press, 1955.

Shirley, Glenn. *Pawnee Bill: A Biography of Major Gordon W. Lillie.* Lincoln: University of Nebraska Press, 1958.

———, ed. *Buckskin Joe.* Lincoln: University of Nebraska Press, 1966.

Spring, Agnes Wright. *Buffalo Bill and His Horses.* Denver: Bradford-Robinson Printing Co., 1968.

Swartwout, Annie Fern. *Missie.* Blanchester, Ohio: Brown Publishing Co., 1947.

Thayer, Stuart. "Tom Mix Circus and Wild West." *Bandwagon* 15 (March-April 1971):18-23; 15 (May-June):4-11.

Thompson, William C. *On the Road with a Circus.* N.p.: Goldmann, 1903.

Thorp, N. Howard (Jack), and Clark, Neil M. *Pardner of the Wind.* Caldwell, Idaho: Caxton Printers, 1945.

Thorp, Raymond W. *Spirit Gun of the West. The Story of Doc W. F. Carver.* Glendale, Calif.: Arthur H. Clark Co., 1957.

Tompkins, Charles H. "Gabriel Brothers Wild West Show." *Westerners Brand Book* 13 (October 1956):64.

Towne, Charles Wayland. "Preacher's Son on the Loose with Buffalo Bill Cody." *Montana, The Magazine of Western History* 18 (Autumn 1968):40-55.

Vestal, Stanley [Walter S. Campbell]. *Sitting Bull: Champion of the Sioux.* 1932. New ed. Norman: University of Oklahoma Press, 1957.

Walsh, Richard J., in collaboration with Milton S. Salsbury. *The Making of Buffalo Bill.* Indianapolis: Bobbs-Merrill Co., 1928.

Watson, Elmo Scott. "The Photographs of Sitting Bull." *Westerners Brand Book* 6 (August 1949):43, 47-48.

Webb, Harry E. "My Years with Buffalo Bill's Wild West Show." *Real West* 13 (January 1970):12-14, 52-55.

The Westerners Brand Book 1945-46. Chicago: Westerners, 1947.

The West of Buffalo Bill. Introduction by Harold McCracken. New York: Harry N. Abrams, n.d.

Wetmore, Helen Cody. *Last of the Great Scouts.* Duluth, Minn.: Duluth Press Publishing Co., 1899.

Wilstach, John. "Buffalo Bill's Last Stands." *Esquire* 21 (June 1944):46-47, 126.

Winch, Frank. *Thrilling Lives of Buffalo Bill and Pawnee Bill.* New York: S. L. Parsons and Co., 1911.

Yellow Rob, Chauncey. "The Menace of the Wild West Show." *Quarterly Journal of the Society of American Indians* 2 (July-September 1914): 224-28.

Yost, Nellie Snyder. *Buffalo Bill: His Family, Friends, Fame, Failures, and Fortunes.* Chicago: The Swallow Press (Sage Books), 1979.

CHAPTER 5

The Dime Museum and
P. T. Barnum

HISTORICAL SUMMARY

Prior to the American Revolution, strolling exhibitors of curiosities operated in the colonies along with numerous other mountebanks and itinerant entertainers. They presented crude and disorganized entertainments— animals, freaks, mechanical and scientific oddities, wax figures, peep shows, and the like. By the beginning of the nineteenth century, showmen had begun to organize such exhibits into "museums" or "cabinets of curiosities," with little competition from legitimate or serious museums. By mid-century the so-called dime museum was established as a major center of American entertainment, and the first formidable American showman emerged, Phineas Taylor Barnum, entrepreneur of the American Museum in New York, beginning in 1841.

Barnum has rightly been called "the father of American show business," "the patron saint of promoters," and the "Prince of Humbugs." Although he was capable of promoting serious exhibits and art, his true talent was in selling marvelous deceptions to a gullible public. The public still associates the name Barnum with the history of the American circus, although his contributions were quite late and relatively minor compared to his major involvements and ultimate contributions to American entertainment. Barnum was the first entertainment entrepreneur in the United States to seize on the potential of a relatively new and restless urban audience. Between 1830 and 1860, the period of his greatest activity, the American population doubled. By 1850 there were some 85 cities with populations exceeding 8,000; eight cities were over 100,000, and by 1860 New York City had already exceeded 900,000, more than doubling its 1840 population. Barnum, in an uncanny way, and more than any of his contemporaries, understood the tastes and desires of the American public and was able to squeeze more money from the middle-class American pocket than any other showman had done before.

Barnum's "humbugging" ways began in 1835, after years of clerking in general stores, organizing lotteries, and running a small newspaper, when he purchased Joice Heth, a black woman who claimed to be 161 years old and the former nurse of George Washington. His techniques for advertising and enticing an audience were evident immediately. To make his attraction even more alluring, after a sensational advertising campaign, Barnum planted a letter in a newspaper claiming that Joice was actually a rubber dummy and that her owner was a ventriloquist. The ruse worked and crowds flocked to see for themselves whether or not she was fake or for real. When Joice died that year, the post mortem indicated that she was no more than eighty years of age; Barnum feigned innocence, of course, and, as he was to do many times in the future, found a public quick to forgive and more eager to be amused, no matter what lengths he might go to. During his fascinating career, Barnum often used unscrupulous and exaggerated means to publicize and promote attractions, many of which were quite legitimate and unique, including Tom Thumb, Jenny Lind, Chang and Eng the Siamese Twins, and Jumbo the elephant. But to this list must be added such attractions as the Feejee Mermaid, a hairy embalmed creature supposedly half-human and half-fish, and his great model of Niagara Falls, which turned out to be only eighteen inches high.

Following Joice Heth and the short-lived furor that accompanied her, Barnum experienced a number of lean years until in 1841 he purchased John Scudder's American Museum collection at Broadway and Ann Street. Barnum took this unimpressive collection of historical and scientific "curiosities," renamed the edifice Barnum's American Museum, and launched it as a profitable concern and national institution. Barnum knew that the established theater in New York was virtually off limits to a large portion of the population, especially those of the lower classes who could not afford the price of admission, those immigrants who found language a major barrier, and those who held fundamentalist religious beliefs or were from very proper and conservative families. Barnum offered them entertainment that on the surface had no taint, required little education, and had something for all ages. The amusements at his establishment ran the gamut—human curiosities, an Indian village, variety acts, a 3,000-seat playhouse, which he called a "lecture room" to free it from any association with "theater," and much, much more. By 1849 Barnum claimed to have

600,000 curiosities on view, including a wax works devoted to the "Horrors and Penalties of Intemperance."

Barnum's museum was not unique in concept, but it was in execution. Before mid-century there were no public, free museums, although private collectors did attempt to attract patrons to see their legitimate exhibits with little success. In order to hype their exhibits, legitimate museums were forced to offer sensational novelties. Charles Willson Peale's Museum and Gallery of Fine Arts in New York City, for example, featured a magician, a fake mind reader, and an anaconda that swallowed live fowl in order to attract patrons into the museum. Barnum, on the other hand, had no ulterior motives other than to amuse and to make money. As Brooks McNamara points out in "The Rise and Fall of the Dime Museum," "Better than any of his rivals, he understood how to create the complex mixture of novelty, piety, pedantry, and outright fraud that spelled spectacular success in the museum business."

Barnum, therefore, although not the first museum proprietor, through his phenomenal sense of publicity and organization, created the prototype of a new form of American entertainment and began what became a rage for similar museums throughout the country. However, none could compete with Barnum's in size and diversity of attractions. A patron at Barnum's could see all kinds of freaks and curiosities; a visit to the Lecture Room offered the visitor a constant stream of variety entertainment and popular theater fare, usually billed as "edifying." Variety was not new, but Barnum developed it to a new scale and promoted it with a barrage of pious advertising.

It was not until the American Museum burned down for the second time in 1868 that Barnum's name was associated with the circus. Once more, despite a number of setbacks, including bankruptcy and moments of public outrage at his frauds during his museum career, Barnum's sense of showmanship paid off. The supreme showmanship of Barnum remains one of the great mystiques of our popular culture. When he died in 1891, an obituary proclaimed rightly, "His name is a proverb already, and a proverb it will continue." The 1980s success of the Broadway musical *Barnum* will no doubt help popularize the name of Barnum for an even greater number of Americans, while at the same time it perpetuates the myth of the man and adds new misconceptions to his life and accomplishments.

The phenomenon exploited by Barnum, operating under the thin veneer of culture and learning, soon spread to every medium-sized city in America. Only a few, like the Eden Museum in New York City and the Boston Museum, both of which drew a largely conservative middle-class audience, could compete in any way with the size and scope of Barnum's. A larger group, less legitimate perhaps but far more colorful and attractive to a lower-middle-class patron, lowered their prices to a dime by streamlining their entertainment. Whereas Barnum and the Boston Museum had fine theater stock companies, these museums specialized in continuous showings of variety entertainment or condensed plays and cheap amusement devices. McNamara says that by the 1880s such an establishment had a penny arcade on the first floor, a menagerie on the second, and a so-called "Curio Hall" (platforms around a room with freaks on display) on the third floor. The featured attraction was frequently placed in another room and could be viewed for an additional fee. From the Curio Hall the patron would descend to the "Theatorium," again for an additional fee, to view a condensed play or a variety show. Such museums in the larger cities remained major centers of amusement until vaudeville houses and motion pictures theaters began to lure patrons away.

At the bottom of the ladder were the small, traveling versions of the dime museum, which became the auxiliary show or sideshow of most carnivals and circuses and were adjuncts of many amusement parks (I saw my first dime museum or sideshow at Coney Island in the early 1950s). Other traveling museums set up business in empty stores located on the main business artery in modest neighborhoods or in areas devoted to cheap entertainment. The Bowery in New York was such an area, with numerous store shows, beer gardens, amusement arcades, concert saloons, and cheap melodrama theaters. Many of these smaller museums were unsavory places and fronts for gambling, prostitution, or quack doctors. By the end of the nineteenth century, the principle attraction of most dime museums was the freak show, preying on a public's insatiable curiosity for the bizarre, the maimed, and the horrible. Certainly the dominant sideshow at the carnival and the circus was the freak show.

Even the cheapest and shabbiest form of the dime museum filled a void; unsophisticated Americans and recent immigrants, in particular, could find here cheap and comprehensible entertainment that was seemingly acceptable on moral and religious grounds including mechanical and optical entertainment devices billed as "scientific marvels." The dime museum survived as a uniquely American institution until World War I; after which it all but vanished, save for carnival or circus sideshows, although Hubert's in New York persisted as a regular dime museum with platform acts and a flea circus until the 1960s. Today, only a handful of sideshows are on the road; the nearest equivalent to the dime museum is the wax museum. The first permanent wax museum in this country was not established until 1949 when George L. Potter opened Potter's Wax Museum in St. Augustine, Florida. The 1970s witnessed a resurgence of interest in wax museums located in major tourist areas. Currently there are more than forty wax museum attracting several million Americans each year, but as a middle-class diversion they are a far cry from Barnum's American Museum with its variegated and wondrous attractions.

SURVEY OF SOURCES

The dime museum tradition has received less attention than any other American entertainment institution. The best survey to date is Brooks McNamara's " 'A Congress of Wonders': The Rise and Fall of the Dime Museum." McNamara also includes frequent references to dime museums in *Step Right Up: An Illustrated History of the American Medicine Show.* A recent essay, Robert C. Allen's "B. F. Keith and the Origins of American Vaudeville," traces Keith's version of clean vaudeville to the dime museum tradition in Boston and, while doing so, offers a useful survey of early dime museums. Two scholarly essays investigate aspects of Barnum's American Museum: William W. Appleton's "The Marvelous Museum of P. T. Barnum" and John Rickards Betts's "P. T. Barnum and the Popularization of Natural History." Appleton defines the museum's appeal as "the lure of the wonderful," and Betts includes a good assessment of Barnum's recognition of the appeal of both science and religion to men and women of the Victorian age and the moral overtones of natural history in his displays. Also useful for its analysis of Barnum's techniques is John Dizikes's "P. T. Barnum: Games and Hoaxing." A serviceable summary of the history of early museums, including Barnum's, Scudder's, and Gardiner Baker's Tammany Museum (late 1790s) can be found in Loyd Haberly's "The American Museum from Baker to Barnum."

Herbert and Marjorie Katz's *Museums, U.S.A.* provides an excellent introduction to the history of the American museum and places entertainment museums, such as Barnum's or the Boston Museum, in relationship to the evolution of "serious" collections. For a useful history of museums in New York prior to Barnum, Robert M. and Gale S. McClung's "Tammany's Remarkable Gardiner Baker" is recommended. Joseph Mitchell's *McSorley's Wonderful Saloon* and William Knight Northall's *Before and Behind the Curtain, or Fifteen Years' Observation Among the Theatres of New York* include interesting and informative sections on dime museums in New York City. Charles Willson Peale's Museum is covered extensively in Charles Coleman Sellers's *Mr. Peale's Museum.* Barnum's various guides to his museum are fascinating documents and useful sources, if approached discriminantly. Recommended is the 1860 guide, *An Illustrated Catalogue and Guide Book to Barnum's American Museum. A Cabinet of Curiosities: Five Episodes in the Evolution of American Museums* provides a series of essays on the American museum, including coverage of William Clark's Indian Museum in St. Louis and The Western Museum in Cincinnati.

Additional sources on dime museums, and Barnum's in particular, can be found in the standard sources on the American theater, a list of which can be found in Don B. Wilmeth's *The American Stage to World War I* and other bibliographies on the American theater (see sources in chapters 1 and 12).

Material on Phineas Taylor Barnum and his principal attractions is more plentiful. A useful bibliography of material on Barnum and specifically the collection at the Bridgeport Public Library is Nelle Neafie's *A P. T. Barnum Bibliography.* By far the best documented study of Barnum's career, especially in its social, economic, entertainment, and intellectual contexts, is Neil Harris's *Humbug: The Art of P. T. Barnum.* Harris's notes and bibliographical essay is an excellent guide to sources not listed in this guide. Irving Wallace's *The Fabulous Showman,* although a popularized biography, is still useful and fairly reliable. For years the standard biography was M. R. Werner's *Barnum,* now superseded by Harris and Wallace's works. Other biographical sources worth consultation are the following: Joel Benton, *Life of Phineas T. Barnum,* basically a reworking of Barnum's own autobiography, and his essay, "P. T. Barnum, Showman and Humorist"; Paul J. Boxell, "P. T. Barnum's Lecture for Londoners" (on "The Art of Money-Getting"); Gamaliel Bradford, "Phineas Taylor Barnum"; J. Bryan III, *The World's Greatest Showman. The Life of P. T. Barnum* (a biography for younger readers); Helen Ferris, *Here Comes Barnum,* Barnum's life collected from his various writings; Raymund Fitzsimons, *Barnum in London,* the most complete study of this phase of his career; Gene Fowler and Bess Meredyth, *The Mighty Barnum,* the screenplay of the 1935 film with Wallace Beery (the first film script to be published); George W. Haines, *Plays, Players & Playgoers! Being Reminiscences of P. T. Barnum and His Museum* (written by Barnum's special advertising agent for public relations purposes); Harvey W. Root, *The Unknown Barnum,* a discussion of the traits and abilities that set Barnum apart; Constance Rourke, *Trumpets of Jubilee,* which includes a good treatment of the myth around Barnum; and Helen Wells, *Barnum, Showman of America.*

Of those attractions exploited by Barnum, the following sources shed light on a number of these, as well as on his operation and techniques. Charles S. Stratton, better known as Tom Thumb, is given reasonably good coverage in Alice Curtis Desmond's *Barnum Presents General Tom Thumb.* More information of his wife, Lavinia Warren, can be found in Mertie E. Romaine's *General Tom Thumb and His Lady; The Autobiography of Mrs. Tom Thumb,* a superbly edited volume by A. H. Saxon; and Theodore James, Jr.'s "Tom Thumb's Giant Wedding." Sources on Chang and Eng, known as the Siamese Twins, include the following: Irving and Amy Wallace, *The Two: The Story of the Original Siamese Twins,* the definitive full-length biographical study; and Kay Hunter, *Duet for a Lifetime,* a more superficial treatment. Jenny Lind, the "Swedish Nightingale" who toured under Barnum's management, is given exhaustive treatment by the following: S. P. Avery, *The Life and Genius of Jenny Lind,* including her appearances at Castle Garden in New York; Laura Benet, *Enchanting Jenny Lind,* a popular biography; Joan Bulman, *Jenny Lind, A Biography,* a reliable study; Frances Cavanah, *Jenny Lind's America;* Ruth Hume, "Selling the Swedish Nightingale. Jenny Lind and P. T. Barnum," a useful summary of their association; C. G. Rosenberg, *Jenny Lind: Her Life, Her Struggles, and Her Triumphs* and *Jenny Lind in America;* and W. Porter Ware and Thaddeus C. Lockard, Jr., *P. T. Barnum Presents Jenny Lind: The American Tour of the Swedish Nightingale,* the most recent book on Lind and the most detailed study of her American tour. In addition to the sources on Jumbo the elephant (Haley and Scott), in chapter 3 on the circus, H. A. Ardman's "Phineas T. Barnum's Charming Beast" is recommended.

Barnum's own prodigious writings are frequently full of puffery and exaggerations but still of value in understanding the man and his accomplishments. Three works that went through many editions and minor revisions are recommended: *The Humbugs of the World, Struggles and Triumphs; or, The Life of P. T. Barnum, Written by Himself,* and *Dollars and Sense, or How to Get On.*

The larger subject of freaks has been a topic of curiosity dealt with in varying degrees of seriousness by many writers through the years. Among the earliest sources are W. L. Alden's *Among the Freaks,* which communicates a good sense of nineteenth-century sensibilities toward human curiosities; F. T. Buckland's four-volume study *Curiosities of Natural History* (especially the last volume); George M. Gould and Walter L. Pyle's *Anomalies and Curiosities of Medicine,* encyclopedic in scope but quite dated; and Edward J. Wood's *Giants and Dwarfs.* Among the more contemporary studies, though not necessarily limited to freaks in American dime museums or sideshows, are the following: Richard D. Altick, *The Shows of London;* Walter Bodin and Burnet Hershey, *It's a Small World. All About Midgets;* Hy Roth and Robert Cromie, *The Little People;* Bill Carmichael, *Incredible Collectors, Weird Antiques, and Odd Hobbies;* Richard Carrington, "The Natural History of the Giant"; Lee Cavin, *There Were Giants on the Earth;* Colin Clair, *Human Curiosities,* a useful exploration of the insatiable desire to view human freaks of nature; Pete Collins, *No People Like Show People;* Marie Delcourt, *Hermaphrodite. Myths and Rites on the Bisexual Figure in Classical Antiquity* (useful for background information); Eric John Dingwall, *Some Human Oddities,* of peripheral interest only; Frank Edwards, *Strange People;* Frederick Fadner, assisted by Harold F. Wadlow, *The Gentleman Giant* (the life of Robert Pershing Wadlow); Barbara Franco, "The Cardiff Giant: A Hundred Year

Old Hoax'' (a famous fossilized freak fraud); Palmer Howard Futcher, *Giants and Dwarfs: A Study of the Anterior Lobe of the Hypophysis,* a scientific investigation into giantism and dwarfism; Alvin Goldfarb, ''Gigantic and Miniscule Actors on the Nineteenth-Century American Stage''; Giovanni Juliani, *Freaks: A Collector's Edition of Nature's Human Oddities, Past and Present,* a photographic collection of freaks; Polly J. Lee, *Giant: The Pictorial History of the Human Colossus;* Harry Lewiston as told to Jerry Holtman, *Freak Show Man;* John Money, *Sex Erros of the Body:* Cheryl C. Sullivan, ''A Strange Kind of Bondage'' (on the Siamese twins Millie and Christina); C.J.S. Thompson, *The Mystery and Lore of Monsters. With Accounts of Some Giants, Dwarfs, and Prodigies,* an authoritative study of freaks; and Marcello Truzzi, ''Lilliputians in Gulliver's Land: The Social Role of the Dwarf.'' For the best sense of the freak in the world of entertainment, the work of three authors is most highly recommended, though for very different reasons. The most stimulating and provocative study of the freak to date, with virtually no aspect of the ''other'' left unexamined, is Leslie Fiedler's *Freaks: Myths & Images of the Secret Self* (see also the essence of his book in ''The Fascination of Freaks''). Frederick Drimmer's *Very Special People: The Struggles, Loves and Triumphs of Human Oddities* is a much publicized popularized study of freaks, whom the author prefers to call very special people. *We Who Are Not As Others,* by Daniel Mannix, though documented only in passing and written for a popular audience, brings understanding and first-hand observation to this survey of freaks.

Although ''The Elephant Man,'' a much discussed nineteenth-century freak, never appeared in America, his story, recently popularized by a successful Broadway play and a most effective film, is worth consideration for its insight into the plight of some human oddities and the atmosphere of nineteenth-century sideshows in England. Three useful sources are available: the standard source, recently released in a paperback edition, is Ashley Montagu's *The Elephant Man: A Study in Human Dignity,* based largely on Frederick Treves's account of Joseph Merrick (incorrectly called John in Montagu's book and other accounts); Christine Sparks's *The Elephant Man,* a fictionalized version of his story based on the Paramount film; and Michael Howell and Peter Ford's *The True History of the Elephant Man,* the most recent and definitive study, correcting a number of major errors perpetuated by Montagu (and Treves). Bernard Pomerance's play *The Elephant Man* is a strong portrayal of the human spirit, though not particularly factual.

Other sources on the sideshow at carnivals and circuses can be found in the chapters dealing with those topics. Indeed, most general sources on these forms of entertainment include some mention of sideshows. One older source of unique interest is worth citing here: William G. FitzGerald's

"Side-Shows," a fascinating survey of types of attractions during the nineteenth century, including natural freaks and man-made freaks, such as contortionists, human claw hammers, and the like. Tattooees as freaks in sideshows and dime museums, including a brief history of the phenomenon in the United States, is covered extensively in Albert Parry's *Tattoo: Secrets of a Strange Art.* Also relevant is the more recent *Pushing Ink: The Fine Art of Tattooing* by Spider Webb.

Sources on wax museums in the United States are rare, although Gene Gurney's mostly pictorial *America in Wax* includes a brief but reliable essay on the history of wax museums in Europe and America. The definitive reference and bibliographical work on wax modellers is E. J. Pyke's *A Biographical Dictionary of Wax Modellers.* The famous Madame Tussaud's Wax Museum, and its impact, is covered in John T. Tussaud's *The Romance of Madame Tussaud's* and the superior study by Leonard Cottrell, *Madame Tussaud.* Richard D. Altick's *The Shows of London* is a superb source on early wax museums in England.

The more elaborate dime museums, such as Barnum's, featured in addition to live performers and the more common type of curiosities, a variety of early optical and mechanical entertainments, as well as stage productions dependent on dioramas or panoramas. Many of these, of course, also were seen outside of the museum environment as independent entertainments. Additional sources, especially on English equivalents, can be found in Don B. Wilmeth's *American and English Popular Entertainment.* Because the illusions of American stage magicians are closely related to the sources on optical entertainments, chapter 11 on stage magic should be consulted.

The American exhibit of dioramas and panoramas, terms frequently used interchangeably in this country (see Altick for a clear explanation of their original differences), can be found in the following: Llewellyn Hubbard Hedgbeth, "Extant American Panoramas: Moving Entertainment of the Nineteenth Century," an excellent scholarly study that includes a general history of panoramas and gives the detailed history and description of eight extant examples; Joseph Earl Arrington, "Leon D. Pomarede's Original Panorama of the Mississippi River," "The Story of Stockwell's Panorama," and "Lewis and Bartholomew's Mechanical Panorama of the Battle of Bunker Hill"; Theodore C. Blegen, "The 'Fashionable Tour' on the Upper Mississippi," on the panorama's influence on travel, its attempt at realism, and its great popularity; Roy A. Boe, "The Panoramas of the Mississippi"; Wolfgang Born, "The Panoramic Landscape as an American Art Form"; Robert L. Carothers and John L. Marsh, "The Whale and the Panorama"; Curtis Dahl, "Panoramas of Antiquity," "Artemus Ward; Comic Panoramist," and "Mark Twain and the Moving Panorama"; Dorothy Dondore, "Banvard's Panorama and The Flowering of New England"; John Hanners, "The Adventures of an Artist: John Banvard

(1815-1891) and His Mississippi Panorama''; Bertha L. Heilbron, ''Henry Lewis' 'Das Illustrirte Mississippithal'; A Contemporary Advertisement'' and ''Documentary Panorama'' (on a Minnesota panorama painted by John Stevens); John Francis McDermott, ''Banvard's Mississippi Panorama Pamphlets,'' ''Henry Lewis' Das Illustrirte Mississippithal','' and *The Lost Panoramas of the Mississippi,* the latter the definitive study of the origins and early history of the American panorama of the 1840s; Richard McLanathan, *The American Tradition in the Arts,* which includes a survey of panoramas in the United States; John L. Marsh, ''The Moving Panorama'' and ''Captain E. C. Williams and the Panoramic School of Acting''; Lee Parry, ''Landscape Theatre in America''; Perry T. Rathbone, editor, *Mississippi Panorama: The Life and Landscape of the Father of Waters and Its Great Tributary, The Missouri* (a guide to an exhibit with 188 illustrations); Charles van Ravenswaay, ''Our Cover'' (on Henry Lewis and his panorama); Richard Carl Wickman, ''An Evaluation of the Employment of Panoramic Scenery in the Nineteenth-Century Theatre''; and Victor Wolfgang Von Hagen, *Frederick Catherwood, Architect* (on his early career as a panoramist).

Since this study is not concerned with the early motion picture, the following very selected sources will serve only as a basic introduction to early optical and mechanical devices germane to the coverage of this guide, such as peep shows, magic lanterns, and automatons. Most histories of the motion picture contain coverage of early optical devices and should be consulted as well if a thorough investigation is desired. Of the numerous sources available, the following provide a balanced cross section and can be recommended: Richard L. Arnold's ''Animated Scenery'' is an informative essay on effects that gave animation to otherwise static settings; Wolfgang Born's ''Early Peep-Shows and the Renaissance Stage,'' although not immediately germane to American forms, provides a good survey of the earliest peep show devices; Charles Michael Carroll's *The Great Chess Automation* remains the definitive history of one of the most famous of the automata; C. W. Ceram's *Archaeology of the Cinema* is a history of the genesis of the cinema to 1897 and is a valuable introduction to early optical entertainments (magic lanterns, dioramas and panoramas, and so forth); Alfred Chapuis and Edmund Droz's *Automata* remains a standard study of mechanical devices for entertainment from antiquity to the 1940s; Olive Cook's *Movement in Two Dimensions. A Study of the Animated and Projected Pictures Which Preceded the Invention of Cinematography* includes clear explanations of peep shows, panoramas, Far Eastern shadows, Chinese shades or shadow shows, and the magic lantern. Also useful are: Conrad William Cooke's *Automata Old and New,* a dated, brief, but still classic work; Henry Dircks's *The Ghost! As Produced in the Spectre Drama . . . By the Apparatus Called the Dircksian Phantasmagoria* on the so-called "Pepper's Ghost" and George Speaight's explanation with illustrations of the evolution and methodology of this magic lantern device, "Professor Pepper's Ghost"; Lesley Gordon's *Peepshow Into Paradise: A History of Children's Toys,* with its coverage of automata; J. F. Heather's *Optical Instruments,* an early source on the magic lantern; Mary Hillier's *Automata and Mechanical Toys—An Illustrated History,* with a useful chapter entitled "Wizards and Showmen"; Albert A. Hopkins's *Magic: Stage Illusions and Scientific Diversions Including Trick Photography,* not only an important historical document on magic but a useful compendium on optical illusions and mechanical devices; Edita Lausanne's *The Golden Age of Toys,* with good coverage of optical devices; Arthur W.J.G. Ord-Hume's *Clockwork Music,* a not always reliable illustrated history of mechanical instruments; and Martin Quigley's *Magic Shadows: The Story of the Original Motion Picture,* a valuable summary of the evolution of optical entertainment.

As is evident from the wide range of topics included under the dime museum, the entertainment offered the patron was a true cornucopia of delights, overlapping other entertainment forms covered in this guide. Most of the major sources on the carnival, the circus, variety and vaudeville, stage magic, and minstrelsy can be consulted as supplements to the more specific sources discussed in this chapter. And certainly the numerous sources on popular American theater offer insights into the types of plays offered the patrons of the larger museums. In order to include these sources, another volume, or several, would be needed. In lieu of this, the user of this guide is urged to consult the bibliographies on American theater and drama discussed in the first and final chapters of this volume.

BIBLIOGRAPHY

Alden, W. L. *Among the Freaks.* London, New York, and Bombay: Longmans, Green, and Co., 1896.

Allen, Robert C. "B. F. Keith and the Origins of American Vaudeville." *Theatre Survey* 21 (November 1980):105-15.

Altick, Richard D. *The Shows of London: A Panoramic History of Exhibitions, 1600-1862.* Cambridge, Mass. and London: Harvard University Press, Belknap Press, 1978.

Appleton, William W. "The Marvelous Museum of P. T. Barnum." *Revue d'Histoire du Theatre* 15 (January-March 1963):57-62.

Ardman, H. A. "Phineas T. Barnum's Charming Beast." *Natural History* 82 (February 1973):46-50, 55-57.

Arnold, Richard L. "Animated Scenery." *Educational Theatre Journal* 16 (October 1964):249-52.

Arrington, Joseph Earl. "Leon D. Pomarede's Original Panorama of the Mississippi River." *Missouri Historical Society Bulletin* 9 (April 1953):261-73.

_____. "The Story of Stockwell's Panorama." *Minnesota History* 33 (Autumn 1953):284–90.

_____. "Lewis and Bartholomew's Mechanical Panorama of the Battle of Bunker Hill." *Old-Time New England* 52 (Fall 1961):50-58, 81-89.

Avery, S. P. *The Life and Genius of Jenny Lind, With Beautiful Engravings.* New York: W. F. Burgess, 1850.

Barnum, Phineas T. *The Humbugs of the World.* 1865. Reprint. Detroit: Singing Tree Press, 1970.

_____. *Struggles and Triumphs; or, The Life of P. T. Barnum, Written by Himself.* 1869. Reprint. New York: Arno Press, 1970.

_____. *Dollars and Sense, or How to Get On. The Whole Secret in a Nut Shell.* . . . Boston: Eastern Publishing Co., 1890.

Benet, Laura. *Enchanting Jenny Lind.* New York: Dodd, Mead, and Co., 1940.

Benton, Joel. *Life of Phineas T. Barnum.* New York: Edgewood Publishing Co., 1891.

_____. "P. T. Barnum, Showman and Humorist." *The Century Magazine* 64 (August 1902):580-92.

Betts, John Rickards. "P. T. Barnum and the Popularization of Natural History." *Journal of the History of Ideas* 20 (June-September 1959):353-68.

Blegen, Theodore C. "The 'Fashionable Tour' on the Upper Mississippi." *Minnesota History* 20 (December 1939):377-96.

Bodin, Walter, and Hershey, Burnet. *It's a Small World. All About Midgets.* New York: Coward-McCann, 1934.

Boe, Roy A. "The Panoramas of the Mississippi." *Mississippi Quarterly* 16 (Fall 1963):203-19.

Born, Wolfgang. "Early Peep-Shows and the Renaissance Stage." *Connoisseur* 107 (February 1941):67-71; 107 (April 1941):161-64, 180.

_____. "The Panoramic Landscape as an American Art Form." *Art in America* 36 (1948):3-19.

Boxell, Paul J. "P. T. Barnum's Lecture for Londoners." *Quarterly Journal of Speech* 54 (April 1968):140-46.

Bradford, Gamaliel. "Phineas Taylor Barnum." *Atlantic Monthly* 130 (July 1922): 82-92.

Bryan, J. III. *The World's Greatest Showman. The Life of P. T. Barnum.* New York: Random House, 1956.

Buckland, F. T. *Curiosities of Natural History.* 4 vols. London: Richard Bentley and Sons, 1890.

Bulman, Joan. *Jenny Lind, A Biography.* London: James Barrie Press, 1956.

A Cabinet of Curiosities: Five Episodes in the Evolution of American Museums. Introduction by Walter Muir Whitehill. Charlottesville: University Press of Virginia, 1967.

Carmichael, Bill. *Incredible Collectors, Weird Antiques, and Odd Hobbies.* Englewood Cliffs, N.J.: Prentice-Hall, 1971.

Carothers, Robert L., and Marsh, John L. "The Whale and the Panorama." *Nineteenth-Century Fiction* 26 (December 1971):319-28.

Carrington, Richard. "The Natural History of the Giant." In *The Saturday Book 17,* edited by John Hadfield. New York: Macmillan Co., 1957.

Carroll, Charles Michael. *The Great Chess Automation.* New York: Dover Publications, 1975.

Cavanah, Frances. *Jenny Lind's America.* New York: Chilton Book Co., 1969.

Cavin, Lee. *There Were Giants on the Earth.* Seville, Ohio: Chronicle, 1959.

Ceram, C. W. [Kurt W. Marek]. *Archaelogy of the Cinema.* Translated by Richard Winston. New York: Harcourt, Brace, and World, [1965].

Chapuis, Alfred, and Droz, Edmund. *Automata.* Translated by Alec Reid. New York: Central Book Co., 1958.

Clair, Colin. *Human Curiosities.* New York: Abelard-Schuman, 1968.

Collins, Pete. *No People Like Show People.* London: Frederick Muller, 1957.

Cook, Olive. *Movement in Two Dimensions. A Study of the Animated and Projected Pictures Which Preceded the Invention of Cinematography.* London: Hutchinson and Co., 1963.

Cooke, Conrad William. *Automata Old and New.* London: Cheswick Press, 1893.

Cottrell, Leonard. *Madame Tussaud.* London: Evans Brothers, 1951.

Dahl, Curtis. "Panoramas of Antiquity." *Archaeology* 12 (Winter 1959):258-63.

_____. "Artemus Ward: Comic Panoramist." *New England Quarterly* 32 (December 1959):476-85.

_____. "Mark Twain and the Moving Panoramas." *American Quarterly* 13 (Spring 1961):20-32.

Delcourt, Marie. *Hermaphrodite. Myths and Rites on the Bisexual Figure in Classical Antiquity.* Translated by Jennifer Nicholson. London: Studio Books, 1961.

Desmond, Alice Curtis. *Barnum Presents General Tom Thumb.* New York: Macmillan Co., 1954.

Dingwall, Eric John. *Some Human Oddities.* London: Home and Van Thal, 1947.

Dircks, Henry. *The Ghost! As Produced in the Spectre Drama . . . By the Apparatus Called the Dircksian Phantasmagoria.* London: Spon, 1863.

Dizikes, John. "P. T. Barnum: Games and Hoaxing." *Yale Review* 67 (1978):338-56.

Dondore, Dorothy. "Banvard's Panorama and The Flowering of New England." *New England Quarterly* 11 (December 1938):817-26.

Drimmer, Frederick. *Very Special People: The Struggles, Loves and Triumphs of Human Oddities.* New York: Amjon Publishers, 1973. Reprint. New York: Bantam Books, 1976.

Edwards, Frank. *Strange People.* New York: Lyle Stuart, 1961.

Fadner, Frederick, assisted by Harold F. Wadlow. *The Gentleman Giant.* Boston: Bruce Humphries, 1944.

Ferris, Helen. *Here Comes Barnum.* New York: Harcourt, Brace and Co., 1932.

Fiedler, Leslie. "The Fascination of Freaks." *Psychology Today* 11 (August 1977): 56-59, 80-82.

_____. *Freaks: Myths & Images of the Secret Self.* New York: Simon and Schuster, 1978.

FitzGerald, William G. "Side-Shows." *Strand Magazine* 13 (March 1897):318-28; 14 (April 1897): 407-16; 14 (May 1897):521-28; 14 (June 1897):774-80; 14 (July 1897):92-97; 14 (August 1897):152-57.

Fitzsimons, Raymund. *Barnum in London.* London: Geoffrey Books, 1969.

Fowler, Gene, and Meredyth, Bess. *The Mighty Barnum.* New York: Covici-Friede, 1935.

Franco, Barbara "The Cardiff Giant: A Hundred Year Old Hoax." *New York History* 50 (October 1969):420-40.

Futcher, Palmer Howard. *Giants and Dwarfs: A Study of the Anterior Lobe of the Hypophysis.* Cambridge, Mass.: Harvard University Press, 1933.

Goldfarb, Alvin "Gigantic and Miniscule Actors on the Nineteenth-Century American Stage." *Journal of Popular Culture* 10 (Fall 1976):267-79.

Gordon, Lesley. *Peepshow into Paradise: A History of Children's Toys.* New York: J. DeGraff, 1953.

Gould, George M., and Pyle, Walter L. *Anomalies and Curiosities of Medicine.* 1896. Reprint. New York: Julian Press, 1956.

Gurney, Gene *America in Wax.* New York: Crown Publishers, 1977.

Haberly, Loyd. "The American Museum from Baker to Barnum." *New York Historical Society Quarterly* 43 (July 1959):273-87.

Haines, George W. *Plays, Players & Playgoers! Being Reminiscences of P. T. Barnum and His Museums.* New York: Bruce, Haines and Co., 1874.

Hanners, John. "The Adventures of an Artist: John Banvard (1815-1891) and His Mississippi Panorama." Ph.D. dissertation, Michigan State University, 1979.

Harris, Neil. *Humbug: The Art of P. T. Barnum.* Boston: Little, Brown and Co., 1973.

Heather, J. F. *Optical Insturments.* London: Lockwood, 1888.

Hedgbeth, Llewellyn Hubbard. "Extant American Panoramas: Moving Entertainments of the Nineteenth Century." Ph.D. dissertation, New York University, 1977.

Heibron, Bertha L. "Henry Lewis' 'Das Illustrirte Mississippithal'; A Contemporary Advertisement." *Bibliographic Society of American Papers* 43 (3d quarterly, 1949):244-45.

_____. "Documentary Panorama." *Minnesota History* 20 (March 1949):14-24.

Hillier, Mary. *Automata and Mechanical Toys—An Illustrated History.* London: Jupiter Books, 1976.

Hopkins, Albert A. *Magic: Stage Illusions and Scientific Diversions Including Trick Photography.* 1897. Reprint. New York: Arno Press, 1977.

Howell, Michael, and Ford, Peter. *The True History of the Elephant Man.* New York: Schocken Books, 1980.

Hume, Ruth. "Selling the Swedish Nightingale. Jenny Lind and P. T. Barnum." *American Heritage* 28 (October 1977):98-107.

Hunter, Kay. *Duet for a Lifetime.* New York: Coward-McCann, 1964.

An Illustrated Catalogue and Guide Book to Barnum's American Museum. New York: Published by Barnum, [circa 1860].

James, Theodore, Jr. "Tom Thumb's Giant Wedding." *Smithsonian* 4 (September 1973):56-62.

Juliani, Giovanni. *Freaks: A Collector's Edition of Nature's Human Oddities, Past and Present.* Montreal: By the author, n.d.

Katz, Herbert, and Katz, Marjorie. *Museums, U.S.A.* Garden City, N.Y.: Doubleday and Co., 1965.

Lausanne, Edita. *The Golden Age of Toys.* London: Patrick Stephens, 1967.

Lee, Polly J. *Giant: The Pictorial History of the Human Colossus.* South Brunswick, N.J. and New York: A. S. Barnes and Co., 1970.

Lewiston, Harry, as told to Jerry Holtman. *Freak Show Man.* Los Angeles: Holloway House, 1968.

McClung, Robert M. and McClung, Gale S. "Tammany's Remarkable Gardiner Baker." *New York Historical Society Quarterly* 42 (April 1958):143-69.

McDermott, John Francis. "Banvard's Mississippi Panorama Pamphlets." *Bibliographic Society of America Papers* 43 (1st quarter, 1949):48-62.

_____. "Henry Lewis' 'Das Illustrirte Mississippithal." *Bibliographic Society of America Papers* 45 (2d quarter, 1951):152-55.

_____. *The Lost Panoramas of the Mississippi,.* Chicago: University of Chicago Press, 1958.

McLanathan, Richard. *The American Tradition in the Arts.* New York: Harcourt, Brace and World, 1968.

McNamara, Brooks. " 'A Congress of Wonders': The Rise and Fall of the Dime Museum." *Emerson Society Quarterly* 20 (3d quarter, 1974):216-32.

_____. *Step Right Up: An Illustrated History of the American Medicine Show.* Garden City, N.Y.: Doubleday and Co., 1976.

Mannix, Daniel. *We Who Are Not As Others.* New York: Pocket Books, 1976.

Marsh, John L. "The Moving Panorama." *Players, The Magazine of American Theatre* 45 (August-September 1970):272-75.

_____. "Captain E. C. Williams and the Panoramic School of Acting." *Educational Theatre Journal* 23 (October 1971):289-97.

Mitchell, Joseph. *McSorley's Wonderful Saloon.* 1943. Reprint. New York: Grosset, 1959.

Money, John. *Sex Errors of the Body.* Baltimore: Johns Hopkins University Press, 1968.

Montagu, Ashley, and Treves, Frederick. *The Elephant Man: A Study in Human Dignity.* 1971. Reprint. New York: E. P. Dutton, 1979.

Neafie, Nelle. *A P. T. Barnum Bibliography.* Lexington: University of Kentucky, 1965.

Northall, William Knight. *Before and Behind the Curtain, or Fifteen Years' Observation Among the Theatres of New York.* New York: W. F. Burgess, 1851.

Ord-Hume, Arthur W.J.G. *Clockwork Music.* New York: Crown Publishers, 1973.

Parry, Albert. *Tattoo: Secrets of a Strange Art.* 1933. Reprint. New York: Macmillan Co., 1971.

Parry, Lee. "Landscape Theatre in America." *Art in America* 59 (November-December 1971):52-61.

Pomerance, Bernard. *The Elephant Man.* New York: Grove Press, 1979.

Pyke, E. J. *A Biographical Dictionary of Wax Modellers.* Oxford: Oxford University Press, 1973.

Quigley, Martin. *Magic Shadows: The Story of the Original Motion Picture.* 1948. Reprint. New York: Quigley Publishing, 1960.

Rathbone, Perry, ed. *Mississippi Panorama: The Life and Landscape of the Father of Waters and Its Great Tributary, The Missouri.* St. Louis: City Art Museum, 1949.

Romaine, Mertie E. *General Tom Thumb and His Lady.* Taunton, Mass.: William S. Sullwold Publishing, 1976.

Root, Harvey W. *The Unknown Barnum.* New York: Harper and Bros., 1927.

Rosenberg, C. G. *Jenny Lind: Her Life, Her Struggles and Her Triumphs.* New York: Stringer and Townsend, 1850.

_____. *Jenny Lind in America.* New York: Stringer and Townsend, 1851.

Roth, Hy, and Cromie, Robert. *The Little People.* New York: Everest House, 1980.

Rourke, Constance. *Trumpets of Jubilee.* New York: Harcourt, Brace and Co., 1927.

Saxon, A. H., ed. *The Autobiography of Mrs. Tom Thumb.* Hamden, Conn.: Archon Books (The Shoe String Press), 1979.

Sellers, Charles Coleman. *Mr. Peale's Museum.* New York. W. W. Norton and Co., 1979.

Sparks, Christine. *The Elephant Man.* New York: Ballantine Books. 1980.

Speaight, George. "Professor Pepper's Ghost." *Revue d'Histoire du Theatre* 15 (January-March 1963):48-56.

Sullivan, Cheryl C. "A Strange Kind of Bondage." *American History Illustrated* 14 (November 1979):48-49.

Thompson, C.J.S. *The Mystery and Lore of Monsters. With Accounts of Some Giants, Dwarfs, and Prodigies.* New York: Citadel Press, 1970.

Truzzi, Marcello. "Lilliputians in Gulliver's Land: The Social Role of the Dwarf." In *Sociology and Everyday Life,* edited by Marcello Truzzi. Englewood Cliffs, N.J.: Prentice-Hall, 1968.

Tussaud, John T. *The Romance of Madame Tussaud's.* London: Odhams Press, 1921.

van Ravenswaay, Charles, "Our Cover." *Missouri Historical Society Journal* 4 (July 1948):196.

Von Hagen, Victor Wolfgang. *Frederick Catherwood, Architect.* New York: Oxford University Press, 1950.

Wallace, Irving. *The Fabulous Showman.* New York: Alfred A. Knopf, 1959.

_____, and Wallace, Amy. *The Two: The Story of the Original Siamese Twins.* New York: Simon and Schuster, 1978.

Ware, W. Porter, and Lockard, Thaddeus C., Jr. *P. T. Barnum Presents Jenny Lind: The American Tour of the Swedish Nightingale.* Baton Rouge: Louisiana State University Press, 1980.

Webb, Spider, with Marco Vassi. *Pushing Ink: The Fine Art of Tattooing.* New York: Simon and Schuster, 1979.

Wells, Helen. *Barnum, Showman of America.* New York: David McKay, 1957.

Werner, M. R. *Barnum.* New York: Harcourt, Brace and Co., 1923.

Wickman, Richard Carl. "An Evaluation of the Employment of Panoramic
    Scenery in the Nineteenth-Century Theatre." Ph.D. dissertation, Ohio State
    University, 1961.
Wilmeth, Don B., ed. *The American Stage to World War I: A Guide to Information
    Sources.* Detroit: Gale Research Co., 1978.
_____, ed. *American and English Popular Entertainment: A Guide to Information
    Sources.* Detroit: Gale Research Co., 1980.
Wood, Edward J. *Giants and Dwarfs.* London: Richard Bentley, 1868.

CHAPTER 6

The Medicine Show

HISTORICAL SUMMARY

The medicine show, a very American institution, although it evolved from the age-old quack doctor and mountebank performers of Europe, was designed to sell patent medicines and other miscellaneous cheap articles. Such shows flourished in the mid-nineteenth century, although the tradition continued well into this century. Their success paralleled the phenomenal growth of the American patent medicine industry as a major business in the nineteenth century. Before the turn of the nineteenth century, the traveling medicine show, with its pitchman and frequent humbug Indian spectaculars, was a flourishing form of entertainment, borrowing everything that was taking place in the American theater and adapting it to its own needs.

The medicine show was an important diversion in rural American; many shows provided the only entertainment in small, out-of-the-way towns and were greeted by the townspeople with great eagerness when the show wagon rolled into town. The size and extravagance of these shows ran the gamut from a quack and a single musician performing on the tailgate of a wagon to very elaborate productions with large numbers of entertainers, and Indians, performing on more sophisticated stages erected in tents or surrounded by canvas walls. Although the entertainment attracted the audience, ultimately the important moment was the spiel by the "Doc" and the sale of goods.

It was no small wonder that medicine showmen succeeded so well in their trade. The American frontier offered previously unexploited potential suckers. Medical care was still quite primitive in the early nineteenth century. In 1775 there were only 400 trained doctors with university medical degrees; hospitals were available only in major cities, and even apothecary shops were rare. Circuit doctors traveled on horseback to isolated areas bringing with them primitive drugs that could be prepared by patients in their own homes, including quinine, caolomel, salts, aloes, sassafras and bergamot. Even if more advanced drugs had been available, few physicians could diagnose with any exactitude the causes of most illnesses. Even the germ theory of disease would not be proven until the late nineteenth century. A medicine show quack, with wonder elixirs, salves, and tonics advertised to cure all ailments was a welcomed sight. The great marvel was that the partial acceptance of their patent medicines continued well after modern science had disproven their pseudocures.

The term "patent medicine" did not mean that the concoction had been registered with the U.S. Patent Office; indeed, such medicines were merely proprietary medicines or mixtures devised by the manufacturer as a curative. Most often, such a cure was nothing more than a mixture of herbs, spices, or snake oil. Legally, the seller of the cure was free from any restraints.

Although the selling of patent medicine was a big business for proprietors of apothecary shops in fixed locations and a prime source of advertising revenue for smaller newspapers, it was the showman cum medicine man who saw the lucrative possibilities on the road, taking his wares to rural areas where the people lacked both adequate medical care and entertainment. From one-man shows during the early nineteenth century, the medicine showman soon added other performers to his entourage—banjo players, comic actors, and dancers. Entertainment to entice the patrons included not only variety acts but shortened versions of popular plays, such as *Uncle Tom's Cabin* or *The Drunkard*. After the Civil War, the Indian medicine show developed, with more nearly universal appeal for all regions of the country, and capitalized on the belief that Indians possessed special powers as healers. Naturally, the patent medicine industry quickly gave their cures Indian names and medicine men posed as Indian doctors. By the 1880s the medicine show had become big business, thanks largely to John E. Healy and his Kickapoo Indian Medicine Company in New Haven, Connecticut, which produced millions of bottles of Indian Sagwa. Healy's "Kick" shows, which toured the East and the Midwest, became legendary in the medicine-show business. Small independent troupes and lone pitchmen, selling their own concoctions or standard remedies like Ayer's Sarsaparilla or Lydia E. Pinkham's Vegetable Compound, were now forced to compete with large stage shows sent out by Healy or other big firms like the Hamlin Company of Chicago, manufacturer of Wizard Oil.

Mary Calhoun describes in *Medicine Show* a typical kickapoo show with twelve performers (six Indians and six other performers). This unit traveled from town to town, pitching their tents in empty lots. "On stage the Indians would sit in a half circle around Oliver [Ned Oliver, the leader of the troupe, inpersonated an "Indian Agent"], who, in Western scout costume, introduced each Indian. One Indian would then make an impassioned speech in his native language, which Oliver interpreted as a glowing tale of the marvelous properties of their medicines." At the end of the pitch, three entertainers broke into fast music while "three Indians would shout war whoops and beat their tom-toms and the other six would circulate through the crowd to sell" Indian Sagwa.

Hamlin, Healy's major competitor, took a more refined and distinguished approach. Hamlin's Wizard Oil was sold from wagons drawn from town to town by handsome four- or six-horse teams. Each wagon carried a driver, a lecturer, a vocal-instrumental quartet, and a parlor organ built onto the wagon. Without Healy's ballyhoo, Hamlin attempted to promote local goodwill and relatively long engagements, hoping to return to the same location each year.

By the late nineteenth century the traveling medicine show, like other forms of traveling amusements of the period, was an established and flourishing entertainment enterprise. When the Indian medicine show began to lose it novel appeal, showmen quickly looked for a new gimmick. Jim Ferdon, for example, developed the Quaker Medicine Company, capitalizing on the trust most Americans placed in the Quakers. Another enterprising showman formed the Shaker Medicine Company, although in this case the Shakers of Lebanon, Pennsylvania, actually did supply the formulas for the medicines and carefully watched the actions of the troupes selling their patent medicine.

As the medicine show moved into the twentieth century, its format remained much the same. Small-time medicine men, providing the spiel and the entertainment, continued to travel into rural areas in buggies. More ambitious showmen, however, offered much more; in fact, some shows were so large that they traveled by railway cars. Shows like those of the Big Sensation Medicine Company and the Ton-Ko-Ko Medicine Show played under canvas tents or at local opera houses and theaters, charging admission fees as well as fees for medicines. Such shows, actually traveling variety shows, added gimmicks common to the American circus such as free parades and concerts. Entertainment ran the gamut from strong-man acts to ballet dancers, fire-eaters to stand-up comics, comedy skits to song-and-dance routines. Most shows, however, continued the practice of offering free shows in order to entice the customers to buy their products.

Like most forms of traveling entertainment dependent on small-town and rural areas, the medicine show had begun its decline by World War I. Improved travel, better communication, the motion picture, and medical advances were creating a less impressionable audience. New governmental regulations, beginning in 1906, curtailed the patent medicine business, making it far more difficult to operate within more stringent restrictions.

Although the bigger shows prospered until the late 1920s, even the shows produced by the titans of the business gradually shrank in size and splendor. By the 1930s medicine-show routes were limited primarily to the rural areas of the South and the Midwest. By World War II those few medicine showmen who managed to subsist in remote areas were virtually ignored in locales that previously had welcomed them. The 1940s witnessed gasoline rationing that further curtailed the mobility of the few remaining medicine shows. In *Step Right Up* Brooks McNamara estimates that through the forties about two dozen medicine show troupes continued to struggle along. By the 1950s it was rare to find even a small medicine show on the road.

During the last throes of the medicine-show tradition, one enterprising entrepreneur, Dudley J. LeBlanc, a Cajun and one-time Louisiana state senator, created a brief flurry of interest with his wonder drug, Hadacol, and made a fortune for himself. Although Hadacol was more sophisticated than earlier patent medicines, it was not that different, containing B-complex vitamins, iron, calcium, and honey on a base of 12 percent alcohol. In order to ballyhoo his concoction, LeBlanc staged a gigantic medicine show that toured 3,800 miles of the South and featured major performers, including Mickey Rooney, Burns and Allen, and Roy Acuff. But even LeBlanc could not compete with radio entertainment and early television— forms, as McNamara points out, that medicine shows helped to create. Indeed, the formula of free entertainment in order to sell a product continues to be the stock in trade of commercial radio and television.

SURVEY OF SOURCES

Little serious attention has been given to the theatrical and entertainment format of the American medicine show, despite the fact that it belongs to a rich tradition of mountebanks, charletans, and quack doctors selling tonics and elixirs mixed with attention-getting free entertainment that dates back to the Middle Ages. The most thorough documented history and analysis of the form is Brooks McNamara's *Step Right Up: An Illustrated History of the American Medicine Show,* which is not only a definitive study but an excellent reference for additional sources on patent medicine and related topics, examples of medicine show skits, and a glossary of pitchmen's terms. His essays on the subject, although to a large extent incorporated into the longer work, are also recommended. These include "The Indian Medicine Show" and "Medicine Shows: American Vaudeville in the Marketplace."

Other major sources, though not comparable to McNamara's carefully researched work, include the following: Graydon Freeman's *The Medicine*

Showman, written by the son of a medicine show operator whose show was modeled after the Kickapoo Indian Show (the major part of the book is devoted to proprietary medicines sold by showmen up to 1900); Thomas Kelley's *The Fabulous Kelley,* covering the fifty-year career of "Doc" Kelley (1865-1931) as a medicine-show entrepreneur in thirty-seven states and every province in Canada; Malcolm Webber's fictionalized reminiscences, *Medicine Show,* about a traveling show in the 1900s; Mary Calhoun's *Medicine Show: Conning People and Making Them Like It,* a juvenile book which nonetheless captures the essentials of the medicine show and its history; and Violet McNeal's *Four White Horses and a Brass Band,* the life of one of the few female medicine show operators (Princess Lotus Blossom) and an excellent source on the caste system among medicine shows. The chapter called "Troupers and Pitchmen" in Ann Banks's *First-Person America* includes insightful interviews with a small-time pitchman and a medicine showman (part of a Federal Writers' Project collected between 1938 and 1942).

Mae Noell, one of the last surviving female medicine show performers and a frequent traveler on the rural circuits, has written two essays that are informative and extremely entertaining, "Some Memories of a Medicine Show Performer" and "Recollections of Medicine Show Life." Other recommended sources on specific medicine showmen and their methods are the following: Bob Barton's *Old Covered Wagon Show Days,* primarily about the circus but with good coverage of the old-time medicine show; Jean Brand's "Picturesque Medicine Shows Combined Entertainment with Salesmanship," on shows in Missouri in the late-nineteenth century and attempts to control medicine showmen; William P. Burt's very useful "Back Stage with a Medicine Show Fifty Years Ago," on John Austin Hamlin, his Wizard Oil, and his show during the Civil War; F. J. Clifford's brief survey of medicine shows, "The Medicine Show," which recounts a classic "ghost" routine; Richard Donovan and Dwight Whitney's "Painless Parker—Last of America's Tooth Plumbers," covering the fifty-nine-year career of a dental medicine showman in a very entertaining and vivid series of articles; W.A.S. Douglas's "Pitch Doctors," with a focus on medicine shows in the 1920s; David Edstrom's *The Testament of Caliban* (condensed as "Medicine Men of the '80s"), which discusses Dr. Lamereux's Indian Medicine Show; William Price Fox's "The Late Great Medicine Show," a brief but atmospheric look at the medicine show of Doc Milton Bartok (and his foray into the circus); Arrell M. Gibson's "Medicine Show," a good overview of medicine-show entertainment, especially on the frontier; Mary Hardgrove Hebberd's "Notes on Dr. David Franklin Powell, Known as 'White Beaver'," a showman and manufacturer of patent medicines; Kay Haugaard's "Medicine Show," based in part on Malcolm Webber's previously discussed book, and an interesting look at the medicine show as "a kind of backwoods vaudeville"; Winifred Johnston's "Medicine Show," a brief history of medicine shows from the Middle Ages with a section on traveling medicine shows in Texas and Mississippi around 1886 and in Oklahoma in the 1930s; Thomas J. LeBlanc's "The Medicine Show," a recreation of the show's yearly visit to a small American town; Doc Art Miller's "Medicine Show Tonight!" with coverage of a show's structure; George Jean Nathan's exploration of a show's methods and the selling of Indian Sagwa in "The Medicine Man"; N. T. Oliver and Wesley Winans Stout's "Med Show" and "Alagazam, The Story of Pitchmen, High and Low," which provide good first-hand observations of Nevada Ned, a big-time showman, and other operations; Joe Sappington's "The Passing of the Medicine Show," the memoirs of one patron of the Great Mohawk Herb Remedy Co.; Jim Tully's "The Giver of Life," on Jonathan Maloney, who toured a small medicine show; and Sisley Barnes's "Medicine Shows: Duped, Delighted," a fairly recent survey of various medicine-show doctors, their cures and entertainment.

The medicine show has frequently appeared in fictional work. For example, Robert Lewis Taylor's *A Journey to Matecumb* (his tale of Dr. Ewing T. Snodgrass and his medicine showboat on the Mississippi) is based in part on actual medicine shows; Harry Leon Wilson's *Professor How Could You?* provides a good account of a medicine show's structure and audience reaction; and Will Rose's *The Vanishing Village,* set in Woodstock Valley, New York, between 1896 and 1903, includes the visit of a medicine show. The more contemporary medicine show, in particular that of Dudley LeBlanc, is given adequate coverage in Jerry C. Brigham and Karlie K. Kenyon's "Hadacol: The Last Great Medicine Show" and James Harvey Young's "The Hadacol Phenomenon." Long John Nebel provides an interesting comparison between radio and television advertising and the old-time medicine show pitch in "The Pitchman." The language of the pitchman and medicine shows is given extensive coverage in Don. B. Wilmeth's *The Language of American Popular Entertainment.*

Patent medicine and its relation to the medicine show has been studied quite thoroughly in the work of James Harvey Young. Those sources by Young that incorporate some coverage of medicine shows include the following: "Patent Medicines: The Early Post-Frontier Phase," "Patent Medicines and Indians," *The Toadstool Millionaires, A Social History of Patent Medicines in America Before Federal Regulation,* and *The Medical Messiahs,* a sequel to *The Toadstool Millionaires* (which covers the period from colonial days to 1906) and a study of the rise in the twentieth century of modern medical science and of pseudomedical nonsense (LeBlanc and "Hadacol" are included). For background, Young's "American Medical Quackery in the Age of the Common Man" is also recommended.

The historical roots of the American patent medicine industry and the quack doctor are covered in the following recommended sources: Grete de Francesco, *The Power of the Charlatan,* which contains a section on American quackery by Miriam Beard; Eric Jameson, *The Natural History of Quackery,* a history of cures and nostrums from the sixteenth century; C.J.S. Thompson, *The Quacks of Old London;* and John Camp, "The Golden Age of Quackery," a useful summary of eighteenth-century quackery in England.

Various aspects of American quack medicine and the patent medicine industry in this country, in addition to those sources by Young, have been studied in the following: Gerald Carson's *One for a Man, Two for a Horse: A Pictorial History, Grave and Comic, of Patent Medicines,* and "Sweet Extract of Hokum," the story of Lydia Pinkham's and other patent medicines of the late 1800s and early 1900s (both sources have excellent illustrations); Stewart H. Holbrook's *The Golden Age of Quackery,* which includes a great deal on medicine shows; Adelaide Hechtlinger's *The Great Patent Medicine Era,* an intriguing collection of illustrations and texts of books, and advertisements on patent medicine; William J. Petersen's "Patent Medicine Advertising Cards"; Madge E. Pickard and R. Caryle Buley's *The Midwest Pioneer, His Ills, Cures, and Doctors;* Dorothea D. Reeves's "Come All for the Cure-all: Patent Medicines; Nineteenth Century Bonanza"; and Julian B. Roebuck and Robert Bruce Hunter's "Medical Quackery as Deviant Behavior," a sociological study which attempts to construct an operational definition of several forms of medical quackery and to evolve an empirical typology of deviant practices within the broader field of medical quackery, including a discussion of LeBlanc and Hadacol and Lydia Pinkham and her products.

BIBLIOGRAPHY

Banks, Ann, ed. *First-Person America.* New York: Alfred A. Knopf, 1980.

Barnes, Sisley. "Medicine Shows: Duped, Delighted." *Smithsonian* 5 (January 1975):50–54.

Barton, Bob, as told to G. Ernest Thomas. *Old Covered Wagon Show Days.* New York: E. P. Dutton and Co., 1939.

[Brand, Jean]. "Picturesque Medicine Shows Combined Entertainment with Salesmanship." *Missouri Historical Review* 45 (July 1951):374-76.

Brigham, Jerry C., and Kenyon, Karlie K. "Hadacol: The Last Great Medicine Show." *Journal of Popular Culture* 10 (Winter 1976):520-33.

Burt, William P. "Back Stage with a Medicine Show Fifty Years Ago." *Colorado Magazine,* July 1942, pp. 127-36.

Calhoun, Mary. *Medicine Show: Conning People and Making Them Like It.* New York: Harper and Row, 1976.

Camp, John. "The Golden Age of Quackery." *British History Illustrated* 5 (June-July 1978):54-61.

Carson, Gerald. *One for a Man, Two for a Horse: A Pictorial History, Grave and Comic, of Patent Medicines.* Garden City, N.Y.: Doubleday and Co., 1961.
_____. "Sweet Extract of Hokum." *American Heritage* 22 (June 1971):19-27, 108-10.
Clifford, F. J. "The Medicine Show." *Frontier Times,* November 1930, pp. 92-96.
Donovan, Richard, and Whitney, Dwight. "Painless Parker—Last of America's Tooth Plumbers." *Collier's* 129, 5 January 1952, pp. 7-9, 54-55; 129, 12 January 1952, pp. 20, 43-45; 129, 19 January 1952, pp. 26, 27, 38-40.
Douglas, W.A.S. "Pitch Doctors." *American Mercury* 10 (February 1927):222-26.
Edstrom, David. *The Testament of Caliban.* New York: Funk and Wagnalls, 1927. Condensed as "Medicine Men of the '80s." *Readers Digest* 32 (June 1938): 77-78.
Fox, William Price. "The Late Great Medicine Show." *Travel and Leisure,* December 1974, pp. 6, 10, 14-15.
Francesco, Grete de. *The Power of the Charlatan.* Translated by Miriam Beard. New Haven: Yale University Press, 1939.
Freeman, Graydon La Verne. *The Medicine Showman.* Watkins Glen, N.Y.: Century House, 1957.
Gibson, Avrell M. "Medicine Show." *The American West* 4 (February 1967):34-39, 74-79.
Haugaard, Kay. "Medicine Show." *True West,* January-February 1964, pp. 26-27, 46.
Hebberd, Mary Hardgrove. "Notes on Dr. David Franklin Powell, Known as 'White Beaver'." *Wisconsin Magazine of History* 35 (Summer 1952):306-9.
Hechtlinger, Adelaide. *The Great Patent Medicine Era.* New York: Grosset and Dunlap, 1970.
Holbrook, Stewart H. *The Golden Age of Quackery.* New York: Macmillan Co., 1959.
Jameson, Eric. *The Natural History of Quackery.* Springfield, Ill.: Charles C. Thomas, 1961.
Johnston, Winifred. "Medicine Show." *Southwest Review* 21 (July 1936):390-99.
Kelley, Thomas P., Jr. *The Fabulous Kelley: He Was King of the Medicine Men.* New York: Pocket Books, 1968.
LeBlanc, Thomas J. "The Medicine Show." *American Mercury* 5 (June 1925): 232-37.
McNamara, Brooks. "The Indian Medicine Show." *Educational Theatre Journal,* 23 (December 1971):431-45.
_____. "Medicine Shows: American Vaudeville in the Marketplace." *Theatre Quarterly* 4 (May-July 1974):19-30.
_____. *Step Right Up: An Illustrated History of the American Medicine Show.* Garden City, N.Y.: Doubleday and Co., 1976.
McNeal, Violet. *Four White Horses and a Brass Band.* New York: Doubleday and Co., 1947.
Miller, Doc Art. "Medicine Show Tonight!" *Bandwagon* 16 (July-August 1972): 20-22.
Nathan, George Jean. "The Medicine Men." *Harper's Weekly,* September 1911, p. 24.
Nebel, Long John. "The Pitchman." *Harper's* 222 (May 1961):50-54.

Noell, Mae. "Some Memories of a Medicine Show Performer." *Theatre Quarterly,* 4 (May-July 1974):25-30.

———. "Recollections of Medicine Show Life." In *American Popular Entertainment,* edited by Myron Matlaw. Westport, Conn. and London: Greenwood Press, 1979.

Oliver, N. T., as told to Wesley Winans Stout. "Med Show." *Saturday Evening Post,* 14 September 1929, pp. 12, 166, 169, 173-74.

———. "Alagazam, The Story of Pitchmen, High and Low." *Saturday Evening Post,* 19 October 1929, p. 12.

Petersen, William J. "Patent Medicine Advertising Cards." *Palimpsest* 50 (June 1969):317-31.

Pickard, Madge E., and Buley, R. Caryle. *The Midwest Pioneer, His Ills, Cures, and Doctors.* New York: Henry Schuman, 1946.

Reeves, Dorothea D., "Come All for the Cure-all: Patent Medicines; Nineteenth Century Bonanza." *Harvard Library Bulletin* 15 (July 1967):253-72.

Roebuck, Julian B., and Hunter, Robert Bruce. "Medical Quackery as Deviant Behavior." In *Deviant Occupational and Organizational Bases,* edited by Clifton D. Bryant. Chicago: Rand McNally College Publishing Co., 1974.

Rose, Will. *The Vanishing Village.* New York: Citadel Press, 1963.

Sappington, Joe. "The Passing of the Medicine Show." *Frontier Times,* February 1930, pp. 229-30.

Shafer, Henry B. *The American Medical Profession, 1783 to 1850.* New York: Columbia University Press, 1937.

Taylor, Robert Lewis. *A Journey to Matecumb.* New York: McGraw-Hill, 1961.

Thompson, C.J.S. *The Quacks of Old London.* New York, London, and Paris: Brentano's, 1928.

Tully, Jim. "The Giver of Life." *American Mercury* 14 (June 1928):154-60.

Webber, Malcolm. *Medicine Show.* Caldwell, Idaho: Caxton Printers, 1941.

Wilmeth, Don B. *The Language of American Popular Entertainment: A Glossary of Argot, Slang, and Terminology.* Westport, Conn. and London: Greenwood Press, 1981.

Wilson, Harry Leon. *Professor How Could You?* New York: Grosset and Dunlap, 1924.

Young, James Harvey. "The Hadacol Phenomenon." *Emory University Quarterly* 7 (June 1951):72-86.

———. "Patent Medicines: The Early Post-Frontier Phase." *Illinois State Historical Journal* 46 (Autumn 1953):254-64.

———. "American Medical Quackery in the Age of the Common Man." *Mississippi Valley Historical Review* 47 (March 1961):579-93.

———. "Patent Medicines and Indians." *Emory University Quarterly* 17 (Summer 1961):86-92.

———. *The Toadstool Millionaires, A Social History of Patent Medicines in America Before Federal Regulation.* Princeton, N.J.: Princeton University Press, 1961.

———. "The Patent Medicine Almanac." *Wisconsin Magazine of History* 45 (Spring 1962):159-63.

———. *The Medical Messiahs.* Princeton, N.J.: Princeton University Press, 1967.

CHAPTER 7

The Minstrel Show

HISTORICAL SUMMARY

Of the major forms of stage entertainment, the minstrel show is usually considered the first uniquely American show-business form. Beginning in the 1840s, blackface minstrelsy literally swept the nation, producing in time a tremendous impact on subsequent forms, in particular vaudeville and burlesque. Using what the white performers claimed were credible black dialects, songs, dances, and jokes, showmen in blackface created extremely popular and entertaining shows while at the same time perpetuating negative stereotypes of blacks that endured in American popular thought long after the show had vanished. Robert C. Toll, in his important study *Blacking Up,* has analyzed the form thoroughly and concludes that minstrelsy went far beyond being just a show. In his essay ''Showbiz in Blackface'' Toll writes:

> It was no accident that when slavery and race threatened to tear America apart, white men blacked up their faces and literally acted out images of black people that satisfied great masses of white Americans, especially in the North where early minstrel shows were most popular. It was also no accident that after the Civil War when white America made crucial decisions about the rights and status of black people, the blackface minstrel show dominated American show business. There were, then, deep-seated racial and sociological reasons for the popularity and longevity of the minstrel show.

Toll is quick to point out, however, that the minstrel show was also dynamite entertainment, expanding at a time when America was experiencing its first urban population explosion and the creation of a large audience of working-class people. In chapter 5 on the dime museum it was noted that P. T. Barnum was the first major showman to capitalize on this new audience. Minstrel showmen were not far behind (and Barnum was quick to capitalize on the minstrelsy rage at his museum).

During the 1820s the unique culture of black Americans took its place along with other aspects of American folklore that appealed to common people as a regular feature of variety turns between the acts of virtually every play produced in most major cities and as acts in the circus. The popularity of such acts grew so rapidly that white performers began to specialize in blackface routines.

Historically, the popularity of the black native character portrayed by whites in blackface dates from about 1828 when Thomas Dartmouth Rice created, almost by accident, his "Jim Crow" song and dance routine. Tradition has it that Rice witnessed a crippled Negro at a stable owned by a man named Crow. The slave had taken the surname of his master and called himself Jim Crow. Rice, who was performing with Samuel Drake's company, possibly in Louisville, Kentucky, watched the man sweeping out the stables, singing a catchy song accompanied by a dance with short hopping and spinning motions. The song ended with the refrain:

> Weel about, and turn about
> And do jis so;
> Eb-ry time I weel about
> I jump Jim Crow.

Rice, who had an eye for what would appeal to the public taste, saw the comic possibilities in the song and dance. After purchasing the man's shabby clothes, he learned the dance and song, which he embellished with new verses (in time, well over fifty). After performing his act for several years on the road, Rice took his Jim Crow routine to New York's Bowery Theatre on November 12, 1832. In Rice's hands, the "Ethiopian delineator" (the name given to early blackfaced white entertainers), graduated from a simple entr'acte spot to a major attraction. Rice began to write farces for his character, called "Ethiopian Operas," with such titles as *Long Island Juba, Where's My Head?, Virginia Mummy,* and *Bone Squash Diavolo.* Rice's popularity by the mid-1830s was established in New York and London, and he became the first major blackface star.

Other white performers, such as Barney Williams, Jack Diamond, Bill Keller, and Bob Farrell, quickly began to imitate Rice's concept, with songs, dances, and comedy. The next step in the evolution of the minstrel show was to find an innovation that would exploit the potential to its fullest. In 1843, four performers calling themselves the Virginia Minstrels and organized by Dan Emmett developed the first full-length example of the new entertainment that would be called the minstrel show. The group had chosen the name "Virginia" to underscore the supposed authenticity of their material and their impersonations of Southern blacks. They called themselves "minstrels" in order to cash in on the recent popularity of the Tyrolese Minstrel Family, a group of touring European singers. Soon a flood of competitors followed. In 1846 E. P. Christy gave the minstrel show its distinctive three-part structure: repartee between the master of ceremonies, or interlocutor, and the endmen (Bruder Tambo and Bruder Bones) sitting on either end of a semicircular arrangement of the company, followed by the "olio" or the variety section, and culminating with a one-act skit (an outgrowth of the "Ethiopian Opera"). By the 1850s such an arrangement was commonplace in most minstrel shows.

Like the imitators of Jim Rice, groups of blackface showmen banned together to form minstrel troupes in imitation of these early, successful companies. Almost over night, the minstrel show became a national entertainment. Its popularity survived for over fifty years; as an amateur pastime, minstrel shows continued to perpetuate negative stereotypes well into this century. Despite the detrimental aspects of the minstrel show, which cannot be denied, the popularity of such shows should not be too surprising. Minstrelsy was the first major stage entertainment to avoid the elitist reputation of legitimate drama and commit itself, quite consciously, to the new common-man audience. It was immediate, unpretentious, and devoted to fun, the emotional outlet that its urban patrons needed so desperately. Its appeal was especially strong in the major cities of the Northeast, where the minstrel show, as Toll explains, provided the white audience with a non-threatening way to work out their feelings about race and slavery. Everything possible was done in the minstrel show to emphasize the differences between whites and blacks and thus reinforce the status and identity of the patrons. Although public concerns and anxieties were addressed by minstrels, it was its use of music and comedy that created its greatest appeal and most lasting influence. With its endmen and interlocutor, the audience was engulfed in an endless string of puns, malapropisms, riddles, and jokes, delivered as rapid-fire exchanges and carried over into the later urban humor of vaudeville, burlesque, and even radio, motion pictures, and television.

Before the Civil War, the theatrical impact of the black mask and the adaptability of the form captivated its audience. The newness of the form, with its carefree attitude, created maximum audience rapport and empathy, verging on active participation. Furthermore, the reinforcement of traditional values and the naked, uncluttered emotionality of the songs gave the audience a very comfortable feeling. The master of the minstrel musical form, although given little credit at the time, was Stephen Collins Foster, who, better than anyone, was able to blend those elements characteristic of minstrel music—modified Afro-American rhythms, the Euro-American folk song tradition, and genteel melodies of a more original creation.

In the 1860s, and especially during the period immediately after the Civil War when the country swelled with a second major wave of immigrants, most of whom settled in the cities, the minstrel show was confronted with competition from entertainment forms less limited in scope and more capable of attracting audiences with a European orientation. Variety shows, which by the 1870s were dominated by immigrant humor, musicals, and burlesque, each provided new structures and outlets for entertainers. Furthermore, no longer were minstrel companies limited to white performers; entire troupes of blacks began to break into show business via the minstrel form. As a result of these and other factors, in order to remain competitive the minstrel show expanded in diversity and scope, incorporating elements from the newer forms of entertainment, and reached its peak in 1870. The westward population shift of this period, coupled with an improved national transportation system, made it possible for minstrel companies to travel into heretofore unexplored areas where the minstrel show might have a greater appeal to a whole new audience less jaded and sophisticated but also less willing to tolerate controversial material and disinterested in issue-based content. Minstrel shows became more lavish, typified by the productions of J. H. Haverly, more generalized in subject matter and specificity, and generally more refined, thus moving farther and farther away from minstrelsy's roots. Finally, though these changes had prolonged the life of minstrelsy for a short time, its uniqueness was destroyed. Other than by its name, the minstrel show frequently was indistinguishable from other variety forms or spectacular musical productions. The troupe of George Primrose and Billy West, for example, epitomized this final step. Their show, though financially successful for a time, virtually eliminated all those unique characteristics of the minstrel show, including dialects, blackface, and topics and music associated with Southern (or even Northern) blacks.

By 1896 only ten minstrel companies remained, and the minstrel show was no longer America's major stage entertainment; its replacement was the new refined version of variety, vaudeville. All that was left, other than its central image of the caricatured black, were individual performers such as Al Jolson, Eddie Cantor, and Bert Williams (a black who was forced to appear in burnt cork), who specialized in blackface routines as part of a complex vaudeville bill.

SURVEY OF SOURCES

The most comprehensive history and analysis of the minstrel show to date is Robert C. Toll's *Blacking Up,* which, in addition to its stimulating text, provides a chronological listing of minstrel troupes with black performers for the period 1855-1890 and a superb bibliography of primary and secondary sources. Abbreviated versions of his full-length study (with some new information) can be found in "Behind the Blackface: Minstrel Men and Minstrel Myths," "Show Biz in Blackface: The Evolution of the Minstrel Show as a Theatrical Form," and chapter 4 of *On with the Show* ("The Minstrel Show: Show Biz in Blackface"). Along with Francis Lee Utley, Toll has edited *Old Slacks's Reminiscences and Pocket History of the Colored Profession From 1865 to 1891* by Ike Simond, originally published circa 1892, which incorporates a useful preface by Utley and introduction by Toll, plus a knowledgeable account of nineteenth-century black performers (including a list of over one thousand names).

Two recent sources should be mentioned before turning to more dated material. Henry T. Sampson's *Blacks in Blackface: A Source Book on Early Black Musical Shows* is an impressive compendium of information on every phase of the black musical show, including a good historical overview of the early black musical and going back to its roots in the minstrel show; like Sampson's, Charles Hamm's *Yesterdays: Popular Song in America* is a broad study that surveys the American popular song over a two-hundred-year period and includes an excellent chapter on the music of the minstrel show (older sources with similar coverage are discussed in chapter 10).

Of the more dated sources on the minstrel show, the following are still useful surveys. Carl Wittke's *Tambo and Bones* remains a good basic history and explanation of minstrelsy form. Dailey Paskman's *"Gentlemen, Be Seated!"* (originally published in 1928) has been revised recently by Paskman and updated to include recent offshoots of minstrelsy. It remains, however, a romanticized history but with good examples of music, sample minstrel routines, and good illustrations. Edward Rice's *Monarchs of Minstrelsy* supplies biographical sketches of minstrel specialists, an index of minstrels, and a list of minstrel organizations up to 1911. Other books and essays that survey minstrelsy that can be recommended include the following: Richard Moody's "Negro Minstrelsy," which provides a good appraisal of minstrelsy largely as a romantic invention of Northern whites; Alain Locke's *The Negro and His Music & Negro Art,* with several informative chapters on minstrelsy; Brander Matthews's "The Rise and Fall of Negro Minstrelsy," a brief but useful older summary; and Harry Reynolds's *Minstrel Memories: The Story of Burnt Cork Minstrelsy in Great Britain from 1836-1927,* which chronicles the tremendous impact of minstrelsy in England.

A number of more scholarly studies should be of special interest. Two doctoral dissertations on minstrelsy and songsters have added scholarly credibility to the topic: Frank Davidson's "The Rise, Development, Decline, and Influence of the American Minstrel Show" and Cecil L. Patterson's "A Different Drummer." Patterson also has published a useful essay drawn in large part from his thesis: "A Different Drummer: The

Image of the Negro in Nineteenth Century Songsters." Other more specific scholarly studies include the following: Ray B. Browne, "Shakespeare in American Vaudeville and Negro Minstrelsy"; Charles Haywood, "Negro Minstrelsy and Shakespearean Burlesque" (emphasis on the period 1850 to 1870); George F. Rehin, "The Darker Image: American Negro Minstrelsy through the Historian's Lens," a review of trends in scholarly studies of minstrelsy, and his "Harlequin Jim Crow: Continuity and Convergence in Blackface Clowning," a useful review of the literature of blackface minstrelsy and an explanation of minstrelsy in something other than American terms; Orrin Clayton Suthern II, "Minstrelsy and Popular Culture"; and Jules Zanger, "The Minstrel Show as Theater of Misrule," an analysis of the minstrel show that reveals it had as its target the pieties of genteel culture, education, and art.

The early origins and history of the minstrel show are discussed in the following: T. Allston Brown, "The Origin of Negro Minstrelsy" (in Charles H. Day's *Fun in Black, or Sketches of Minstrel Life,* which is less useful in its totality than Brown's essay); W. P. Eaton, "Dramatic Evolution and the Popular Theatre: Playhouse Roots of our Drama," which focuses on the influence of minstrelsy in the American theater; Isaac J. Greenwood, *The Circus: Its Origin and Growth Prior to 1835, With a Sketch on Negro Minstrelsy;* Alan W.C. Green, " 'Jim Crow,' 'Zip Coon'; The Northern Origins of Negro Minstrelsy," a discussion of pre-1800 stage Negroes in American plays, early specialty acts and performers (J. D. Rice and George Washington Dixon), and the full-fledged show; Laurence Hutton, "The Negro on the Stage"; Olive Logan, "The Ancestry of Brudder Bones," a discussion of George Christy and Dan Bryant, followed by an attempt to show parallels between American minstrelsy and medieval bas-reliefs of musicians and ancient instruments; J. J. Trux, "Negro Minstrelsy—Ancient and Modern"; and Hans Nathan, "The First Negro Minstrel Band and Its Origin" (on the formation of the Virginia Minstrels in 1843).

Specific minstrel showmen are covered in the following recommended sources. T. D. Rice's career is effectively summarized by Molly Ramshaw in "Jump, Jim Crow! A Biographical Sketch of Thomas D. Rice" and by James H. Dormon in "The Strange Career of Jim Crow Rice." Hans Nathan's *Dan Emmett and the Rise of Early Negro Minstrelsy* chronicles the life of this minstrel specialist and the early period of minstrelsy from the point of view of a musicologist (other sources on music are discussed below). Other useful sources include the following: John Jay Daly, *A Song in His Heart* (James Bland as composer and performer); Ralph Keeler, "Three Years a Negro Minstrel" and *Vagabond Adventures;* Henry A. Kmen, "Old Corn Meal: A Forgotten Urban Negro Folksinger" (on a performer that the author considers a direct influence on the minstrel show); Eddie Leonard, *What a Life I'm Telling You,* the career of a latter-day minstrel; Frank Oakman Spinney, "A New Hampshire Minstrel Tours the Coast" (on Rhodolphus Hall and his tour of California in the mid-1860s); and Marian Winter, "Juba and American Minstrelsy" (on William Henry "Juba" Lane).

Regional histories of the minstrel show include the following: Horace G. Belcher, "Mr. Tambo and Mr. Bones: Rhode Island in Negro Minstrelsy"; Elbert R. Bowen, "Negro Minstrels in Early Rural Missouri"; Francis Garvin Davenport, *Cultural Life in Nashville on the Eve of the Civil War* (for the period 1850-1860); Harry R. Edwall, "The Golden Era of Minstrelsy in Memphis: A Reconstruction"; Harvey G. Gaul, "The Minstrel of the Alleghenies," with a focus on the family of Stephen Foster; John Smith Kendall, "New Orleans Negro Minstrels"; "Melodies and Soft Shoes in Blackface" (cursory survey of minstrelsy in Missouri in the nineteenth century); E. T. Sawyer, "Old-Time Minstrels of San Francisco"; and Albert Stoutamire, *Music of the Old South: Colony to Confederacy* (minstrelsy in Richmond, Virginia).

Sources that deal specifically with the music of minstrelsy, in addition to Hamm and Nathan, include the following: H. T. Burleigh, *Negro Minstrel Melodies* (twenty-one minstrel songs with a useful preface); Gilbert Chase, *America's Music from the Pilgrims to the Present* (three informative chapters on minstrelsy); S. Foster Damon, "The Negro in Early American Songsters," a survey from preminstrel days to the blues; W. C. Handy, *Father of the Blues* (includes a list of his books and compositions); Charles Haywood, *A Bibliography of North American Folklore and Folksongs,* with a superb bibliography of minstrel songsters; John Trasker Howard, *Stephen Foster: America's Troubadour,* a definitive, documented biography of Foster; LeRoi Jones, *Blues People: Negro Music in White America,* with considerable insight into black minstrelsy; Kelly Miller, "The Negro 'Stephen Foster'," on James A. Bland; R. P. Nevin, "Stephen C. Foster and Negro Minstrelsy"; and Robert L. Webb, "Banjos in their Saddle Horns." Other less specific sources on music, but still worth consultation, include Rudi Blesh and Harriet Janis's *They All Played Ragtime;* Michael Demarest's "Music to Which the Gold Rushed"; Dena J. Epstein's *Sinful Tunes and Spirituals: Black Folk Music to the Civil War;* Nathan Huggins's *Harlem Renaissance;* Helen L. Kaufmann's *From Jehovah to Jazz;* Lindsay Patterson's edited anthology *The Negro in Music and Art* (which includes Locke's essay mentioned above); and James Monroe Trotter's *Music and Some Highly Musical People,* with a good chapter on "The Georgia Minstrels."

More general studies of blacks in the entertainment world are frequently useful and informative sources. In addition to Sampson's *Blacks in Black-face,* the following are suggested: Tom Fletcher's *100 Years of the Negro in*

Show Business, which places minstrelsy, with a focus on individuals, in the context of black performers over a one-hundred-year period; James Weldon Johnson's *Black Manhattan,* which is more useful on the development of the black musical; Frederick W. Bond's *The Negro and the Drama;* and W. C. Handy's *Negro Authors and Composers of the United States.* Other sources on blacks in the entertainment world are discussed in chapters 1, 8, 9, and 10.

Many nineteenth-century memoirs of performers and managers include mention of minstrel shows and minstrel entertainments. The list is too extensive to include here, but the following are especially relevant: Al G. Field's *Watch Yourself Go By* and M. B. Leavitt's *Fifty Years in Theatrical Management, 1859-1909.* As with memoirs, most general histories of American theater and entertainment incorporate the minstrel show in the coverage. Richard Moody's *America Takes the Stage* and *Dramas from the American Theatre, 1762-1909* are among the most perceptive on the minstrel show, and the latter includes examples of minstrel material. Other miscellaneous essays of value are Ralph Ellison's "Change the Joke and Slip the Yoke"; J. Kinnard's "Who Are Our National Poets?" (the corruption of plantation sources on the minstrel stage); Newman White's "The White Man in the Woodpile" (blackface minstrel influences on Negro secular folk-songs); and Stanley White's "The Burnt-Cork Illusion of the 1920s in America: A Study in Nostalgia" (on extensions of the minstrel mode). It should be added that most good sources on variety/vaudeville, the medicine show, the dime museum, and frequently even the American circus include references or sections on blackface entertainers and the minstrel show in those formats.

Numerous "how-to" handbooks on putting on a minstrel show were published, especially during the late nineteenth century. Two that are of interest are Jack Haverly's *Negro Minstrels: A Complete Guide* (written by the successful minstrel manager) and Edward Marble's *The Minstrel Show.* A recent collection of twenty-two minstrel afterpieces, edited by Gary D. Engle (*This Grotesque Essence: Plays from the American Minstrel Show*) provides a good sense of this aspect of the minstrel show from 1833 to 1871.

Minstrel material can be found in various collections containing sources on variety forms, most of which are discussed in chapter 8. Especially strong collections on minstrelsy can be found in the Harris Collection, Brown University, and the Buffalo and Erie County Library, New York. Certainly the researcher in the area of the minstrel show should be cognizant of the wealth of primary sources available, in particular playlets, joke books, and songsters. The serials and periodicals discussed in the next chapter are important reservoirs for reconstruction of minstrelsy's history and uniqueness.

BIBLIOGRAPHY

Belcher, Horace G. "Mr. Tambo and Mr. Bones: Rhode Island in Negro Minstrelsy." *Rhode Island History* 8 (October 1949):47-110.

Blesh, Rudi, and Janis, Harriet. *They All Played Ragtime.* New York: Alfred A. Knopf, 1950.

Bond, Frederick W. *The Negro and the Drama.* College Park, Md.: McGrath, 1940.

Bowen, Elbert R. "Negro Minstrels in Early Rural Missouri." *Missouri Historical Review* 47 (January 1953):103-9.

Brown, T. Allston. "The Origin of Negro Minstrelsy." In *Fun in Black, or Sketches of Minstrel Life,* edited by Charles H. Day. New York: Robert M. DeWitt, 1874.

Browne, Ray B. "Shakespeare in American Vaudeville and Negro Minstrelsy." *American Quarterly* 12 (Fall 1960):374-91.

Burleigh, H. T. *Negro Minstrel Melodies.* Preface by W. J. Henderson. New York: G. Shirmer, 1910.

Chase, Gilbert. *America's Music from the Pilgrims to the Present.* New York: McGraw-Hill, 1955.

Daly, John Jay. *A Song in His Heart.* Philadelphia and Toronto: John C. Winston Co., 1951.

Damon, S. Foster. "The Negro in Early American Songsters." *Papers of the Bibliographical Society of America* 28 (1934):132-63.

Davenport, Francis Garvin. *Cultural Life in Nashville on the Eve of the Civil War.* Chapel Hill: University of North Carolina Press, 1941.

Davidson, Frank C. "The Rise, Development, Decline, and Influence of the American Minstrel Show." Ph.D. dissertation, New York University, 1952.

Demarest, Michael. "Music to Which the Gold Rushed." *Opera and Concert* 15 (1950):9-11, 15-16.

Dormon, James H. "The Strange Career of Jim Crow Rice." *Journal of Social History* 3 (Winter 1969-70):109-22.

Eaton, W. P. "Dramatic Evolution and the Popular Theatre: Playhouse Roots of Our Drama." *American Scholar* 4 (Spring 1935):148-59.

Edwall, Harry R. "The Golden Era of Minstrelsy in Memphis: A Reconstruction." *West Tennessee Historical Society Papers,* no. 9 (1955), pp. 29-47.

Ellison, Ralph. "Change the Joke and Slip the Yoke." In *Shadow and Act,* edited by Ralph Ellison. New York: Vintage Books, 1954.

Engle, Gary D., ed. *This Grotesque Essence: Plays from the American Minstrel Show.* Baton Rouge and London: Louisiana State University Press, 1978.

Epstein, Dena J. *Sinful Tunes and Spirituals: Black Folk Music to the Civil War.* Urbana, Chicago, and London: University of Illinois Press, 1977.

Field, A. G. *Watch Yourself Go By.* Columbus, Ohio: Spahr and Glenn, 1912.

Fletcher, Tom, *100 Years of the Negro in Show Business.* New York: Burdge and Co., 1954.

Gaul, Harvey B. "The Minstrel of the Alleghenies." *The Western Pennsylvania History Magazine* 34 (March 1951):1-22; 34 (June 1951):97-118; 34 (September 1951):168-84; (December 1951):239-60.

Green, Alan W.C. " 'Jim Crow,' 'Zip Coon'; The Northern Origins of Negro Minstrelsy." *Massachusetts Review* 11 (Spring 1970):385-97.

Greenwood, Isaac J. *The Circus: Its Origin and Growth Prior to 1835. With a Sketch of Negro Minstrelsy.* 1898. 2d ed. with additions. New York: William Abbatt, 1909.

Hamm, Charles. *Yesterdays: Popular Song in America.* New York and London: W. W. Norton and Co., 1979.

Handy, W. C. *Negro Authors and Composers of the United States.* New York: Handy Brothers Music Co., [ca. 1938].

_____. *Father of the Blues.* Edited by Arna Bontemps. New York: Macmillan Co., 1941.

Haverly, Jack. *Negro Minstrels: A Complete Guide.* 1902. Reprint. Boston: Gregg Press, 1969.

Haywood, Charles. *A Bibliography of North American Folklore and Folksong.* 2 vols. 2d rev. ed. New York: Dover Publications, 1961.

_____. "Negro Minstrelsy and Shakespearean Burlesque." In *Folklore and Society,* edited by Bruce Jackson. Hatboro, Pa.: Folklore Associates, 1966.

Howard, John Trasker. *Stephen Foster: America's Troubadour.* Rev. ed. New York: Thomas Y. Crowell Co., 1954.

Huggins, Nathan. *Harlem Renaissance.* New York: Oxford University Press, 1971.

Hutton, Laurence. "The Negro on the Stage." *Harper's Magazine* 79 (June-November 1889):131-45.

Johnson, James Weldon. *Black Manhattan.* New York: Alfred A. Knopf, 1940.

Jones, LeRoi. *Blues People: Negro Music in White America.* New York: William Morrow and Co.. 1963.

Kaufmann, Helen L. *From Jehovah to Jazz.* New York: Dodd, Mead, and Co., 1937.

Keeler, Ralph. "Three Years a Negro Minstrel." *Atlantic Monthly* 24 (July 1869): 71-85.

_____. *Vagabond Adventures.* Boston: Fields, Osgood and Co., 1870.

Kendall, John Smith. "New Orleans Negro Minstrels." *Louisiana Historical Quarterly* 30 (January 1947):128-48.

Kinnard, J. "Who Are Our National Poets?" *Knickerbocker Magazine* 26 (October 1845):331-41.

Kmen, Henry A. "Old Corn Meal: A Forgotten Urban Negro Folksinger." *Journal of American Folklore* 75 (January-March 1962):29-34.

Leavitt, M. B. *Fifty Years in Theatrical Management, 1859-1909.* New York: Broadway Publishing Co., 1912.

Leonard, Eddie [Lemuel Toney]. *What a Life I'm Telling You.* New York: Eddie Leonard, 1934.

Locke, Alain. *The Negro and His Music & Negro Art: Past and Present.* 1936. Reprint. New York: Arno Press, 1969.

Logan, Olive. "The Ancestry of Brudder Bones." *Harper's Monthly* 58 (April 1879):687-98.

Marble, Edward. *The Minstrel Show.* New York: F. M. Lupton, 1893.

Matthews, Brander. "The Rise and Fall of Negro Minstrelsy." *Scribner's Magazine* 57 (January-June 1915):754-59.

"Melodies and Soft Shoes in Blackface." *Missouri Historical Review* 39 (January 1944):192-95.

Miller, Kelly. "The Negro 'Stephen Foster.' " *Etude* 57 (July 1939):431-32, 472.

Moody, Richard. "Negro Minstrelsy." *Quarterly Journal of Speech* 30 (October 1944):321-28.

_____. *America Takes the Stage.* Bloomington: Indiana University Press, 1955.

_____, ed. *Dramas from the American Theatre, 1762-1909.* Cleveland and New York: World Publishing Co., 1966.

Nathan, Hans. "The First Negro Minstrel Band and Its Origins." *Southern Folklore Quarterly* 16 (June 1952):132-44.

_____. *Dan Emmett and the Rise of Early Negro Minstrelsy.* Norman: University of Oklahoma Press, 1962.

Nevin, R. P. "Stephen C. Foster and Negro Minstrelsy." *Atlantic Monthly* 20 (November 1867):608-16.

Paskman, Dailey [and Sigmund Spaeth]. *"Gentlemen, Be Seated!" A Parade of the Old-Time Minstrels.* 1928. Rev. ed. New York: Clarkson N. Potter, 1976.

Patterson, Cecil L. "A Different Drummer: The Image of the Negro in Nineteenth Century Popular Song Books." Ph.D. dissertation, University of Pennsylvania, 1961.

_____. "A Different Drummer: The Image of the Negro in Nineteenth Century Songsters." *California Language Association* 9 (September 1964):44-50.

Patterson, Lindsay, ed. *The Negro in Music and Art.* 2d rev. ed. New York: Publishers Co. under the auspices of the Association for the Study of Negro Life and History, 1970.

Ramshaw, Molly Niederlander. "Jump, Jim Crow! A Biographical Sketch of Thomas D. Rice." *Theatre Annual* 17 (1960):36-47.

Rehin, George F. "The Darker Image: American Negro Minstrelsy through the Historian's Lens." *Journal of American Studies* 9 (December 1975):365-73.

_____. "Harlequin Jim Crow: Continuity and Convergence in Blackface Clowning." *Journal of Popular Culture* 9 (Winter 1975):682-701.

Reynolds, Harry. *Minstrel Memories: The Story of Burnt Cork Minstrelsy in Great Britain from 1836-1927.* London: Alston Rivers, 1928.

Rice, Edward LeRoy. *Monarchs of Minstrelsy from "Daddy" Rice to Date.* New York: Kenny Publishing Co., 1911.

Sampson, Henry T. *Blacks in Blackface: A Source Book on Early Black Musical Shows.* Metuchen, N.J. and London: The Scarecrow Press, 1980.

Sawyer, E. T. "Old-Time Minstrels of San Francisco. Recollections of a Pioneer." *Overland Monthly* 81 (October 1923):5-7.

Simond, Ike. *Old Slack's Reminiscences and Pocket History of the Colored Profession From 1865 to 1891.* Edited by Robert C. Toll and Francis Lee Utley. Bowling Green, Ohio: Popular Press, 1974.

Spinney, Frank Oakman. "A New Hampshire Minstrel Tours the Coast," *California Historical Society Quarterly* 20 (September 1941):243-58.

Stoutamire, Albert. *Music of the Old South: Colony to Confederacy.* Rutherford, Madison, and Teaneck, N.J.: Fairleigh Dickinson University Press, 1972.

Suthern, Orrin Clayton, II. "Minstrelsy and Popular Culture." *Journal of Popular Culture* 4 (Winter 1971):658-73.

Toll, Robert C. *Blacking Up: The Minstrel Show in Nineteenth Century America.* New York: Oxford University Press, 1974.

_____. "The Minstrel Show: Show Biz in Blackface." In *On with the Show: The First Century of Show Business in America,* by Robert C. Toll. New York: Oxford University Press, 1976.

_____. "Behind the Blackface: Minstrel Men and Minstrel Myths." *American Heritage* 29 (April-May 1978):93-105.

_____. "Show Biz in Blackface: The Evolution of the Minstrel Show as a Theatrical Form." In *American Popular Entertainment,* edited by Myron Matlaw. Westport, Conn. and London: Greenwood Press, 1979.

Trotter, James Monroe. *Music and Some Highly Musical People.* 1881. Reprint. New York: Johnson Reprint, 1968.

Trux, J. J. "Negro Minstrelsy—Ancient and Modern." *Putnam's Monthly* 5 (1885):72-79.

Webb, Robert L. "Banjos on Their Saddle Horns." *American History Illustrated* 11 (May 1976):11-20.

White, Newman. "The White Man in the Woodpile." *American Speech* 4 (February 1929):207-15.

White, Stanley. "The Burnt-Cork Illusion of the 1920s in America: A Study in Nostalgia." *Journal of Popular Culture* 5 (Winter 1971):530-50.

Winter, Marian Hannah. "Juba and American Minstrelsy." *Dance Index* 6 (1947): 28-47.

Wittke, Carl. *Tambo and Bones. A History of the Minstrel Show.* 1930. Reprint. Westport, Conn.: Greenwood Press, 1968.

Zanger, Jules. "The Minstrel Show as Theater of Misrule." *Quarterly Journal of Speech* 60 (February 1974):33-38.

CHAPTER 8

Variety/Vaudeville

HISTORICAL SUMMARY

Like the minstrel show, American vaudeville, although related to variety forms of entertainment in many parts of the world, was largely indigenous, the product of saloon owners' efforts to attract eager and free-spending drinkers by enticing them with free shows. Although special acts were a common appendage to the legitimate theater in America as early as the eighteenth century, an independent tradition of autonomous variety entertainment was growing in prominence by the 1940s and 1950s, reflecting the fragmentation of the American populace into elite and popular components. Variety theaters, spawned from beer gardens, concert saloons, dime museums, and possibly other locales of the earliest staged variety amusement, became habitats of earthy and low-brow entertainment.

The most accepted precursor to variety theater, the concert saloon, developed first across the American frontier as an amusement resort offering liquor, gambling, women, smoke, and shows to induce patronage, and soon spread to most major American cities. On the frontier such establishments catered to a largely, if not exclusively, male audience, with a concomitant overtly masculine, rough, and bawdy atmosphere. The city version, though more polished and less make-shift, differed little from its frontier cousin. Amusing the lower elements of the burgeoning urban population was a natural notion for enterprising saloon owners. Whereas the frontier version became the male social center in unsettled western communities, the urban concert saloon, like the early English music hall of the 1840s, became a late haunt for men of all classes in search of carousing and the lowest sort of amusement.

By the late 1850s and early 1860s concert saloons were well established in New York, where there were soon over 300 such establishments, mainly around Broadway and on the Bowery. In the early 1860s most major cities had at least one concert saloon; by the mid-1860s they had spread to many smaller towns. Those establishments that charged no admission but depended on the sale of drink and food and gambling for their profit became known as "free concert saloons," "honky-tonks," or "free-and-easies." The 1860s brought public outcries against the prostitution and vice that were associated with the concert saloon and especially against the "waiter-girls" who hustled drinks, flirted, and often practiced prostitution on the side. With such loathsome connotations, many concert saloons tried to gain greater respectability by calling themselves "concert rooms," "concert gardens," or "music halls," and adopting such impressive names as The Melodeon or The Alhambra. Finally, the terms "variety halls" or "variety theaters" came into prominence, probably used first around 1849 by William Valentine who ran the Vauxhall Garden. Although these variety theaters continued to serve alcoholic beverages and catered to male audiences, they were beginning to offer a more decent type of entertainment.

After the Civil War variety broke away from the concert saloon, moved into regular theaters, and began to gain some degrees of respectability. At first the changes were superficial and, although more elegant than the saloon, the fare was still quite low and vulgar. The variety entertainment business was nonetheless on the move, establishing entire circuits of variety houses and a great demand for variety performers. The early variety show borrowed a great deal from blackface minstrelsy, including format and a clear intent to entertain and get laughs. Like minstrel performers, variety entertainers were ordinary people playing to a largely common-man audience and using subjects they all understood. What variety did not totally adopt from the minstrel show was the blackface, thus allowing for new themes in the skits, especially those centered around the new European immigrant (by the Civil War there were, for example, 1,700,000 Irish immigrants) and sex. Ethnic humor in variety, focusing on the Irish, the Negro, and the Dutch or German, was robust and generally good natured, although the predominantly male audience continued to find great enjoyment in snickering at off-colored jokes and ogling female forms and the near-naked limbs of dancing girls viewed through the foul, smokey atmosphere.

During the 1870s and 1880s some attempts were made to clean up variety, to make it more respectable in order to appeal to a broader audience. By the 1890s the older variety had been renamed vaudeville, capitalizing on the more elegant sound of the French word for light pastoral plays with musical interludes, but having nothing in common with its French namesake. Instead, vaudeville developed its own brand of a highly organized, nationwide big business. Tony Pastor (1837-1908), the most important vaudeville producer prior to the turn of the century (although he actually preferred the term "variety"), is credited with the first effective efforts to make vaudeville an entertainment where women as well as men could be welcomed and amused. Pastor, who was associated with the "444" variety theater owned by Robert Butler in the early 1860s, took variety performers from this essentially "cheap theater" on tour each summer, playing such legitimate houses as the respectable Boston Museum in 1863 and 1864. Perhaps with the success of variety in such establishments in mind, Pastor opened in 1865 "Tony Pastor's Opera House" on the Bowery as a "beautiful Temple of Amusement." When Pastor took over the Fourteenth Street Theater in 1881 he made the final break with the concert saloon tradition. Variety could now attract an audience without the added attractions of the saloon. As it became a more acceptable form of amusement, vaudeville became a kind of American microcosm, integrating many separate parts into a whole; its performer, as Robert Toll explains in *On with the Show,* was the constant symbol of individual liberty and pioneer endeavor.

Modern vaudeville's heyday lasted a scant fifty years or so, from the 1880s to the early 1930s, but during its time Americans of all classes were amused and found relief from the relatively new industrial complex. Its aim was to amuse or distract and in the process to make as much money as possible. Consequently, vaudeville tended to be anti-intellectual, providing something for everyone. Huge circuits of vaudeville theaters, led by such entrepreneurs and managers as E. F. Albee, B. F. Keith, Marcus Loew, Martin Beck, F. F. Proctor, and Alexander Pantages, were in constant competition and, as rivalries blossomed, vaudeville flourished. To protect their interests, managements formed conglomerates; performers quickly retaliated by founding the White Rats, modeled on the British music hall performers' union, the Water Rats, but with little success.

Vaudeville circuits were divided into two classes: big-time (the best theaters, salaries, and working conditions) and small-time (poor exposure, smaller, out-of-the-way towns, grueling performance schedules). Big-time performers, especially during the first two decades of this century, were able to fill most of a year with engagements and made large salaries (Lillian Russell made as much as $3,000 per week after 1900). By the teens there were more than one thousand theaters playing standard vaudeville acts and in excess of 4,000 small-time theaters. There were some eighty big-time houses in urban centers featuring star attractions. At its height, ten people attended a vaudeville show to everyone who patronized other forms of entertainment; as many as ten to twenty thousand vaudeville acts were competing for bookings.

Although vaudeville appeared to its audiences as an unstructured collection of dissimilar acts, it was actually a meticulously planned and executed balance of "turns" designed to control the audiences' responses and interest, while enhancing the appeal of each act and providing a smorgasbord of the best available entertainment—magic, vocals, juggling, comic routines, animal acts, skits, and even recitations and guest appearances by celebrities of the day. In 1913, for example, the international actress Sarah Bernhardt opened at the Palace Theater in New York City and collected $7,000 for her talents.

The success of the Keith-Albee circuit established a formula for clean vaudeville, aiming at a family audience and eschewing any offensive material, so much so that their theaters became known as "the Sunday School circuit." Keith, who began his career with a Boston dime museum in the 1880s, also developed the "continuous show" in 1885, beginning at 9:30 A.M. and running until about 10:30 P.M. Keith-Albee houses, beginning with the ornate and palatial Colonial Theater in Boston in 1894, also featured luxury. Many vaudeville houses showcased as many as twenty or more acts; Keith-Albee set a standard pattern of eight to ten acts, carefully structuring the bill for maximum effect and making the most of the stage space, thus giving the vaudeville show a pace, rhythm, and unity that enhanced each individual "turn" and gave the whole an almost subliminal cohesiveness. Generally, a successful act during the peak period of vaudeville had to be short and to the point. If a comic routine had not succeeded during its first minute or so, chances were it was doomed. Humor was especially popular in vaudeville, in part because of the need of the audience to laugh during a time of tension and great change. Like the minstrel audience, vaudeville patrons were especially amused by word play and simple, obvious humor, thus a successful comedy team would shoot for the short, pithy joke. All types of humor were possible: male-female teams (most often with the woman potrayed as a dumbbell type), ethnic or dialect comics (a clear reflection of the ethnic diversity of the country, especially the new immigrant groups, as well as second and third generation Irish, German, Italian, and Jewish), and single comics, especially those who developed clearly recognized routines built around one-line jokes or slapstick.

Because of its tremendous popularity, vaudeville helped to dictate morals and attitudes more than any other form of American entertainment during a time of significant changes, whether consciously or not. It certainly did so without trying to deal with important issues or ideas. Ethnic humor, for example, was a powerful force and, although immigrants were aided in their assimilation into the American melting pot by ethnic comics, like Weber and Fields, jokes about them helped to sustain the stereotyped misunderstandings and mythologies that still permeate American culture.

For the first time in America, a form of entertainment was developed that offended virtually no one and appealed to all classes. For a time it served as America's radio, movies, and television, but, significantly, it was live and immediate. By the late teens and the 1920s, other live amusement forms, especially revues and musical comedy, began to steal the better performers from vaudeville, including those that had been featured at The Palace, the leading and most prestigious vaudeville house in America, and to offer major competition for the audiences of vaudeville. Vaudeville retaliated with its own version of a musical/comical revue as one act in a bill that soon began to dominate the performance but could never quite manage to compete with the lavishness and spectacle of an Earl Carroll or a Florenz Ziegfeld revue. Even burlesque, which was quickly growing into a major competitor of vaudeville, became a source of material. Blue material and graduates of burlesque transferred to vaudeville, making what was once big-time entertainment tainted and vulgarized. By the 1920s a major vaudevillian, especially one who did not depend on visual appeal, could expect far greater financial reward by appearing on radio or by making recordings and for far less effort. Radio and records also provided the public with a relatively inexpensive form of entertainment and, in the case of records, one that could be enjoyed over and over again. And, finally, the movies, at first simply one act in a vaudeville bill, supplanted vaudeville's popularity almost completely. By 1907 between 4,000 and 5,000 nickelodeons were attracting over 2 million viewers a day; by 1913 America had approximately 30,000 movie houses, many formerly vaudeville theaters. Although so-called "presentation houses," movie theaters with live acts between movie features, struggled with watered-down variety through the 1940s, vaudeville was clearly dead by 1932, the year the movies took over The Palace.

SURVEY OF SOURCES

In the broadest sense, variety can include all entertainment that depends on a compartmentalized structure; the three most prominent examples, minstrel shows, vaudeville, and burlesque, dominated American popular stage entertainment during their heydays. Each grew out of earlier saloon and variety structures and collectively demonstrate the type of mutation that occurred in American popular stage entertainment. In this section the coverage will concentrate on early variety and vaudeville but will also include basic sources necessary for an in-depth study of American variety entertainment in general and a few selected sources on peripheral amusement centers, such as the night club and the cabaret. These are virtually the only remaining locales for variety acts, other than Las Vegas revues (the revue is dealt with in chapter 10). Strictly speaking, night club and cabaret entertainment, twentieth-century phenomena in America, are not popular in terms of a large base audience of middle-class patrons but have tended to appeal to the wealthy, elite, or upper middle class. Because of the importance of the minstrel show and burlesque, sources on these forms are dealt with separately. Stage magic also relates to variety entertainment but is discussed in its own chapter, as is variety presented on showboats and in tent theaters.

Meaningful research on variety entertainment is still largely dependent on periodicals and serials of the time and special collections. Of the numerous New York newspapers and periodicals of the period, the most valuable are *Billboard* (beginning in 1894), the *New York Clipper* (1900-1918), *Variety* (especially 1905 to 1937), and the *New York Mirror* (1879-1922). Other serials published during the period, however, should not be overlooked: for example, the *New York Dramatic News* (1875-1919), the *Spirit of the Times* (under its various titles between 1856-1902), and *The Theatre* or *The Theatre Magazine* (1900-1931). Indeed, with much research yet to be done on variety and vaudeville, no stone should be left unturned; newspapers and serials from cities other than New York, in particular, provide a wealth of information on vaudeville throughout the country. Some of the more extensive collections on variety forms are located in well-known libraries: the Library of Congress, the Harvard Theatre Collection, the Hoblitzelle Theatre Arts Library of the University of Texas at Austin, the Library of the Performing Arts at Lincoln Center in New York, and the Boston Public Library.

The definitive histories of early variety and the concert saloon have yet to be written, although the following sources have suggested the rich potential as well as dearth of knowledge. Parker Zellers's essay, "The Cradle of Variety: The Concert Saloon," sheds some light on one origin of early variety, as does his full-length study of Tony Pastor, *Tony Pastor: Dean of the Vaudeville Stage*. Lloyd Morris in his chatty book *Incredible New York* discusses the atmosphere, reputation, and dangers of various concert saloons; Eddie Shayne's "oddly constructed melange" *Down Front on the Aisle* compares variety and western concert halls to vaudeville in the form of an interview with an old vaudevillian; M. B. Leavitt's *Fifty Years in Theatrical Management, 1859-1909* is especially good on variety (and minstrelsy); and Joe Laurie, Jr.'s "The Early Days of Vaudeville" surveys early nineteenth-century variety up to the rise of B. F. Keith's vaudeville circuit late in the century.

A number of the better documented and informative sources concentrate on regional variety, including the following recommended sources: Harold E. Briggs, "Early Variety Theatres in the Trans-Mississippi West"; various essays by Eugene K. Bristow, in particular "Look Out for Saturday Night: A Social History of Professional Variety Theatre in Memphis, Tennessee, 1859-1880" (Ph.D. dissertation), "Variety Theatre in Memphis, 1859-1862," "Charley Broom, Variety Manager in Memphis, Tennessee, 1866-1872," and "The Low Varieties Program in Memphis, 1865-1873"; John Russell David, "The Genesis of the Variety Theatre: The Black Crook Comes to St. Louis"; Lawrence James Hill, "A History of Variety-Vaudeville in Minneapolis, Minnesota, From Its Beginning to 1900" (Ph.D. dissertation); Roger Meersman and Robert Boyer, "The National Theatre in Washington: Buildings and Audiences, 1835-1972"; Murray Morgan, *Skid Road: An Informal Portrait of Seattle* (on "Box-houses," 1893-1910); and Clair Eugene Willson, *Mimes and Miners* (variety in the West) and "From Variety Theatre to Coffee Shop" (on the Bird Cage Theatre in Tombstone). Three essays under the general title of "The Variety Stage" in *Harper's Weekly* (1902) provide a useful survey of variety performers and managers: "Early Creators of a Renumerative Vogue," "Some Artists of This and Other Generations," and "Something of Its Early History in New York." Jenifer P. Winsted's "Tripping on the Light Fantastic Toe: Popular Dance of Early Portland, Oregon, 1800-1864" contains a good deal on variety entertainment other than dancing.

Before turning to other sources on specific topics, it would be useful first to discuss major surveys and histories of vaudeville, most of which attempt to deal in varying degrees with concert saloons and early variety as well. Of the general histories of vaudeville during its peak period, John DeMeglio's *Vaudeville U.S.A.* is among the better documented and furnishes the most extensive notes and bibliography of published studies. Also useful are his essays "New York vs. Rural America . . . Who Ruled Vaudeville?" and "Radio's Debt to Vaudeville" (one of few good analyses on the shift of performers from vaudeville into radio). Another useful scholarly study is Frederick Edward Snyder's "American Vaudeville Theatre in a Package: The Origins of Mass Entertainment" and his essay adapted from this study, "Theatre in a Package." Highly recommended is Shirley L. Staples's "From 'Barney's Courtship' to Burns and Allen: Male-Female Comedy Teams in American Vaudeville," which, while a superb analysis of this special type of humor in vaudeville, is also a perceptive history of vaudeville and the factors that affected its change. Several older histories should still be considered essential: Abel Green and Joe Laurie, Jr.'s *Show Biz from Vaude to Video;* Joseph Laurie's *Vaudeville: From the Honky-Tonks to The Palace* (also suggested are his essays "Vaudeville," "Vaudeville's Ideal Bill," and "Is Vaudeville Dead? It's Never Been"); Bernard Sobel's *A Pictorial History of Vaudeville;* and Douglas Gilbert's standard history *American Vaudeville: Its Life and Times* (his *Lost Chords* is useful on songs written for vaudeville). Of other more recent investigations, Albert

McLean's *American Vaudeville as Ritual* represents the most ideological analysis of vaudeville in its social-historical framework and delves below the surface for greater significance. His more recent article, "U.S. Vaudeville and the Urban Comics," is a natural extension of his book. Robert C. Toll's chapter "The Vaudeville Show: Something for Everybody" in *On with the Show* provides a helpful overview, as does the chapter on vaudeville in Allen Churchill's *The Great White Way.*

Other survey sources, more specific in scope, include the following: Franklin P. Adams's "Olympic Days," on the first decade of the nineteenth century; Eugene Clinton Elliott's *A History of Variety-Vaudeville in Seattle* (survey from 1852 to 1914); Gordon C. Green's "Seattle, Former Vaudeville Capital of the World"; and Marian Spitzer's "Morals in the Two-A-Day" and *The Palace* (based in part on a series of essays that appeared in *Saturday Evening Post* in 1924-1925 and the definitive history of the Palace Theater).

Most recent vaudeville studies are offshoots of the nostalgia craze and vary greatly in content and value. Charles and Louise Samuels' *Once Upon a Stage* is an informal and undocumented history and in no way supersedes earlier histories; Bill Smith's *The Vaudevillians* is a rather sad and wistful look at daily life on the vaudeville circuit via interviews with thirty-one former headliners (also see his essay "Vaudeville: Entertainment for the Masses"); and Marcia Keegan's *We Can Still Hear Them Clapping* is a photographic essay, with limited text, recording the impressions and reminiscences of former vaudevillians still living in the Times Square area when the book was written. Abel Green's *The Spice of Variety,* a collection of essays, includes useful entries by or about vaudeville and vaudevillians from the pages of *Variety.*

A large number of essays and books have been written by or about specific individuals associated with vaudeville. Only a representative number can be mentioned here. Tony Pastor has received a considerable amount of attention. In addition to Zellers's book, previously discussed, the following are suggested: Edwin A. Goewey, "Tony Pastor, the Starmaker"; Myron Matlaw, "Pastor and his flock" and "Tony the Trouper: Pastor's Early Years"; Montrose Moses, "Tony Pastor—Father of Vaudeville"; "Tony Pastor, Father of Vaudeville"; and J. Milton Traber, "Pen Sketch of 'Tony' Pastor, the Father of Modern Variety." Other useful sources about specific vaudeville performers or managers (listed here in alphabetical order by name of individual) include: (Fred Allen) Fred Allen, *Much Ado About Me* and John K. Hutchens, "Fred Allen, Comedian's Comedian"; (George Burns and Gracie Allen) Shirley L. Staples's previously discussed thesis, George Burns, *I Love Her That's Why* and *Living It Up; or, They Still Love Me in Altoona,* Laurence Senelick, "Allen, Gracie," and Kate Davy, "An Interview with George Burns";

(Eddie Cantor) Eddie Cantor as told to David Freedman, *My Life Is In Your Hands;* (Gus Edwards) S. J. Woolfe, "Gus Edwards' Academy"; (Eddie Foy) Eddie Foy and Alvin F. Harlow, *Clowning Through Life;* (Ruth Hunter) Ruth Hunter, *Come Back on Tuesday;* (Elsie Janis) Elsie Janis, *So Far, So Good;* (George Jessel) George Jessel, *So Help Me* and *This Way, Miss,* and Jessel and John Austin, *The World I Live In;* (Al Jolson) Michael Freedland, *Jolson;* (Buster Keaton) Rudi Blesh, *Keaton,* Buster Keaton with Charles Samuels, *My Wonderful World of Slapstick,* and David Robinson, *Buster Keaton;* (B. F. Keith and E. F. Albee) Frank B. Copley, "The Story of a Great Vaudeville Manager, E. F. Albee," Walter Prichard Eaton, "The Wizards of Vaudeville," Robert Grau, "B. F. Keith," Donald C. King, "Keith-Albee et al . . . ," Hugh Leamy, "You Ought to Go on the Stage: An Interview with Edward F. Albee," Albert F. McLean, Jr., "Genesis of Vaudeville: Two Letters from B. F. Keith," and Robert C. Allen, "B. F. Keith and the Origins of American Vaudeville"; (Harry Lauder) John B. Kennedy, "I'm a Spendthrift at Heart," "A King of the Vaudeville Stage," and Lauder's four memoirs, especially *Roamin' in the Gloamin';* (Marcus Loew) Arthur Prill, "The 'Small Time' King"; (the Marx Brothers) Joe Adamson, *Groucho, Harpo, Chico—And Sometimes Zeppo,* Kyle Crichton, *The Marx Brothers,* Alva Johnston, "Those Mad Marx Brothers," "Groucho" (interview), Groucho Marx, *Groucho and Me* and *The Grouchophile: An Illustrated Life,* and Hector Arce, *Groucho;* (William Morris) Robert Grau, "A Napoleon of the Vaudeville World"; (Alexander Pantages) Warren E. Crane, "Alexander Pantages" and Ellis Lucia, *Klondike Kate;* (F. F. Proctor) William Marston and John H. Feller, *F. F. Proctor, Vaudeville Pioneer* (one of the more extensive vaudeville biographies) and James S. Moy, "Proctor's Pleasure Palace and Garden of Pleasure 1897-1898" (see also Charles R. Sherlock, "Where Vaudeville Holds the Boards"); (Pat Rooney) John B. Kennedy, "We've Forgotten How to Fight"; (Benny Rubin) Benny Rubin, *Come Backstage With Me;* (Jimmy Savo) Jimmy Savo, *I Bow to the Stones;* (Gus Sun) Richard B. Gehman, "Daddy of the Small Time"; (Sophie Tucker) Sophie Tucker with Dorothy Giles, *Some of These Days;* (Weber and Fields) Felix Isman, *Weber and Fields: Their Tribulations, Triumphs, and Their Associates* and Ada Patterson, "A Dual Interview with Weber and Fields." A useful new reference guide to information on specific vaudevillians is Jeb H. Perry's *Variety Obits,* although not all types of vaudeville performers are included in this index.

A number of memoirs and biographies are of special value because of the perspective and scope of their narratives. Robert Grau's writings touch on many aspects of vaudeville: *Forty Years of Observation of Music and the Drama* (general memoir), "The Origin of Amateur Night," *The Business Man in the Amusement World,* "The Amazing Prosperity of the

Vaudeville Entertainer'' (managers and performers who had become millionaires), and "The Growth of Vaudeville" (from 1892). Grau's *The Stage in the Twentieth Century* includes an important chapter on vaudeville circa 1911. Nora Bayes "Holding My Audience" is an interesting analysis of one performer's formula for success; Leo Carrillo's *The California I Love* provides a classic vaudeville story; Ed Spielman's *The Mighty Atom* treats the career of the strongman Joseph L. Greenstein in vaudeville and other entertainment forms; Will M. Cressy's disjointed memoir *Continuous Vaudeville* touches on virtually all aspects of vaudeville; and George Fuller Golden's *My Lady Vaudeville and Her White Rats* covers Golden's efforts to create a union for vaudeville performers. Elbert Hubbard's *In the Spotlight,* though poorly written, is a valuable memoir of a vaudevillian working primarily on the Orpheum Circuit. Fred Stone's *Rolling Stone* traces the rise of this vaudevillian (of Montgomery and Stone fame) from acrobat to major Broadway star.

Specific sources on humor in vaudeville, especially ethnic comedy, include Paul A. Distler's "The Rise and Fall of the Racial Comics in American Vaudeville," "Exit the Racial Comics," and "Ethnic Comedy in Vaudeville and Burlesque," each a well-documented, scholarly investigation. E. L. Gamble's *Vaudeville Gambols* provides examples of ethnic stage humor. Bill Treadwell's *50 Years of American Comedy* discusses, rather superficially, numerous vaudeville comics from 1900 to 1950. Also perceptive are Staples's study of male-female comedy teams, mentioned previously, "Enter the Italian on the Vaudeville Stage," and Laurence Senelick's "Variety into Vaudeville, The Process Observed in Two Manuscript Gagbooks." One of vaudeville's most famous comic routines is reconstructed by the recently deceased Joe Smith (of Smith and Dale) in "Dr. Kronkite Revisited." Charles Hamm's *Yesterdays* provides a serviceable survey of the musical aspect of vaudeville.

Specific information on the structure of vaudeville, the life of the performer, and vaudeville's methods of operation, in addition to sources already discussed, can be found in the following: Cyrus T. Brady, "A Vaudeville Turn"; "Browsing the Vaudeville Talent" (the role of the agent); Sewell Collins, "Breaking Into Vaudeville" (on writing); Hartley Davis, "In Vaudeville" (popular types of acts), "The Business Side of Vaudeville," and "Tabloid Drama" (one-act plays in vaudeville); Walter DeLeon, "The Wow Finish"; George A. Gottlieb, "Psychology of the American Vaudeville Show. From the Manager's Point of View" (analysis of structure); Helen Green, "The Vaudevillians" (getting into vaudeville); Norman Hapgood, "The Life of a Vaudeville Artiste"; Marsden Hartley, "Vaudeville" (decor and billing) and *Adventures in the Arts;* Clare Maynard Hill, "Sartorial Splendors in Vaudeville"; Arthur S. Hoffman, "Who Writes the Jokes?"; Arthur LeRoy Kaser, *Vaudeville Turns* and

Snappy Vaudeville Jokes (representative of late routines); Bert Levy, *For the Good of the Race and Other Stories* (an act on the circuit described); Jimmy Lyons, *Encyclopedia of Stage Material* (typical joke book); Donald McGregor, "The Supreme Court of the Two a Day" (disputes between performers and managers); William McNally, *Mack's Vaudeville Guide* (typical of information booklets published for vaudevillians); Wallace Irwin, "Country Clubs of Broadway" (on the road); and Edwin Milton Royle, "The Vaudeville Theatre" (on respectable houses). An interesting guide to vaudeville outside of major urban areas is the *Vaudeville Year Book, 1913* (West and South covered). Three additional sources are especially informative. Brett Page's *Writing for Vaudeville* is an excellent and important guide to all aspects of vaudeville, not just writing, as the title suggests. Edward Renton's *The Vaudeville Theatre* is a compendium of specific suggestions covering all physical and managerial aspects. Will Rossiter's *The Vaudeville Prompter,* though essentially a collection of vaudeville material, includes a useful brief essay on various aspects of the business. Rossiter was a prolific writer of skits, songs, monologues, and so forth.

For essays on the decline of vaudeville and more ideological discussions, the following are suggested: "The Apotheosis of Vaudeville" (respectability of vaudeville); Alexander Bakshy, "Vaudeville Must Be Saved" and "Vaudeville's Prestige"; Marshall D. Beuick, "The Vaudeville Philosopher" (vaudeville's limited view of life); Mary C. Canfield, "The Great American Art"; "The Decay of Vaudeville"; "Decline of Vaudeville"; W.A.S. Douglas, "The Passing of Vaudeville"; "The Golden Age of Vaudeville"; June Havoc, "Old Vaudevillians, Where Are You Now?"; Katherine Merrill, "The Elective System and the Vaudeville" (compares vaudeville to the "dissipation of energy" brought about by the elective system in education); Bennett Musson, "Week of One Night Stands" (the strict regimen of a traveling performer); George Jean Nathan, "A Matter of Life and Death" (vaudeville in other media); the various reviews of Nellie Revell in *Theatre Magazine* (and in particular: "Stars in Vaudeville," "The Passing of the Freak Act," "Good Sketches Rare as Radium in Vaudeville," "Yellow Peril Threatens Vaudeville," "When Vaudeville Goes to War," "Speed Mania Afflicts Vaudeville," and "Vaudeville Demands Cheerful Patriotism"); Vadim Uraneff, "Commedia dell' arte and American Vaudeville"; and Maurice Willows, "The Nickel Theatre" (a biased report on the effect of cheap vaudeville). Caroline Caffin and Malins de Zayas's *Vaudeville* is a good source of critical essays on vaudeville as seen by a member of the audience. Oscar Handlin's "Comments on Mass and Popular Culture" analyzes vaudeville in order to reveal significant elements in the difference between popular culture during vaudeville's heyday and in 1960.

Black performers in vaudeville are given exceptionally good coverage in Henry T. Sampson's *Blacks in Blackface,* a recommended source book.

An informative survey is Helen Armstead-Johnson's "Blacks in Vaudeville: Broadway and Beyond." Sammy Davis, Jr.'s autobiography, *Yes I Can,* written with Jane and Burt Boyar, covers the beginning of his career in vaudeville. Also recommended is Jack Schiffman's *Uptown, The Story of Harlem's Apollo,* the fountainhead of black entertainment in New York during the 1930s. Other sources on blacks in vaudeville are included in the chapters on the minstrel show and musical theater (chapters 7 and 10). The special nature of American Yiddish vaudeville is covered in Nahma Sandrow's " 'A Little Letter to Mamma': Traditions in Yiddish Vaudeville."

A sense of the tag-end days of vaudeville, attempts to revive it, and the transition from variety to films, can be found in the following: H. I. Brock, "Vaudeville Still the Same—and Still Going Strong" (1944); Saul Carson, "Theatre: Vaudeville" (1949 revival at The Palace); "Springtime in the 40s"; "If Troupers Make Good They'll Go Back to the Sticks" (1935); Alva Johnston, "Profiles, Vaudeville to Television"; Lawrence Lader, "The Palace Theater: Broadway's Shrine"; Edward Reed, "Vaudeville Again" (1933); and Ken Murray, *Life on a Pogo Stick* ("blackouts" and variety in the 1940s). Vaudeville and its relationship to the cinema, in addition to film sources not covered by this guide, is discussed by Brooks McNamara in " 'Scavengers of the Amusement World': Popular Entertainment and the Birth of the Movies," William Trufant Foster in *Vaudeville and Motion Picture Shows: A Study of Theatre in Portland, Oregon,* Will Irwin in *The House That Shadows Built* (biography of Adolph Zukor), and Nick Grinde in "Where's Vaudeville At?". The phenomenon of the "Presentation House" (variety between motion picture showings) is best dealt with in Ben M. Hall's *The Best Remaining Seats, The Story of the Golden Age of the Movie Palace* and Charles Francisco's *The Radio City Music Hall: An Affectionate History of the World's Greatest Theater.*

The emergence of the Catskills resort area in the 1930s and 1940s as a haven for comics and a training ground for entertainers is discussed vividly in Joey Adams's *From Gags to Riches* and *The Borscht Belt,* the latter written with Henry Tobias. Little serious work has been done on night clubs, although two early histories are both entertaining and surprisingly informative: Stanley Walker's *The Night Club Era* and Jimmy Durante and Jack Kofoed's *Night Clubs* (especially Kofoed's early section on the beginnings of night clubs). Jim Haskins's *The Cotton Club* provides vivid portraits of black entertainers associated with this famous club of the 1930s and 1940s. Julian B. Roebuck and Wolfgang Frese's *The Rendezvous: A Case Study of an After-Hours Club* is a seminal sociological investigation, and Lewis A. Erenberg's *Steppin' Out: New York Nightlife and the Transformation of American Culture* (and his earlier Ph.D. dissertation) covers the pre-World War I dance craze, various entertainers in night clubs, and provides a revealing study of the process of transition in social and sexual values. Few specific, good sources deal with the stand-up comic in America. General sources on clowns (see chapter 3) sometimes touch on the subject, especially the early talking clown. Phil Berger's *The Last Laugh* is a reasonably successful study of the lives, gags, and routines of the major contemporary stand-up comics. William Cahn's *The Laugh Makers* (and the revised version, *A Pictorial History of the Great Comedians*) is one of the better contemporary sources on stand-up comics, although short on analytical text. Green and Laurie's *Show Biz From Vaude to Video,* mentioned earlier in this section, sums up seven great eras of show business up to 1951 and includes selected emphasis on the place of the stand-up comic.

Of specific works by or about individual stand-up comics, most are so chatty and informal as to be almost useless. Joey Adams's books are exceptions, especially the two mentioned previously and *Encyclopedia of Humor.* Steve Allen's *The Funny Men* is a better than average literary effort, and Art Cohn's *The Joker Is Wild* is a fair biography of Joe E. Lewis. Lenny Bruce, the subject of great attention as a controversial and revolutionary comic, has been given good treatment in Albert Goldman's biography *Ladies and Gentlemen, Lenny Bruce!* and John Cohen's *The Essential Lenny Bruce.*

The cabaret, never a major American entertainment institution, has received little important treatment. The best available source to date is Lisa Appignanesi's *The Cabaret,* a useful historical survey and analytical account in English of the cabaret from its Parisian beginnings to its most recent manifestations in London and the United States. And finally, a type of performer almost unique to the cabaret, the female impersonator, is surveyed in Peter Ackroyd's *Dressing Up* and analyzed from an anthropological point of view in Esther Newton's *Mother Camp.*

The nature of variety entertainment has necessitated that this section be rather lengthy, but it should be underscored that only a suggestion of the types and scope of sources available could be recorded in this guide. Many theatrical memoirs of the late nineteenth and early twentieth centuries discuss aspects of variety and vaudeville, and studies of the legitimate theater during the heyday of vaudeville invariably include some coverage but are beyond the parameters of this volume. The user of this guide should investigate these sources as well and note that a large number of the general sources discussed in the opening chapter include vaudeville and reference works cited there and in the final chapter will direct the user to additional sources on popular theater and performers of the time. Performers in revues and early musical comedy frequently appeared in vaudeville and sources in chapter 10 should be consulted.

BIBLIOGRAPHY

BOOKS AND ARTICLES

Ackroyd, Peter. *Dressing Up: Transvestism and Drag: The History of an Obsession.* New York: Simon and Schuster, 1979.

Adams, Franklin P. "Olympic Days." *Saturday Evening Post,* 22 June 1929, pp. 18, 123, 126.

Adams, Joey. *From Gags to Riches.* New York: Frederick Fell, 1946.

_____. *Encyclopedia of Humor.* Indianapolis: Bobbs-Merrill, 1968.

_____, with Henry Tobias. *The Borscht Belt.* New York: Avon Books, 1967.

Adamson, Joe. *Groucho, Harpo, Chico—and Sometimes Zeppo. A History of the Marx Brothers and a Satire on the Rest of the World.* New York: Simon and Schuster, 1973.

Allen, Fred. *Much Ado About Me.* Boston: Little, Brown and Co., 1956.

Allen, Robert C. "B. F. Keith and the Origins of American Vaudeville." *Theatre Survey* 21 (November 1980):105-15.

Allen, Steve. *The Funny Men.* New York: Simon and Schuster, 1956.

"The Apotheosis of Vaudeville." *Current Literature* 33 (November 1902):523.

Appignanesi, Lisa. *The Cabaret.* New York: Universe Books, 1976.

Arce, Hector. *Groucho: The Authorized Biography.* New York: G. P. Putnam's Sons, 1979.

Armstead-Johnson, Helen. "Blacks in Vaudeville: Broadway and Beyond." In *American Popular Entertainment,* edited by Myron Matlaw. Westport, Conn. and London: Greenwood Press, 1979.

Bakshy, Alexander. "Vaudeville Must Be Saved." *Nation,* 24 July 1929, pp. 98, 100.

_____. "Vaudeville's Prestige." *Nation,* 4 September 1929, p. 258.

Bayes, Nora. "Holding My Audience." *Theatre Magazine* 26 (September 1917):128.

Berger, Phil. *The Last Laugh: The World of Stand-up Comics.* New York: William Morrow, 1975.

Beuick, Marshall D. "The Vaudeville Philosopher." *Drama* 16 (December 1925): 92-93, 116.

Blesh, Rudi. *Keaton.* New York: Macmillan Co., 1966.

Brady, Cyrus T. "A Vaudeville Turn." *Scribner's Magazine* 30 (September 1901): 351-55.

Briggs, Harold E. "Early Variety Theatres in the Trans-Mississippi West." *Mid-America* 34 (July 1952):188-202.

Bristow, Eugene Kerr. "Look Out for Saturday Night: A Social History of Professional Variety Theatre in Memphis, Tennessee, 1859-1880." Ph.D. dissertation, University of Iowa, 1957.

_____. "The Low Varieties Program in Memphis, 1865-1873." *Quarterly Journal of Speech* 44 (December 1958):423-27.

_____. "Variety Theatre in Memphis, 1859-1862." *West Tennessee Historical Society Papers* 13 (1959):117-27.

_____. "Charley Broom, Variety Manager in Memphis, Tennessee, 1866-1872." *Southern Speech Journal* 25 (Fall 1959):11-20.

Brock, H. I. "Vaudeville Still the Same—and Still Going Strong." *New York Times Magazine,* 16 January 1944, pp. 16-17.

"Browsing the Vaudeville Talent." *Theatre* 20 (December 1914):281-82, 295.

Burns, George. *I Love Her, That's Why.* New York: Simon and Schuster, 1955.

———. *Living It Up; Or, They Still Love Me in Altoona.* New York: Berkeley, 1978.

Caffin, Caroline, and de Zayas, Malins. *Vaudeville.* New York: Mitchell Kemerley, 1914.

Cahn, William. *The Laugh Makers: A Pictorial History of American Comedians.* New York: Bramhall House, 1957.

Canfield, Mary C. "The Great American Art." *New Republic,* 22 November 1922, pp. 334-35.

Cantor, Eddie, as told to David Freedman. *My Life Is In Your Hands.* Foreword by Will Rogers. New York: Blue Ribbon Books, 1932.

Carrillo, Leo. *The California I Love.* Englewood Cliffs, N.J.: Prentice-Hall, 1961.

Carson, Saul. "Theatre: Vaudeville." *New Republic,* 13 June 1949, pp. 19-20.

Churchill, Allen. *The Great White Way.* New York: E. P. Dutton, 1962.

Cohen, John. *The Essential Lenny Bruce.* New York: Ballantine, 1967.

Cohn, Art. *The Joker Is Wild: The Story of Joe E. Lewis.* New York: Random House, 1955.

Collins, Sewell. "Breaking Into Vaudeville." *Colliers,* 20 March 1909, pp. 20, 28.

Copley, Frank B. "The Story of a Great Vaudeville Manager, E. F. Albee." *American Magazine* 94 (December 1922):46-47, 152-53, 154-55.

Crane, Warren E. "Alexander Pantages." *System* 37 (March 1920):501-3.

Cressy, Will M. *Continuous Vaudeville.* Boston: Richard G. Badger, 1914.

Crichton, Kyle. *The Marx Brothers.* Garden City, N.Y.: Doubleday and Co., 1950.

David, John Russell. "The Genesis of the Variety Theatre: The Black Crook Comes to St. Louis." *Missouri Historical Review* 64 (January 1970):133-49.

Davis, Hartley. "In Vaudeville." *Everybody's Magazine* 13 (August 1905):231-40.

———. "The Business Side of Vaudeville." *Everybody's Magazine* 17 (October 1907):527-37.

———. "Tabloid Drama." *Everybody's Magazine* 21 (August 1909):249-57.

Davis, Sammy, Jr., with Jane and Burt Boyar. *Yes I Can: The Story of Sammy Davis, Jr.* New York: Farrar, Straus and Giroux, 1965.

Davy, Kate. "An Interview with George Burns." *Educational Theatre Journal* 27 (October 1975):345-55.

"The Decay of Vaudeville." *American Magazine* 69 (April 1910):840-48.

"Decline of Vaudeville." *Harper's Monthly* 106 (April 1903):811-15.

DeLeon, Walter. "The Wow Finish." *Saturday Evening Post,* 14 February 1925, pp. 16, 44, 47-48.

DiMeglio, John E. "New York vs. Rural America . . . Who Ruled Vaudeville?" *Mankato State College Today* 2 (Fall 1970):8-9.

———. *Vaudeville U.S.A.* Bowling Green, Ohio: Bowling Green University Popular Press, 1973.

———. "Radio's Debt to Vaudeville." *Journal of Popular Culture* 12 (Fall 1978): 228-35.

Distler, Paul A. "The Rise and Fall of the Racial Comics in American Vaudeville."
Ph.D. dissertation, Tulane University, 1963.

_____. "Exit the Racial Comics." *Educational Theatre Journal* 18 (October 1966):
247-54.

_____. "Ethnic Comedy in Vaudeville and Burlesque." In *American Popular
Entertainment,* edited by Myron Matlaw, Westport, Conn. and London:
Greenwood Press, 1979.

Douglas, W.A.S. "The Passing of Vaudeville." *American Mercury* 12 (October
1927):188-94.

Durante, Jimmy, and Kofoed, Jack. *Night Clubs.* New York: Alfred A. Knopf, 1931.

Eaton, Walter Prichard. "The Wizards of Vaudeville." *McClure* 55 (September
1923):43-49.

Elliott, Eugene Clinton. *A History of Variety-Vaudeville in Seattle.* Seattle: University of Washington Press, 1944.

"Enter the Italian on the Vaudeville Stage." *Survey,* 7 May 1910, pp. 198-99.

Erenberg, Lewis Allen. "Urban Nightlife and the Decline of Victorianism: New
York's Restaurant and Cabarets, 1890-1918." Ph.D. dissertation, University
of Michigan, 1974.

_____. *Steppin' Out: New York Nightlife and the Transformation of American
Culture, 1890-1930.* Westport, Conn. and London: Greenwood Press, 1981.

Foster, William Trufant. *Vaudeville and Motion Picture Shows. A Study of Theatre
in Portland, Oregon.* Portland: Reed College, 1914.

Foy, Eddie, and Harlow, Alvin F. *Clowning Through Life.* New York: E. P. Dutton
and Co., 1928. (This first appeared in an abbreviated serialized form in three
issues of the February 1927 *Collier's,* Volume 79.)

Francisco, Charles. *The Radio City Music Hall: An Affectionate History of the
World's Greatest Theater.* New York: E. P. Dutton, 1979.

Freedland, Michael. *Jolson.* New York: Stein and Day, 1972.

Gamble, E. L. *Vaudeville Gambols.* Chicago: T. S. Denison & Co., 1922.

Gehman, Richard D. "Daddy of the Small Time." *Collier's,* 23 September 1950,
pp. 30, 72.

Gilbert, Douglas, *American Vaudeville: Its Life and Times.* 1940. Reprint. New
York: Dover Publications, 1968.

_____. *Lost Chords: The Diverting Story of American Popular Songs.* Garden
City, N.Y.: Doubleday, Doran and Co., 1942.

Goewey, Edwin A. "Tony Pastor, the Starmaker." *Dance Magazine* 12 (August
1929):12-13, 57, 58.

Golden, George Fuller. *My Lady Vaudeville and Her White Rats.* New York:
Broadway Publishing Co., 1909.

"The Golden Age of Vaudeville." *Current Literature* 42 (June 1907):669.

Goldman, Albert. *Ladies and Gentlemen, Lenny Bruce!* New York: Random House,
1971.

[Gotlieb, George A.] "Psychology of the American Vaudeville Show. From the
Manager's Point of View." *Current Literature* 60 (April 1916):257-58.

Grau, Robert. *Forty Years of Observation of Music and the Drama.* New York:
Broadway Publishing Co., 1909.

_____. "The Origin of Amateur Night." *Independent* 69 (20 October 1910):851-52.

_____. "A Napoleon of the Vaudeville World." *Theatre* 12 (October 1910):117, x.

_____. *The Business Man in the Amusement World.* New York: Broadway Publishing Co., 1910.

_____. "The Amazing Prosperity of the Vaudeville Entertainer." *Overland* 57 (June 1911):608-9.

_____. *The Stage in the Twentieth Century.* New York. Broadway Publishing Co., 1912.

_____. "B. F. Keith." *American Magazine* 77 (May 1914):86-88.

_____. "The Growth of Vaudeville." *Overland* 64 (October 1914):392.96.

Green, Abel. *The Spice of Variety.* New York: Henry Holt and Co., 1952.

_____, and Laurie, Joe, Jr. *Show Biz From Vaude to Video.* Garden City, N.Y.: Permabooks, 1953.

Green, Gordon C. "Seattle, Former Vaudeville Capital of the World." *Western Speech Journal* 30 (Winter 1966):26-36.

Green, Helen. "The Vaudevillians." *Collier's,* 23 October 1909, pp. 20, 31-32, 34.

Grinde, Nick. "Where's Vaudeville At?" *Saturday Evening Post,* 11 January 1930, pp. 44, 46, 158, 161.

"Groucho." *Penthouse Magazine* 5 (December 1973):106-8, 112, 132, 189-90.

Hall, Ben M. *The Best Remaining Seats, The Story of the Golden Age of the Movie Palace.* New York: Clarkson N. Potter, 1961.

Hamm, Charles. *Yesterdays: Popular Song in America.* New York and London: W. W. Norton and Co., 1979.

Handlin, Oscar. "Comments on Mass and Popular Culture." In *Culture for the Millions,* edited by Norman Jacobs. Princeton, N.J.: D. Van Nostrand and Co., 1961.

Hapgood, Norman. "The Life of a Vaudeville Artiste." *Cosmopolitan* 30 (February 1901):393-400.

Hartley, Marsden. "Vaudeville." *Dial* 68 (March 1920):335-42.

_____. *Adventures in the Arts.* 1921. Reprint. New York: Hacker Art Books, 1972.

Haskins, Jim. *The Cotton Club: A Pictorial and Social History of the Most Famous Symbol of the Jazz Era.* New York: Random House, 1977.

Havoc, June. "Old Vaudevillians, Where Are You Now?" *Horizon* 1 (July 1959): 112-20.

Henderson, Jerry. "Nashville in the Decline of Southern Legitimate Theatre during the Beginning of the Twentieth Century." *Southern Speech Journal* 29 (Fall 1963):26-33.

Hill, Clare Maynard. "Sartorial Splendors in Vaudeville." *Billboard,* 29 November 1913, pp. 34, 138.

Hill, Lawrence James. "A History of Variety-Vaudeville in Minneapolis, Minnesota, From Its Beginning to 1900." Ph.D. dissertation, University of Minnesota, 1979.

Hoffman, Arthur S. "Who Writes the Jokes?" *Bookman* 26 (October 1907):171-81.

Hubbard, Elbert. *In The Spotlight: Personal Experiences of Elbert Hubbard on the American Stage.* East Aurora, N.Y.: Roycrofters, 1917.

Hunter, Ruth. *Come Back on Tuesday.* New York: Charles Scribner's Sons, 1945.

Hutchens, John K. "Fred Allen, Comedian's Comedian." *Theatre Arts Monthly* 26 (May 1942):307-14.

"If Troupers Make Good They'll Go Back to the Sticks." *Newsweek,* June 1935, p. 23.

Irwin, Wallace, "Country Clubs of Broadway." *Collier's,* 26 October 1912, pp. 10-12, 30.

Irwin, Will. *The House That Shadows Built.* Garden City, N.Y.: Doubleday, Doran and Co., 1928.

Isman, Felix. *Weber and Fields: Their Tribulations, Triumphs, and Their Associates.* New York: Boni and Liveright, 1924.

Janis, Elsie. *So Far, So Good: An Autobiography of Elsie Janis.* New York: E. P. Dutton and Co., 1932.

Jessel, George. *So Help Me: The Autobiography of George Jessel.* New York: Random House, 1943.

––––––. *This Way, Miss.* New York: Henry Holt and Co., 1955.

––––––, with John Austin. *The World I Lived In.* Chicago: Henry Regnery Co., 1975.

Johnston, Alva. "Those Mad Marx Brothers." *Reader's Digest* 29 (October 1936):49-52. (Condensed from *Woman's Home Companion,* September 1936.)

––––––. "Profiles, Vaudeville to Television." *New Yorker,* 28 September 1946, pp. 32-43; 5 October 1946, pp. 34-47; 12 October 1946, pp. 36-46.

Kaser, Arthur LeRoy. *Vaudeville Turns.* Boston: Walter H. Baker Co., 1923.

––––––. *Snappy Vaudeville Jokes.* Dayton: Paine Publishing Co., 1928.

Keaton, Buster, with Charles Samuels. *My Wonderful World of Slapstick.* Garden City, N.Y.: Doubleday and Co., 1960.

Keegan, Marcia. *We Can Still Hear Them Clapping.* New York: Avon Books, 1975.

Kennedy, John B. "I'm a Spendthrift at Heart." *Collier's,* 12 February 1927, pp. 14, 51.

––––––. "We've Forgotten How to Fight." *Collier's,* 11 May 1929, pp. 39-40, 42.

King, Donald C. "Keith-Albee et al . . ." *Marquee* 7 (3d quarter, 1975):3-14.

"A King of the Vaudeville Stage." *Current Literature* 46 (January 1909):84-86.

Lader, Lawrence. "The Palace Theater: Broadway's Shrine." *Coronet* 32 (July 1952):51-54.

Lauder, Harry. *Roamin' in the Gloamin'.* Philadelphia and London: J. B. Lippincott, 1928.

Laurie, Joe, Jr. "The Early Days of Vaudeville." *American Mercury* 62 (February 1946):232-36.

––––––. "Vaudeville." *Theatre Arts* 32 (August-September 1948):54-55.

––––––. "Vaudeville's Ideal Bill." *New York Times Magazine,* 15 May 1949, pp. 24-25.

––––––. "Is Vaudeville Dead? It's Never Been." *New York Times Magazine,* 14 October 1951, pp. 25, 67, 70, 71.

––––––. *Vaudeville: From the Honky-Tonks to The Palace.* 1953. Reprint. Port Washington, N.Y.: Kennikat, 1972.

Leamy, Hugh. "You Ought to Go on the Stage: An Interview with Edward F. Albee." *Collier's,* 1 May 1926, pp. 10, 36.

Leavitt, M. B. *Fifty Years in Theatrical Management, 1859-1909.* New York: Broadway Publishing Co., 1912.

Levy, Bert. *For the Good of the Race and Other Stories.* New York: Ad Press, 1921.

Lucia, Ellis. *Klondike Kate: The Life and Legend of Kitty Rockwell.* New York: Hastings House Publishers, 1962.

Lyons, Jimmy. *Encyclopedia of Stage Material.* Boston: Walter H. Baker Co., 1925.

McGregor, Donald. "The Supreme Court of the Two a Day." *Collier's,* 20 June 1925, p. 38.

McLean, Albert F., Jr. "Genesis of Vaudeville: Two Letters from B. F. Keith." *Theatre Survey* 1 (1960):82-95.

_____. *American Vaudeville As Ritual.* Lexington: University of Kentucky Press, 1965.

_____. "U.S. Vaudeville and the Urban Comics." *Theatre Quarterly* 1 (October-December 1971):50-57.

McNally, William. *Mack's Vaudeville Guide.* New York: Wm. McNally, 1920.

McNamara, Brooks. " 'Scavengers of the Amusement World': Popular Entertainment and the Birth of the Movies." In *American Pastimes.* Brockton, Mass.: Brockton Art Center, 1976.

Marston, William, and Feller, John H. *F. F. Proctor, Vaudeville Pioneer.* New York: Richard R. Smith, 1943.

Marx, Groucho. *Groucho and Me.* New York: Bernard Geis Associates, 1959.

_____. *The Grouchophile. An Illustrated Life.* Indianapolis and New York: Bobbs-Merrill, 1976.

Matlaw, Myron. "Pastor and his flock." *Theatre Arts* 42 (August 1958):20-21.

_____. "Tony the Trouper: Pastor's Early Years." *Theatre Annual* 24 (1968): 70-90.

Meersman, Roger, and Boyer, Robert. "The National Theatre in Washington: Buildings and Audiences, 1835-1972." In *Records of the Columbia Historical Society of Washington, D.C., 1971-1972,* edited by Francis Coleman Rosenberger. Washington, D.C.: Published by the Society, 1973.

Merrill, Katherine. "The Elective System and the Vaudeville." *New England Magazine* 36 (June 1907):298-99.

Morgan, Murray. *Skid Road: An Informal Portrait of Seattle.* New York: The Viking Press, 1952.

Morris, Lloyd. *Incredible New York.* New York: Random House, 1957.

Moses, Montrose. "Tony Pastor—Father of Vaudeville." *Theatre Guild Magazine* 8 (April 1931):32-35.

Moy, James S. "Proctor's Pleasure Palace and Garden of Palms 1895-1898." *Nineteenth-Century Theatre Research* 8 (Spring 1980):17-27.

Murray, Ken. *Life on a Pogo Stick: Autobiography of a Comedian.* Philadelphia and Toronto: The John C. Winston Co., 1960.

Musson, Bennett. "Week of One Night Stands." *American Magazine* 70 (June 1910):203-13.

Nathan, George Jean. "A Matter of Life and Death." *Newsweek,* 17 April 1939, p. 27.

Newton, Esther. *Mother Camp: Female Impersonators in America.* Chicago: University of Chicago Press, 1979.

Page, Brett. *Writing for Vaudeville*. Springfield, Mass.: Home Correspondence School, 1915.

Patterson, Ada. "A Dual Interview with Weber and Fields." *Theatre Magazine* 15 (April 1912):113-16, x.

Perry, Jeb H. *Variety Obits: An Index to Obituaries in Variety, 1905-1978*. Metuchen, N.J. and London: The Scarecrow Press, 1980.

Prill, Arthur. "The 'Small Time' King." *Theatre Magazine* 19 (March 1914): 139-40, 145.

Reed, Edward. "Vaudeville Again." *Theatre Arts Monthly* 17 (October 1933): 803-6.

Renton, Edward. *The Vaudeville Theatre—Building—Operation—Management*. New York: Gotham Press, 1918.

Revell, Nellie. "Stars in Vaudeville." *Theatre Magazine* 19 (April 1914): 199-200, 206, 208.

_____. "The Passing of the Freak Act." *Theatre Magazine* 19 (June 1914):293-94, 316, 317.

_____. "Good Sketches Rare as Radium in Vaudeville." *Theatre Magazine* 24 (November 1916):278, 322.

_____. "Yellow Peril Threatens Vaudeville." *Theatre Magazine* 25 (May 1917): 290, 316.

_____. "When Vaudeville Goes to War." *Theatre Magazine* 25 (June 1917):356.

_____. "Speed Mania Afflicts Vaudeville." *Theatre Magazine* 26 (October 1917):216.

_____. "Vaudeville Demands Cheerful Patriotism." *Theatre Magazine* 26 (December 1917):364.

Robinson, David. *Buster Keaton*. Bloomington and London: Indiana University Press, 1969.

Roebuck, Julian B., and Frese, Wolfgang. *The Rendezvous: A Case Study of an After-Hours Club*. New York: The Free Press, a division of Macmillan Publishing Co., 1976.

Rossiter, Will, compiler. *The Vaudeville Prompter*. Chicago: Will Rossiter Publisher, 1903.

Royle, Edwin Milton. "The Vaudeville Theatre." *Scribner's* 26 (October 1899): 485-95.

Rubin, Benny. *Come Backstage With Me*. Bowling Green, Ohio: Bowling Green University Popular Press, 1972.

Sampson, Henry T. *Blacks in Blackface: A Source Book on Early Black Musical Shows*. Metuchen, N.J. and London: The Scarecrow Press, 1980.

Samuels, Charles, and Samuels, Louise. *Once Upon a Stage: The Merry World of Vaudeville*. New York: Dodd, Mead and Co., 1974.

Sandrow, Nahma. " 'A Little Letter to Mamma': Traditions in Yiddish Vaudeville." In *American Popular Entertainment,* edited by Myron Matlaw. Westport, Conn. and London: Greenwood Press, 1979.

Savo, Jimmy. *I Bow to the Stones*. New York: Howard Frisch, 1963.

Schiffman, Jack. *Uptown, The Story of Harlem's Apollo Theatre*. New York: Cowles Book Co., 1971.

Senelick, Laurence. "Variety into Vaudeville, The Process Observed in Two Manuscript Gagbooks." *Theatre Survey* 19 (May 1978):1-15.

————. "Allen, Gracie." In *Notable American Women: The Modern Period (A Biographical Dictionary)*, edited by Barbara Sicherman et al. Cambridge, Mass. and London: The Belknap Press of Harvard University Press, 1980.

Shayne, Eddie. *Down Front on the Aisle.* Denver: Parkway Publishing Co., 1929.

Sherlock, Charles R. "Where Vaudeville Holds the Boards." *Cosmopolitan* 32 (February 1902):411-20.

Smith, Bill. *The Vaudevillians.* New York: Macmillan Co., 1976.

————. "Vaudeville: Entertainment for the Masses." In *American Popular Entertainment,* edited by Myron Matlaw. Westport, Conn. and London: Greenwood Press, 1979.

Smith, Joe. "Dr. Kronkite Revisited." In *American Popular Entertainment,* edited by Myron Matlaw. Westport, Conn. and London: Greenwood Press, 1979.

Snyder, Frederick Edward. "American Vaudeville Theatre in a Package: The Origins of Mass Entertainment." Ph.D. dissertation, Yale University, 1970.

————. "Theatre in a Package." *Theatre Survey* 12 (May 1971):34-45.

Sobel, Bernard. *A Pictorial History of Vaudeville.* New York: Citadel Press, 1961.

Spielman, Ed. *The Mighty Atom: The Life and Times of Joseph L. Greenstein. Biography of a Superhuman.* New York: The Viking Press, 1979.

Spitzer, Marian. "Morals in the Two-A-Day." *American Mercury* 3 (September 1924):35-39.

————. *The Palace.* New York: Atheneum, 1969. (For an earlier version of this material, see *Saturday Evening Post,* 12 July 1924, 24 May 1924, 7 March 1925, and 22 August 1925.)

"Springtime in the 40s." Newsweek, 30 May 1949, pp. 76-77.

Staples, Shirley L. "From 'Barney's Courtship' to Burns and Allen: Male-Female Comedy Teams in American Vaudeville, 1865-1932." Ph.D. dissertation, Tufts University, 1981.

Stone, Fred. *Rolling Stones.* New York: Whittlesey House, 1945.

Toll, Robert C. "The Vaudeville Show: Something for Everybody" in his *On with the Show: The First Century of Show Business in America.* New York: Oxford University Press, 1976.

"Tony Pastor, Father of Vaudeville." *Harper's Weekly,* 5 September 1908, p. 10.

Traber, J. Milton. "Pen Sketch of 'Tony' Pastor, the Father of Modern Variety." *Billboard,* 18 February 1911, pp. 5, 42.

Treadwell, Bill. *50 Years of American Comedy.* New York: Exposition Press, 1951.

Tucker, Sophie, with Dorothy Giles. *Some of These Days: The Autobiography of Sophie Tucker.* Garden City, N.Y.: Doubleday, Doran, and Co., 1945.

Uraneff, Vadim. "Commedia dell' arte and American Vaudeville." *Theatre Arts Monthly* 7 (October 1923):321-28.

"The Variety Stage: Early Creators of a Remunerative Vogue." *Harper's Weekly,* 29 March 1902, p. 414.

"The Variety Stage: Some Artists of This and Other Generations." *Harper's Weekly,* 12 April 1902, p. 466.

"The Variety Stage: Something of Its Early History in New York," *Harper's Weekly,* 22 March 1902, p. 380.

Vaudeville Year Book, 1913: Published as a Compendium of General Information for the Vaudeville and Tabloid Field in the West and South. Chicago: Vaudeville Year Book, 1913.

Walker, Stanley. *The Night Club Era.* New York: Frederick A. Stokes, 1933.

Willows, Maurice. "The Nickel Theatre." *Annals of the American Academy of Political and Social Sceince* 38 (July 1911):95-99.

Willson, Clair Eugene. "From Variety Theatre to Coffee Shop." *Arizona Historical Review* 6 (April 1935):3-13.

_____. *Mimes and Miners: Theater in Tombstone.* Tucson: University of Arizona Press, 1935.

Winsted, Jenifer P., "Tripping in the Light Fantastic Toe: Popular Dance of Early Portland, Oregon, 1800-1864." In *American Popular Entertainment,* edited by Myron Matlaw. Westport, Conn. and London: Greenwood Press, 1979.

Woolfe, S. J. "Gus Edwards' Academy." *New York Times Magazine,* 23 March 1941, pp. 12, 19.

Zellers, Parker R. "The Cradle of Variety: The Concert Saloon." *Educational Theatre Journal* 20 (December 1968):578-85.

_____. *Tony Pastor: Dean of the Vaudeville Stage.* Ypsilanti: Eastern Michigan University Press, 1971.

SELECT PERIODICALS AND SERIALS

Billboard. Los Angeles, 1894- .

New York Clipper. New York, 1900-1918.

New York Dramatic News. New York, 1875-1919.

New York Mirror. New York, 1879-1922.

Spirit of the Times. New York, 1856-1902.

The Theatre or *The Theatre Magazine.* New York, 1900-1931.

Variety. New York, 1905- .

CHAPTER 9

Burlesque and the Striptease

HISTORICAL SUMMARY

By the turn of the century a new form of American stage entertainment had begun to assert its own unique brand of amusement, burlesque. The origins of burlesque are complex and confusing. Its components can be traced to numerous forms: English and American literary burlesque and parody, the circus, the knockabout farces of the medicine show and dime museums, the farces of such popular theater writers as Edward Harrigan and Charles Hoyt, the sketches of the minstrel show, concert saloons and beer gardens, western honky-tonks, and even the stage Yankee. It is, however, misleading to attach the American form of burlesque to the older and more reputable forms, as a number of scholars and historians continue to do, for American burlesque was clearly rooted in native soil and developed a unique format for success. As William Green explains in his essay on the Minsky era, burlesque, a predominantly male oriented entertainment form, had as its aim "to incite audiences to laughter and delight through appeal to the rougher side within the human being. If nature abhors a vacuum, the vacuum that the burlesque show filled in the popular entertainment world was a type of show frankly sexual in nature." In other words, the essence of burlesque was the recognition that a segment of the American public would be attracted by an entertainment form that sought "fun related to the animalistic side of man and for an appreciation and display of female beauty."

Historians usually date burlesque's true beginnings to the 1860s, when in 1866 a troupe of stranded ballet dancers were incorporated into a musical extravaganza called *The Black Crook* at Niblo's Gardens in New York, followed in 1869 by Lydia Thompson and her "British Blondes" appearing in literary burlesques that emphasized feminine charms more than parody, the previous thrust of such burlesque. Recent research has suggested that these episodes in the American theater, and in particular the efforts of Lydia Thompson, have received too much attention as precursors of American burlesque. There is, however, little doubt but that they indicated to showmen the potential of scantily clad women on the stage, and after *The Black Crook* numerous hybrid forms of exhibitions and novelty shows emerged that featured dancers in tights as a major attraction. Certainly female entertainers of a rather low sort were soon part of the honky-tonk and concert saloon traditions. As early as 1894, Koster and Bial's Concert Hall, prior to its becoming a respectable vaudeville house, provides us with one of the earliest instances of the "strip," where the police raided a show after observing two women disrobe to the waist and continue to entertain their audience, without the benefit of a body stocking or other undergarment.

It was not primarily, then, the isolated parodies that spawned burlesque but more importantly the influence of the honky-tonk, half beer hall and half brothel, with its variety entertainments of the most vulgar sort. The audiences were unsophisticated, and the rough and convivial atmosphere was similar to that of the early English music hall, as pointed out in the last chapter on early variety and vaudeville. In such an atmosphere, the entertainer learned to depend on his personal inventiveness and wit and not a scripted, inviolate text. Instead, stock situations for comic routines evolved, and such flexible skits became the stock-in-trade of burlesque humor.

The first American burlesque impresario, M. B. Leavitt, who began his "burlesque" career in the 1870s, combined the atmosphere of the honky-tonk and concert saloon with the structure of the minstrel show, took it out of the saloon, and put it into theaters. Soon burlesque assumed its standard format: variety acts and "bits" mingled with musical numbers, featuring beautiful women and bawdy humor. Leavitt, a Barnum-inspired producer and promoter, established the Rentz-Stanley Novelty and Burlesque Company, taking the name of the successful Continental Rentz's Circus. Leavitt's first show, *Mm. Rentz's Female Minstrels* (1879) replaced the familiar minstrel circle of men with provocatively dressed women. Leavitt ultimately dropped the minstrel pretense and called his companies "burlesque troupes," but compared to the similarly structured shows of the honky-tonks and concert saloons, the content was relatively clean and, although the female performers showed their legs, blatant nudity was not part of the program. Leavitt's format led to the establishment of what might be considered "clean" burlesque and a focus on energetic and good-natured comedy.

By the turn of the century the comedian was the center of a burlesque performance, despite the slow but constant increase of interest in the sensuous presence of the female form, made more prominent beginning with Little Egypt's "cooch dancing" at the St. Louis World's Fair in 1904. The comic retained his central position, however, until the advent of the striptease in the early 1930s.

The "golden age" of burlesque began in 1905 with the organization of the Columbia circuit or wheel under the tutelage of Samuel Scribner and began to change in the 1920s when the new Mutual Burlesque Association directed by I. Herk added greater permissiveness. With an increase in its sexual overtones burlesque, although dominated by male patrons from the beginning, came to appeal even more to male audiences, reaching its height of popularity just prior to World War I. It should be stressed again, however, that during the teens and twenties the heart of burlesque was the comic. The prime attraction was the short scene or "bit" played by a troupe of performers, invariably including two comedians, a straight man, a character man, a prima donna, an ingenue, and a soubrette. Although the origin of the "bits" (well over 1,800 are known) is obscure, the enterprising burlesque comic clearly took his material from whatever source was at hand—minstrel skits, legitimate plays, vaudeville acts, fiction, and classical mythology—and made it his own. Most bits were designed to last, at least during the Mutual era, no more than fifteen minutes; the comics depended on their memories, not written texts, and could put together a show within half an hour of the curtain. Important ingredients of burlesque humor's uniqueness were its spontaneousness and flexibility, developing the routine around an established premise as the skit progressed.

Burlesque humor, unlike that of vaudeville, avoided sentiment, was unsophisticated, rowdy, and, by the 1930s quite scatological. Ralph Allen in "Our Native Theatre" explains that the comedian always played "the child of nature." Furthermore, "he represents man stripped of inhibitions, free of moral pretense, lazy, selfish, frequently a victim, but never a pathetic one, because in nine bits out of ten, he blunders into some kind of dubious success." Allen believes that much of the burlesque comic's appeal was his resilence and ability to overthrow authority, thus satisfying the audience's desire to renounce will and intelligence for instinct and appealing to an inner passion for anarchy.

With the rise of the Mutual circuit in the 1920s, the relatively clean fare of the Columbia circuit lost out and permissiveness took over. In the 1930s the Mutual circuit virtually collapsed. The efforts of a number of theater owners under the management of Izzy Hirst led to the formation of a new "wheel," the Hirst circuit, which dominated burlesque through the 1930s, although competition from "stock" burlesque houses was on the rise. Erotic stimulation began to replace bawdy humor; audiences became jaded and bored, much as they had with vaudeville. American burlesque, with the comic as king, fell on bad days. Without its basically cheerful humor, never bitter or moralistic, burlesque, like the minstrel show before it, lost its identity and its uniqueness.

As circuits diminished and permanent stock burlesque theaters increased, the role of the female performer took more and more prominence. After dirty shows defeated the clean shows, resident stock burlesque companies assumed the lead in presenting an eager audience more salacious shows than the remaining touring organizations could or would offer.

To many, the name burlesque is synonymous with the Minsky brothers (Billy, Abe, Herbert, and Morton). The Minskys, who established the major stock theaters in New York in the mid-1920s, began to revolutionize burlesque, glorifying the striptease, eliminating the three-part structure, wedding performer and audience with the runway, and to a large extent changing the nature of the audience from one predominantly working-class male to a mixed audience of all classes and professions. In the 1920s Minsky's National Winter Garden Theater, located on the Lower East Side, became "the high temple of American burlesque." In 1931 Billy Minsky opened the Republic Theater on 42nd Street, introducing Broadway to the burlesque industry and featuring admittedly dirty burlesque for a depression audience composed primarily of out-of-work men with little money and little to do with what they did have. After a lowpoint in the history of burlesque in the late 1920s, when Broadway revues presented more nudity than burlesque, styles became so revealing as to diminish the attraction of burlesque, and the skit had become so stale as to amuse very few, a novelty was needed—that novelty was the striptease.

As has been noted, female performers had been stripping in one way or another long before the Minsky's installed their first runway. What brought prosperity to many performers and entrepreneurs before it led to the form's demise was the "tease." By 1925 a typical burlesque show was including nude tableaux, aping the success of such a gimmick in revues; within a year or two performers began to move out of their frozen tableaux. Enterprising strippers began to devise techniques for removing a couple of garments and promising more. It is impossible to name the first stripteaser; the term is credited to two Minsky press agents, Mike Goldreyer and George Alabama. What is clear, however, is that with the depression attractive girls who could find jobs nowhere else began to replace the former burlesque "beef trust" chorus girls and thus helped to attract a new clientele. By the 1930s, then, the striptease brought burlesque to the top line of the popular entertainment business. Since it was obvious that the strip was the major attraction, producers gave it the most prominent position in the shows, eventually centering everything else on the striptease acts.

With burlesque prominently situated in the Broadway district of New York, opposition began to grow. Battles ensued back and forth for a number of years until 1937, when pressured by property owners, legitimate theater owners, clergymen, and politicians, Mayor Fiorello LaGuardia temporarily closed all New York burlesque houses. The use of the Minsky name or the word "burlesque" was prohibited in advertising. For a brief time a new form of burlesque, called vaudesque, tried to revive the form, offering stripping without nudity and comedy bits without obscenity, thus offering little to attract an audience. Theater owners were issued short-term licenses that were constantly cut shorter; in 1942, License Commissioner Paul Moss, acting under Mayor LaGuardia's orders, refused to renew any burlesque theater licenses. Burlesque was not able to recover from this final blow, exiled from the city that had given birth to it.

Although burlesque survived for a time in other cities (in the past half dozen years the last remaining burlesque houses of note have closed), the form went into further decline until all the talent save the strippers and an occasional fourth-rate comic sought other places of employment. The great stars of the striptease, whenever possible, departed for the greener pastures of nightclubs or cabarets. With nothing left but raunchy dancers, performing awkward bumps and grinds, burlesque became nothing more than a strip show.

Today, live sex shows, the last vestiges of the girlie show and certainly far removed from the Columbia Era of burlesque, exist in strip clubs and topless joints in virtually every major city in the United States. The "go-go" years of the 1960s produced an estimated 8,000 topless dancers; during the late 1960s there were still as many as 7,000 so-called strippers. Today's establishments, however, have more in common with the nineteenth-century concert saloon than with the glory days of burlesque. Cheap booze is sold and the shows, when there is a show, make no bones about their purely exploitive nature. There is no comedy, no tease, and frequently no stripping; instead blatant nudity appeals to the most purient motives. In areas where restrictions are carefully enforced, pasties and G-strings are still worn; in hard-core establishments the sexuality of the performer is demonstrated in a very explicit manner, frequently offering simulated or actual sex acts, or performers risk life and injury as they allow the customers to touch and fondle them. With nudity now commonplace in films and magazines, the striptease, which lost its artistry long ago, can no longer satisfy the insatiable appetite of its audience; today's stripper is merely pornographic.

While burlesque offered its audience varied entertainment in addition to the exploitation of the female performer, it prospered; with the exclusion of the comical, musical, and variety ingredients, burlesque limited its scope and became a form of entertainment that, unlike vaudeville, could never find full acceptance. Thus its ultimate demise was predictable. The late 1970s, ironically, has brought an entirely new twist to the striptease, a reversal of roles, placing male strippers on the runway and predominantly female patrons in the audience.

No other form of American popular stage entertainment underwent as drastic a change as did burlesque. The recent recreated burlesque musical *Sugar Babies* provides a vivid contrast to today's grind houses operating under the guise of burlesque. *Sugar Babies* is an unpretentious production with humor at the center and absolutely no nudity or stripping to be seen; instead, the audience is more than satisfied by the "bit," a magnificently executed fan dance, lovely high-kicking chorus girls, a belly dancer, and other energetic variety acts. It is the suggestion that makes the impact. Ann Corio's *This Was Burlesque,* though a bit more sexually oriented, accomplishes a similar effect. After seeing what a big-time burlesque show had to offer, it is easy to understand why some historians would say that burlesque was the most popular of all stage entertainments in America during the first three decades of this century. And, like vaudeville theaters, burlesque theaters dotted the United States. Today most of these have been torn down or converted into film houses.

SURVEY OF SOURCES

Burlesque has received little serious scholarly treatment and is invariably admixed with the striptease show, which actually spelled the demise of true American burlesque. Fortunately, this situation is beginning to change. A number of important doctoral dissertations have been written on burlesque, several well-documented essays have appeared within the past several years, and sociologists have begun to look at the stripper as one of the most obvious of female deviant occupations. Other significant studies are promised; Ralph G. Allen, one of the more knowledgeable authorities on burlesque humor and the author of the Broadway musical revue *Sugar Babies,* is currently working on a full-length study of burlesque comedy.

American burlesque should not be confused with the literary tradition, which has been effectively dissected (in its English and American forms) by V. C. Clinton-Baddeley in *The Burlesque Tradition in the English Theatre After 1600,* Leland A. Groghan in "New York Burlesque: 1840-1870," John Alden Degen III in "A History of Burlesque-Extravaganza in Nineteenth-Century England," George Kummer in "The Americanization of Burlesque, 1840-1860," Claudia D. Johnson in "Burlesque of Shakespeare: The Democratic American's 'Light Artillery'," Rita M. Plotnicki in "John Brougham: The Aristophanes of American Burlesque," Richard Grant White in "The Age of Burlesque," and Harley Granville-Barker in "Exit Planché—Enter Gilbert," among many other sources.

American burlesque as dealt with in this guide has only one fairly comprehensive history, Irving Zeidman's *The American Burlesque Show,* a somewhat biased account with puritanical overtones and no documentation. The autobiography of early impresario Michael B. Leavitt is useful for insights into the earliest organized companies using the name burlesque.

Recommended published scholarly studies on burlesque include: Ralph G. Allen's "Our Native Theatre: Honky-Tonk, Minstrel Shows, Burlesque," William Green's "Strippers and Coochers—the Quintessence of American Burlesque" and "The Audiences of the American Burlesque Show of the Minsky Era (ca. 1920-40)," and David Dressler's "Burlesque As a Cultural Phenomenon." Other scholarly studies of note (unpublished) include Joel Harvey's "American Burlesque as Reflected Through the Career of Kitty Madison, 1916-1931," William Green's "A Survey of the Development of Burlesque in America," and Patricia Sandberg Conner's "Steve Mills and the Twentieth Century American Burlesque Show. A Backstage History and A Perspective." The latter's published interview with Steve Mills (written under the name Trish Sandberg), "An Interview with Steve Mills," is quite revealing (Mills was Ann Cario's top banana in *This Was Burlesque*).

The standard sources on burlesque, generally weak on historical fact and the separation of striptease from true burlesque, but nonetheless informative, are Ann Corio's *This Was Burlesque* (with Joe DiMona) and Bernard Sobel's *Burleyque: An Underground History of Burlesque Days* and *A Pictorial History of Burlesque*. Sobel's "Take 'Em Off!" provides a brief summary of the American burlesque show, as does Helen Lawrenson's "Where Sex Was Fun: An Examination of Burlesque in America." Rowland Barber's *The Night They Raided Minsky's,* a fanciful account of burlesque in the 1920s, nonetheless provides a sense of the transition from true burlesque to striptease.

The contributions of Lydia Thompson to burlesque are challenged effectively by Marilyn A. Moses in "Lydia Thompson and the 'British Blondes' in the United States." Other points of view can be found in the standard histories of burlesque and in virtually all histories of the American musical (see chapter 10). Other miscellaneous sources on burlesque that offer insights into various aspects of the form include the following: Joseph Bigelow, "Where is Burly Headed?" (on the changing nature of burlesque in the 1930s); e.e. cummings, "Burlesque, I Love It!" (a fascinating appraisal by the poet of the Howard Theater, the National Winter Garden, and the Irving Place Theater); Stewart H. Holbrook, "Boston's Temple of Burlesque" (the Howard); Olive Logan, *Before the Footlights and Behind the Scenes* and *The Mimic World, and Public Exhibitions* (on the morality of preburlesque days); Frances Park, "Burlesque's Last Stand" (the transference of burlesque to 42nd Street); and Edmund Wilson, *The Shores of Light* (stimulating comment on various burlesque topics by this important literary critic).

A 1920s burlesque show is vividly and entertainingly recreated by Ralph G. Allen in "At My Mother's Knee (and Other Low Joints)." A sense of the "bit," in addition to being discussed in Allen's essay, can be gleaned from Richard J. Anobile's *Who's On First? Verbal and Visual Gems from the Films of Abbott and Costello,* Steve Mills's " 'An Artist's Studio'; A Comic Scene from Burlesque," and C. Lee Jenner's "Cornography." In addition to Green's essays, already cited, the Minsky era is discussed in Henry F. Pringle's "The Minsky Kids," Gilbert Seldes's "Fat Ladies," Roy Newquist's *Showcase* (in particular, an interview with Ann Corio), and especially in Morton Minsky, Joey Faye, Judi Faye, and Eleanore Treiber's "Modern Burlesque," which includes both discussions and texts of selected burlesque skits. The Howard in Boston, in addition to being covered in those sources mentioned, receives attention by Stewart Holbrook in his collection of essays, *Little Annie Oakley and Other Rugged People.*

Sources on the striptease and the latter days of burlesque are somewhat more plentiful, in part because today stripping more appropriately belongs to the world of carnivals, fairs, strip clubs, and striptease cabarets. Nevertheless, as an offshoot of burlesque it deserves inclusion and, surprisingly, the subject has begun to stimulate intriguing sociological and psychological investigations. Stripping as an autonomous performing form also lacks a comprehensive history, although Richard Wortley's *A Pictorial History of Striptease* makes a somewhat feeble effort. Susan Meiselas's *Carnival Strippers* is a more forthright and honest pictorial essay on the stripper, as is Roswell Angier's *A Kind of Life,* which combines pictorial and textual insights into the life of strippers in Boston's "Combat Zone." The early history of the striptease and burlesque of the 1930s is briefly chronicled in H. L. Alexander's *Striptease, The Vanished Art of Burlesque.*

Few of the numerous memoirs of strippers are worthy of consideration, although two stand apart from the others: Gypsy Rose Lee's memoirs (*Gypsy*) are coherent and offer good backstage atmosphere, as does her novel, *The G-String Murders;* and Georgia Sothern's *Georgia: My Life in Burlesque* is the best of its ilk—witty, entertaining, and provocative. Herschel C. Logan's *Buckskin and Satin* concerns Mlle. Morlacchi, credited by the author with the introduction of one European forebearer of the striptease, the can-can. Other biographies and essays by or about specific striptease artists include the following: Annabel Batistella (Fanne Fox), *Fanne Fox*; "Candy Barr: Burlesque Queen, Ex-Con, Jack Ruby's Pal, Porno's First (reluctant) Star and a Real Lady"; Honey Bruce, *Honey: The Life and Loves of Lenny's Shady Lady;* Richard Joseph, "Blaze Starr," Don Lee Keith, "America's Almost First Lady Blaze Starr," and her own autobiography, *Blaze Starr: My Life;* and Lois O'Connor, *The Bare Facts.*

Striptease-dominated burlesque and offshoots of striptease of the last thirty years are covered in the following: A. Owen Aldridge, "American Burlesque at Home and Abroad: Together with the Etymology of Go-Go Girl"; Sheldon Bart, "Topless Clubs: A Backroom Exposé"; Jean Christensen, "The K. C. Strip"; "Grinding to a Halt" (on the state of the art in the 1970s); Libby Jones, *Striptease* (a 1960s how-to book); Bernard Lipnitski, "God Save the Queen"; "Minsky's Hideaway" (rise of Lili St. Cyr and the increase of "exotic dancers"); "Strippers' Retreat" (demise of the old burlesque house); and "Le Striptease" (the American art form in Paris). Burlesque's evolution from the 1930s to the 1950s is vividly captured in the work of the artist Reginald Marsh. Sources on Marsh and his illustrations include Lloyd Goodrich, *Reginald Marsh,* Edward Laning, "Reginald Marsh," and Norman Sasowsky, *The Prints of Reginald Marsh.*

By far, the most stimulating and indepth studies of the stripper have been undertaken by sociologists and psychologists. Investigations into strippers' morality and the sociological-psychological implications of their profession have been published by James Skipper, Jr., Charles McCaghy, Marilyn Salutin, Jacqueline Boles, Albeno P. Garbin, Charles Davis, Leszek Kolakowski, Gale Miller, Robert Prus, Styllianoss Irini, Sandra Carey, Robert Peterson, and Louis Sharpe, with varying degrees of success. Skipper and McCaghy have published the most significant studies, including the following: "Stripteasers: The Anatomy and Career Contingencies of a Deviant Occupation," "Stripteasing: A Sex Oriented Occupation," "Lesbian Behavior as an Adaptation to the Occupation of Stripping," "Stripping: The anatomy of a deviant life style," and "The Stripteaser," the latter a good summary of their earlier work. Their essay "Respondents' Intrusion Upon the Situation: The Problem of Interviewing Subjects with Special Qualities" provides a useful analysis of the problems involved in the interview situation of strippers, based on their own experiences.

Nightclub strippers have been investigated in Jacqueline Boles and A. P. Garbin's "Stripping for a Living: An Occupational Study of Nightclub Strippers" and "The Strip Club and Stripper-Customer Patterns of Interaction." Also useful is Boles's dissertation, "The Night Club Stripper: A Sociological Study of an Occupation." Carey, Peterson, and Sharpe's essay, "A Study of Recruitment and Socialization into Two Deviant Female Occupations," compares data from samples of strippers with data from a similar sample of go-go girls; Charles Davis's "Striptease: More than Meets the Eye" is a theologian's analysis of patrons of the art, basically an expansion on the ideas of Leszek Kolakowski in "An Epistemology of the Striptease"; Marilyn Salutin's "Stripper Morality" investigates the motivations and corporeal ideologies of strippers; Gale Miller's *Odd Jobs: The World of Deviant Work* includes a chapter on "Entertainment as Deviant Work" (the stripper and the female impersonator); and finally, Prus and Irini's *Hookers, Rounders, and Desk Clerks,* a sociological study of the social organization of the hotel community, is a very useful source, focusing in its chapter on entertainment on the strippers or exotic dancers in the bar area.

There are few specific collections dealing with burlesque. The repositories discussed in the chapter on variety/vaudeville (chapter 8) contain some material. In addition, the Curtis Theatre Collection in the Hillman Library of the University of Pittsburgh includes about one hundred burlesque skits and bits formerly belonging to the comics Billy Hagan, Billy Fields, and Billy Foster. Recently, Jennie Lee, a former stripper, has established the Exotic Dancers League (and museum) in Los Angeles. The serials and periodicals listed in the variety/vaudeville chapter are useful for burlesque as well, though coverage is far less extensive.

BIBLIOGRAPHY

Aldridge, A. Owen. "American Burlesque at Home and Abroad: Together with the Etymology of Go-Go Girl." *Journal of Popular Culture* 5 (Winter 1971): 565-75.

Alexander, H. L. *Striptease, The Vanished Art of Burlesque.* New York: Knight Publications, 1938.

Allen, Ralph G. "Our Native Theatre: Honky-Tonk, Minstrel Shows, Burlesque." In *The American Theatre: A Sum of Its Parts,* edited by Henry B. Williams. New York: Samuel French, 1971.

_____. "At My Mother's Knee (and Other Low Joints)." In *American Popular Entertainment,* edited by Myron Matlaw. Westport, Conn. and London: Greenwood Press, 1979.

Angier, Roswell. *A Kind of Life: Conversations in the Combat Zone.* Danbury, N.H.: Addison House, distributed by Light Impressions, Rochester, N.Y., 1976.

Anobile, Richard J., ed. *Who's On First? Verbal and Visual Gems from the Films of Abbott and Costello.* New York: Avon, 1972.

Barber, Rowland. *The Night They Raided Minsky's.* New York: Simon and Schuster, 1960.

Bart, Sheldon. "Topless Clubs: A Backroom Exposé." *Gallery* 5 (March 1977): 37-39, 114.

Batistella, Annabel (Fanne Fox), with Yvonne Dunleavy. *Fanne Fox.* New York: Pinnacle Books, 1976.

Bigelow, Joseph. "Where is Burly Headed?" *Variety,* 3 May 1936, p. 15.

Boles, Jacqueline. "The Night Club Stripper: A Sociological Study of an Occupation." Ph.D. dissertation, University of Georgia, 1971.

_____, and Garbin, Albeno P. "Stripping for a Living: An Occupational Study of Nightclub Strippers." In *Deviant Behavior,* edited by Clifton D. Bryant. Chicago: Rand McNally, 1974.

_____. "The Strip Club and Stripper-Customer Patterns of Interaction." *Sociology and Social Research* 58 (1974):136-43.

Bruce, Honey, with Dana Benenson. *Honey: The Life and Loves of Lenny's Shady Lady.* Edited by Bob McKendrick. Chicago: Playboy Press, 1976.

"Candy Bar: Burlesque Queen, Ex-con, Jack Ruby's Pal, Porno's First (reluctant) Star and a Real Lady." *Oui* 5 (June 1976):79-84, 110-13.

Carey, Sandra Harley; Peterson, Robert A.; and Sharpe, Louis K. "A Study of Recruitment and Socialization into Two Deviant Female Occupations." *Sociological Symposium,* no. 11 (Spring 1974), pp. 11-24.

Christensen, Jean. "The K. C. Strip." *The Kansas City Star,* 10 October 1976, Sec. C, pp. 1, 8, 9, 10.

Clinton-Baddeley, V. C. *The Burlesque Tradition in the English Theatre After 1660.* London: Methuen and Co., 1952.

Conner, Patricia Sandberg. "Steve Mills and the Twentieth Century American Burlesque Show. A Backstage History and A Perspective." Ph.D. dissertation, University of Illinois at Urbana, 1979.

Corio, Ann, with Joe DiMona. *This Was Burlesque.* New York: Grosset and Dunlap, 1968.

Croghan, Leland A. "New York Burlesque: 1840-1870." Ph.D. dissertation, New York University, 1968.

cummings, e.e. "Burlesque I Love It!" In *E.E. Cummings: A Miscellany Revised,* edited by George J. Firmage. New York: October House, 1965.

Davis, Charles. "Striptease: More than Meets the Eye." *Commonweal* 99 (2 November 1973):106-8.

Degen, John Alden, III. "A History of Burlesque-Extravaganza in Nineteenth-Century England." Ph.D. dissertation, Indiana University, 1977.

Dressler, David. "Burlesque As A Cultural Phenomenon." Ph.D. dissertation, New York University, 1937.

Goodrich, Lloyd. *Reginald Marsh.* New York: Harry N. Abrams, [1972].

Granville-Barker, Harley. "Exit Planché—Enter Gilbert." In *The Eighteen-Sixties,* edited by John Drinkwater. Cambridge: Cambridge University Press, 1932.

Green, William. "A Survey of the Development of Burlesque in America." M.A. thesis, Columbia University, 1950.

————. "Strippers and Coochers—the Quintessence of American Burlesque." In *Western Popular Theatre,* edited by David Mayer and Kenneth Richards. London: Methuen and Co., 1977.

————. "The Audiences of the American Burlesque Show of the Minsky Era (ca. 1920-40)." In *Das Theater und Sein Publikum.* Vienna: Verlag der Osterreichischen Akadimie der Wissenschaften, 1977.

"Grinding to a Halt." *Time,* 27 April 1970, p. 56.

Harvey, Joel. "American Burlesque as Reflected Through the Career of Kitty Madison, 1916-1931." Ph.D. dissertation, Florida State University, 1980.

Holbrook, Stewart H. "Boston's Temple of Burlesque." *American Mercury* 58 (April 1944):411-16.

————. *Little Annie Oakley and Other Rugged People.* New York: Macmillan Co., 1948.

Jenner, C. Lee. "Cornography." *Other Stages,* 6 November 1980, p. 3.

Johnson, Claudia D. "Burlesques of Shakespeare: The Democratic American's 'Light Artillery'." *Theatre Survey* 21 (May 1980):49-62.

Jones, Libby. *Striptease.* New York: Parallax Publishing Co., distributed by Simon and Schuster, 1967.

Joseph, Richard. "Blaze Starr." *Esquire* 67 (July 1964):58-62.

Keith, Don Lee. "America's Almost First Lady Blaze Starr." *Gallery* 4 (December 1976):65-68, 100, 102.

Kolakowski, Leszek. "An Epistemology of the Striptease." *TriQuarterly* 22 (Fall 1971), pp. 49-67.

Kummer, George. "The Americanization of Burlesque, 1840-1860." *Theatre Annual* 27 (1971-1972):47-56. Reprinted in *Popular Literature in America.* Edited by James C. Austin and Donald A. Koch. Bowling Green, Ohio: Bowling Green Popular Press, 1972.

Laning, Edward. "Reginald Marsh." *American Heritage* 23 (October 1972): 14-35, 93.

Lawrenson, Helen. "Where Sex Was Fun: An Examination of Burlesque in America." *Show* 4 (March 1964):62-63, 87-88.

Leavitt, Michael B. *Fifty Years in Theatrical Management.* New York: Broadway Publishing Co., 1912.

Lee, Gypsy Rose. *The G-String Murders.* Cleveland and New York: World Publishing, 1941.

_____. *Gypsy: A Memoir.* New York: Harper and Bros., 1957.

Lipnitski, Bernard. "God Save the Queen." *Esquire* 72 (August 1969):104-7.

Logan, Herschel C. *Buckskin and Satin: The True Drama of Texas Jack and Mlle Morlacchi, Premiere Danseuse, Originator of the Can Can in America.* Harrisburg, Pa.: Stackpole Co., 1954.

Logan, Olive. *Before the Footlights and Behind the Scenes.* Philadelphia: Parmelee and Co., 1870.

_____. *The Mimic World, and Public Exhibitions.* Philadelphia: New-Word Publishing Co., 1878.

McCaghy, Charles H., and Skipper, James K., Jr. "Lesbian Behavior as an Adaptation to the Occupation of Stripping." *Social Problems* 17 (Fall 1969):262-70.

_____. "The Stripteaser." *Sexual Behavior* 1 (June 1971):78-87.

_____. "Stripping: The anatomy of a deviant life style." In *Life Styles: Diversity in American Society,* edited by Saul D. Feldman and Gerald W. Thielbar. Boston: Little, Brown and Co., 1972.

(See Also under Skipper below)

Meiselas, Susan. *Carnival Strippers.* New York: F., S., and G. Publishing Co. (Farrar, Straus, and Giroux), 1976.

Miller, Gale. *Odd Jobs: The World of Deviant Work.* Englewood Cliffs, N.J.: Prentice-Hall, 1978.

Mills, Steve. " 'An Artist's Studio'; A Comic Scene from Burlesque." *Educational Theatre Journal* 27 (October 1975):342-44.

Minsky, Morton; Faye, Joey; Faye, Judi; and Treiber, Eleanore. "Modern Burlesque (Discussions and Skits)." In *American Popular Entertainment,* edited by Myron Matlaw. Westport, Conn. and London: Greenwood Press, 1979.

"Minsky's Hideaway." *Newsweek,* 8 November 1954, pp. 95-97.

Moses, Marilyn A. Stolzman. "Lydia Thompson and the 'British Blondes' in the United States." Ph.D. dissertation, University of Oregon, 1978.

Newquist, Roy. *Showcase.* New York: Willaim Morrow and Co., 1966.

O'Connor, Lois. *The Bare Facts: Candid Confessions of a Stripper.* New York: MacFadden Books, 1964.

Park, Frances. "Burlesque's Last Stand." *Theatre Magazine,* December 1931, pp. 34-35.

Plotnicki, Rita M. "John Brougham: The Aristophanes of American Burlesque." *Journal of Popular Culture* 12 (1978):442-31.

Pringle, Henry F. "The Minsky Kids." *Collier's,* 6 March 1937, pp. 10, 15, 60.

Prus, Robert, and Irini, Styllianoss. *Hookers, Rounders, and Desk Clerks.* Toronto: Gage Publishing, 1980.

Salutin, Marilyn. "Stripper Morality." *Transaction* 8 (June 1971):12-22.

Sandberg, Trish. "An Interview with Steve Mills." *Educational Theatre Journal* 27 (October 1975):331-41.

Sasowsky, Norman. *The Prints of Reginald Marsh.* New York: Clarkson N. Potter, 1976.

Seldes, Gilbert. "Fat Ladies." *New Republic,* 30 March 1932, pp. 182-83.

Skipper, James K., Jr., and McCaghy, Charles H. "Stripteasers: The Anatomy and Career Contingencies of a Deviant Occupation." *Social Problems* 17 (Winter 1970):391-405.

_____. "Stripteasing: A Sex Oriented Occupation." In *Studies in the Sociology of Sex,* edited by James Henslin. New York: Appleton-Century-Crofts, 1971.

_____. "Respondents' Intrusion Upon the Situation: The Problems of Interviewing Subjects with Special Qualities." *Sociological Quarterly* 12 (1972):237-43.

Sobel, Bernard. *Burleyque: An Underground History of Burlesque Days.* 1931. Reprint. New York: Burt Franklin, 1975.

_____. "Take 'Em Off!" *Saturday Review of Literature,* 18 August 1945, pp. 22-24.

_____. *A Pictorial History of Burlesque.* New York: Putnam, 1956.

Sothern, Georgia. *Georgia. My Life in Burlesque.* New York: Signet Books, 1972.

Starr, Blaze, and Perry, Hue. *Blaze Starr: My Life.* New York: Warner Paperback Library, 1975.

"Strippers' Retreat." *Newsweek,* 11 January 1954, pp. 72-73.

"Le Striptease." *Newsweek,* October 1961, pp. 98-99.

White, Richard Grant. "The Age of Burlesque." *Galaxy* 8 (August 1869):256-66.

Wilson, Edmund. *The Shores of Light.* New York: Farrar, Straus, and Young, 1952.

Wortley, Richard. *A Pictorial History of Striptease: 100 Years of Undressing to Music.* Seacaucus, N.J.: Chartwell Books, distributed by Book Sales, 1976.

Zeidman, Irving. *The American Burlesque Show.* New York: Hawthorn Books, 1967.

The Musical Revue and Early Musical Theater

HISTORICAL SUMMARY

American variety entertainment's final mutation as a major popular amusement was the revue form, which, to some, represented little more than "high-class burlesque" with vaudeville acts placed in spectacular settings. Unquestionably, the revue contributed to the demise of both vaudeville and burlesque. American musical theater, in the broadest sense of that term, might be considered the last strong effort to create a form of amusement that would appeal to a large popular audience, although cutting across class lines. The subject of the American musical, which evolved into a unique form of theater unparalleled in any other nation of the world, is an enormous one, capable of filling hundreds of volumes, as indeed it has. In a guide of this sort, only the briefest of outlines can be proffered. Because of the prominent place of variety-type entertainment in the revue, the evolution of this form will be stressed over the development of the more conventional "book" musical. In order to restrict the following discussion, musical theater will be examined during its early stages, roughly until the emergence of the integrated musical, in which music, book, lyrics, and dance or choreography each play a vital role in producing a unified whole, and briefly brought up the present.

First, it might be helpful to define the revue. As does the more conventional musical, many early revues, until about 1915, built their productions around a story line that was frequently tenuous and incidental to its prime aim, to entertain. The revue, which reached its apogee during the first quarter of this century, used a single group of performers to present sketches, songs, dance numbers, and sometimes dialogue, built around a theme or current political, social, or theatrical events. Unlike vaudeville, the program was not simply a string of specialty acts but was devised especially for the production.

Both the musical and the revue grew out of a blend of elitist European culture and American popular entertainment. The progenitors of the American musical flowed into a complex melting pot into which both European and American stage entertainments, with music as an important ingredient of each, played critical roles. From Europe came such diverse forms as the ballad opera, ballet, extravaganza, operetta, opera bouffe, and the singspiel; the American contribution included the minstrel show, vaudeville, and burlesque, in the sense of parody or travesty. By the 1890s, after the success of *The Black Crook* (1866), a musical extravaganza by Charles M. Barras; George L. Fox's pantomime extravaganza *Humpty Dumpty* (1868); the parody *Evangeline* with musical adaptations by Giuseppe Operti in 1874; Kiralfy's production of *Around the World in 80 Days* (1875); *The Brook,* an 1879 production with Nate Salsbury's "Troubadours" and incorporating vernacular music and dance; and numerous other early musical experiments; an American form of the book musical slowly began to evolve.

In 1879 two American artists, Edward Harrigan and David Brahm, who might well be called the American Gilbert and Sullivan, introduced their immigrant and city low-life characters in a series of Mulligan Guard plays with popular music. This more American trend toward musicals, or plays with music, about urban life was continued into this century by such writers as Charles H. Hoyt and George M. Cohan, moving the mainstream of American musicals away from the more obvious European traditions. Other composers, most notably Victor Herbert, Sigmund Romberg, and Rudolf Friml, continued to follow the tradition of the older European operetta, a generally romantic form dominated by singing. By World War I several important composers, such as Jerome Kern and Irving Berlin, helped to shape a naturalized American form of musical comedy.

Before the turn of the century, however, the revue began to assert itself as a major competing entertainment form. The first revue to appear in the United States was *The Passing Show* in 1894, presented by George Lederer at the Casino Theater. This seminal revue, inspired by the Parisian vogue for topical revues, began a fashion in American musical theater that continued until the last of George White's "Scandals" in 1939, although isolated revues have caught the public's imagination on occasion since then. The prime period of the revue was, in fact, 1907 (the first Ziegfeld show) to 1929 when the depression swept the United States. During this peak period, several editions of this form of light entertainment were seen each spring and summer. American writers and producers saw the revue and the developing musical comedy as more homegrown forms than operetta, the reigning musical theater form of the time. They therefore chose to concentrate their efforts on American revues and musical comedies.

The revue, which might be considered the last true vestige of popular variety entertainment, grew primarily out of the same roots as vaudeville and burlesque; twentieth-century musical comedy, tremendously popular, soon took its place as part of the mainstream. The revue reflected a particular time, and to a large extent a particular place—New York City. Beginning with the opening in 1905 of the New York Hippodrome, the home of early lavish circusy revues with a $2 top admission price, the revue became a unique, dazzling, and universally appealing form, the epitome of how showmen saw New York glamour of the early twentieth century. The shows featured the biggest stars, many graduates of vaudeville, the most expensive sets and costumes, and the best current musical talent in the world. Many revues chose not to call themselves by that name, but instead selected designations such as "spectacular drama," "extravaganza," "spectacular musical production," or "jumble of jollification." The unquestioned king of the form was Florenz Ziegfeld, Jr., who, in 1907, unfurled his first "Follies," which continued annually until 1932. The 1920s and 1930s saw a wave of revue series cashing in on Ziegfield's success. Foremost among them were "The Passing Show" (1912-1924, and no relation to the one in 1894), "Greenwich Village Follies" (1919-1924), George White's "Scandals" (1919-1939), "The Music Box Revues" (1921-1924), and Earl Carroll's "Vanities" (1923-1932).

Ziegfeld's efforts represented the archetypal revue, "glorifying the American girl," and offering its audience a winning combination: a musical revue with songs, skits, and blackouts, talented comedians and singers, and a showcase of beautiful girls, scantily clad but with the extreme elegance of costume and decor giving dignity to their near-nakedness. The whole was raised far above the level of burlesque but made some of the same elements more universally acceptable.

Ziegfeld began as a small-time entrepreneur in Chicago, presenting one of the most popular exhibits at the Columbian Exposition in 1893, the strong man Eugene Sandow, billed as "the Great Sandow." After meeting Anna Held, his first wife and female star, in Europe, Ziegfeld established his trademark, the surrounding of his star with beautiful girls. By the time Held left Ziegfeld in 1912 the "Follies" was well-established. Ziegfeld was lavish with his money on and off stage, handling his theaters and his charges with a tyrannical hand, generous to his Ziegfeld girls, as long as they were ladylike in all situations, and arrogant to the true creative artists in his employ, especially the composers. Despite his many faults, Ziegfeld promoted an astonishing list of performers, composers, lyricists, and scenic and costume artists, including Lillian Lorraine, Marilyn Miller,

Fanny Brice, Will Rogers, Eddie Cantor, W. C. Fields, George Gershwin, Richard Rodgers, Lorenz Hart, Billie Burke (his last wife), Bert Williams (the first great black artist accepted into an entertainment that was not predominantly black), Al Jolson, Fred Allen, Cole Porter, Joseph Urban, and scores of others.

In almost every instance involving an artistic decision, Ziegfeld's taste was superb and his selection of talent quite amazing. Ziegfeld, unlike some of his contemporaries, stressed implied rather than revealed sensuality, with only rare moments of nudity. Earl Carroll, on the other hand, who produced fifteen editions of his "Vanities," operated with the motto "Through these portals pass the most beautiful women in the world" and was far less shy about blatant, but elegant, nudity.

The depression and the movie musical brought the end of the spectacular stage revue, although, ironically, the major producers of the form, including Ziegfeld, Carroll, and White, refused to accept the financial restrictions of that period and failed to recognize the increasing irrelevance of their extravagant productions. Despite later efforts to perpetuate the revue, the great days of Ziegfeld and Earl Carroll, mixing radiant showgirls, humor, and spectacle on the level of sophistication and wit but still retaining a popular appeal, could never again be repeated, despite the success of small revues in New York and the garish revues of Las Vegas (the latter operating like the old concert saloon—presenting a free or inexpensive show in order to attract gamblers to the casinos). The true contribution of the revue was its propelling of artists, especially songwriters and individual stars, into new avenues of show business.

During the years of the revue's rapid demise, American musical comedy was on the rise. In 1927 Jerome Kern and Oscar Hammerstein II's *Show Boat* (produced, somewhat surprisingly, by Flo Ziegfeld) became a major milestone in the development of the American musical, or, perhaps as Gerald Bordman has recently proposed in *American Operetta,* "the first totally American operetta." *Show Boat* was a landmark in a number of respects: its authors were all native, its setting was American, its principals were real people, its music depended heavily on native patterns, its plot was dramatic, its lyrics and dialogue were colloquial, and, as Bordman suggests, "its unstated philosophic premises discarded fundamentally snobbish European sensibilities and puritanism." The impact of this innovative musical suggested other possibilities for the form to creators of musical comedies. In 1931 George and Ira Gershwin and George S. Kaufman collaborated on *Of Thee I Sing,* the first musical with American political satire as its premise and the first musical to win the Pulitzer Prize for drama, thus establishing the musical as a source for serious as well as comic treatment.

The success of these early important collaborations led to subsequent teams of composers and lyricists, the latter often writing the books as well. The movement was toward more carefully integrated use of all elements. Richard Rodgers and Lorenz Hart in *Pal Joey* (1940) introduced a scoundrel hero, a clear reversal of the norm. No longer would the musical comedy be a simple form following an established formula. The variety of approaches and subjects would be limited only by the artists' imaginations; even the term "musical comedy" would be deceptive. From the 1930s to the present, variety entertainment has played an insignificant role in the musical, with some notable exceptions such as *Sugar Babies* and *Barnum,* or musicals capitalizing on nostalgia or on a renewed interest in a specific composer from the immediate past (such as Duke Ellington's music in *Sophisticated Ladies*). The 1930s and early 1940s added many names to the list of important composers and lyricists: Arthur Swartz, Howard Dietz, Marc Blitzstein, Kurt Weill, Cole Porter, Vincent Youmans, Otto Harbach, E. Y. Harburg, and Arthur Freed, to mention a few.

The beginning of the era of the modern musical is usually considered 1943, the year Richard Rodgers and Oscar Hammerstein II collaborated on *Oklahoma!* They followed with some of the most popular musicals of the first sixty years of this century: *Carousel* (1945), *South Pacific* (1949), *The King and I* (1951), and *The Sound of Music* (1959). Other successful collaborators during this golden era of the musical included Frederick Loewe and Alan Jay Lerner (*Brigadoon,* 1947, *My Fair Lady,* 1956, *Camelot,* 1960); Richard Adler and Jerry Ross (*The Pajama Game,* 1954 and *Damn Yankees,* 1955); Leonard Bernstein and Stephen Sondheim (*West Side Story,* 1957); Jerry Bock and Sheldon Harnick (*Fiddler on the Roof,* 1964). Successful collaborations continue to be the norm, as witnessed recently in the work of Tim Rice and Andrew Lloyd-Webber (*Jesus Christ Superstar,* 1971, and *Evita,* 1979).

Unlike most live popular stage forms, the musical's success has not diminished but continues unabated. The 1960s and 1970s saw a strong influence from youthful unrest and disillusionment, as in *Hair* (1967), and a return to nostalgia, which has continued into the 1980s, both in original musicals and frequent revivals, including the old revue format (*Follies, Inner City, Jacques Brel Is Alive and Well and Living in Paris, Dancin',* and others). In the 1970s the musical also attempted to raise its social consciousness and deal with current issues. Emerging from this period as the most vital and creative force in the American musical theater has been Stephen Sondheim, working frequently with the producer/director Harold Prince. Sondheim has been the creative force behind some of the most innovative musicals of the past decade, including *Company* (1970), *A Little Night Music* (1973), and *Sweeney Todd* (1979).

The past few seasons have seen few notable new musicals, although *A Chorus Line,* which opened in 1975 and is still running in 1982, helped to revitalize the American musical and provided an optimistic sign for this very American theatrical genre. *Chorus Line* also reflects one important trend in today's musicals, the rediscovered importance of the dancer and the choreographer, evidenced today by the number of major director-choreographers who have dominated musical production, most notably Michael Bennett, Bob Fosse, Tommy Tune, Jerome Robbins, and the late Gower Champion, whose last directorial assignment, the revival of *42nd Street,* is currently the most expensive musical theater ticket in New York.

Ultimately, what stands out today is the eclectic nature of the musical, both in form, subject matter, and production values. With the rising cost of production, the last true popular American theater form faces potential disaster, much as the revue form during the depression. Unlike the revue, however, the American musical is such a hybrid that it has succeeded in remaining one of America's major forms of escapist theater.

SURVEY OF SOURCES

The American musical has been the subject of a vast outpouring of books and essays. Its acceptability as a serious subject for research and investigation has recently been underscored by a major conference on the musical theater cosponsored by the American Society for Theatre Research, the Theatre Library Association, and the Sonneck Society at C. W. Post Center of Long Island University, with a wide-ranging selection of topics on the history of the American musical, performance, and techniques. It is hoped that the proceedings of this conference will be published and thus made more widely accessible. In this guide, there is space only for major sources on the musical form, a few select sources on early musical theater, and major musical biographies and autobiographies that shed light on the development of musical form. A number of the sources discussed here include extensive bibliographies that can be consulted for additional study. Sources on other variety forms covered in this guide should be consulted for the American origins of musical theater, in addition to the specific sources surveyed in this chapter. The focus in this guide is the nineteenth and early twentieth centuries.

The best general sources on the American musical are still the standard works, with several important recent additions to this list. Certainly an adequate understanding of the evolution of the American musical can be gleaned from the following: Cecil Smith, *Musical Comedy in America,* one of the more comprehensive histories (and recently updated by Glenn Litton); Stanley Green, *The World of Musical Comedy* (in a new fourth edition) and *The Encyclopaedia of the Musical Theatre;* and David Ewen, *The Story of*

America's Musical Theatre and *New Complete Book of the American Musical Theatre,* the latter an excellent reference work for the histories of major musicals. Certainly deserving a major place next to these older studies is Gerald Bordman's recent surveys, *American Musical Theatre: A Chronicle* and *American Operetta: From H.M.S. Pinafore To Sweeney Todd.* Martin Gottfried's *Broadway Musicals,* though an up-to-date survey and a beautifully produced volume, is less authoritative, and Ethan Mordden's *Better Foot Forward: The History of American Theatre,* though it contains the essential information, is a pretentious and aggravating volume due to its author's precious style.

A number of reference sources or histories on American music in a more general sense are useful for specific data and detailed facts. Of these, the following can be recommended: Julius Mattfeld's *Variety Music Cavalcade,* which provides a chronological checklist of popular music, including theater music in the United States from the Pilgrims to 1969; Jacques Barzun's *Music in America;* David Ewen's *The Life and Death of Tin Pan Alley* and *Great Men of American Popular Song;* Graydon La Verne Freeman's *The Melodies Linger On: Fifty Years of Popular Song* (1900 to 1950); Jack Burton's *Blue Book of Broadway Musicals,* which includes time-span essays and data on individual major musicals; Isaac Goldberg's *Tin Pan Alley;* Charles Hamm's *Yesterdays: Popular Song in America;* Richard Lewine and Alfred Simon's *Encyclopedia of Theatre Music* (1900-1950) and *Songs of the American Theater: A Comprehensive Listing of More Than 12,000 Songs,* a revision of the *Encyclopedia;* Cecil Smith's *Worlds of Music;* Sigmund Spaeth's *A History of Popular Music in America;* Irwin Stambler's *Encyclopedia of Popular Music;* and Alec Wilder's *American Popular Song, The Innovators 1900-1950,* with separate chapters on major musical theater composers. Arthur Jackson's *The Best Musicals From Show Boat to a Chorus Line,* although not an even work, can serve as a compendium of information on musical theater; in scope and design it is a cross between a handsome and entertaining coffee-table book and a reference work. Abe Laufe's *Broadway's Greatest Musicals* is a serviceable survey from 1884 to the 1970s but not highly recommended. Mark Lubbock's *The Complete Book of Light Opera* includes a large section on American light opera. The work of Lehman Engel is generally trustworthy and valuable for his knowledgeable musical analysis. Three of his books are recommended: *The American Musical Theatre, Words With Music,* and *The Words Are Music: The Great Theater Lyricists and Their Lyrics.* Edward Bennett Marks's early surveys, *They All Sang: From Tony Pastor to Rudy Vallee* and *They All Had Glamour: From the Swedish Nightingale to the Naked Lady,* though not limited to musical theatre, are useful and entertaining. Raymond Mander and Joe Mitchenson's *Musical*

Comedy, though concerned primarily with English musicals, is still valuable, especially for its 240 photographs. Robert L. Barlow's "Under My Skin" is an adequate, brief survey of the musical's evolution.

The early history of the American musical, prior to 1800, is carefully treated by Julian Mates in his standard history, *The American Musical Stage Before 1800* and in his excellent summary essay with a useful select bibliography, "American Musical Theatre: Beginnings to 1900." The significance of *The Black Crook* is examined in his "The Black Crook Myth." Other sources on *The Black Crook* include Joseph Whitton's *"The Naked Truth",* which remains a major history of the extravaganza, William L. Slout's "The Black Crook: First of the Super Nudies," and Barbara M. Barker's "Maria Bonfanti and *The Black Crook.*" Her essay "The Case of Augusta Sohlke vs. John DePol" is an interesting look at a successor of *The Black Crook.* Other early American musicals, each promoted at one time or another as the "first" native American musical comedy in the modern sense are discussed in the following: Irene Comer's *"Little Nell and the Marchioness:* Milestone in the Development of American Musical Comedy"; Susan Day's "Productions at Niblo's Garden Theatre, 1862-1868, During the Management of William Wheatley" (*The Black Crook* and *The White Faun*); Roger Allan Hall's "Nate Salsbury and His Troubadors: Popular American Farce and Musical Comedy, 1875-1887" and his shorter essay "The Brook: America's Germinal Musical"; and Allan S. Jackson's "Edward Everett Rice and Musical Burlesque" and "Evangeline: Forgotten American Musical."

An additional number of scholarly dissertations and essays shed light on aspects of early American musical theater. Recommended are: Marilyn A. Moses's "Lydia Thompson and the 'British Blondes' in the United States," a useful reassessment of Thompson; Laurence Senelick's "George L. Fox and American Pantomime"; Reuel Keith Olin's "A History and Interpretation of the Princess Theatre Musical Plays, 1915-1919," the most thorough investigation into this early series; Eugenia Schoettler's "From a Chorus Line to *A Chorus Line*: The Emergence of Dance in the American Musical Theatre," a useful survey from the early twentieth century to the present; Earl F. Bargainnier's edited issue of the *Journal of Popular Culture* ("In Depth: Musical Theatre"), containing seventeen useful essays, covering all aspects of the musical; Barbara Naomi Cohen's "The Dance Direction of Ned Wayburn: Selected Topics in Musical Staging, 1901-1923," a fascinating study of an early choreographer in virtually every form of musical stage entertainment; Sally R. Sommer's "Loie Fuller: From the Theatre of Popular Entertainment to the Parisian Avant Garde"; Frank Martin Lerche's "The Growth and Development of Scenic Design for the Professional Musical Comedy Stage in New York from 1866 to 1920," an examination of one hundred key productions, including revues; Robert Friedman's "The Contributions of Harry Bache Smith (1860-1936) to the American Musical Theatre," covering the career of a prolific but little known early librettist and lyricist; and James J. Spurrier's "The Integration of Music and Lyrics with the Book in the American Musical," a useful perspective on the modern musical.

Harrigan and Hart (and the composer David Brahm) were first studied in detail in E. J. Kahn's *The Merry Partners,* a work that has been partially superseded by Richard Moody's *Ned Harrigan: From Colear's Hook to Herald Square,* although neither dissects the Harrigan/Brahm partnership satisfactorily. Of the several biographies of George M. Cohan available, John McCabe's *George M. Cohan: The Man Who Owned Broadway* is the most reliable. Others include Ward Morehouse's *George M. Cohan: Prince of the American Theatre* and Cohan's *Twenty Years on Broadway; And the Years It Took to Get There.*

The revue, especially Ziegfeld's contributions, has been the subject of a number of popularized studies. Robert Baral's *Revue: The Great Broadway Period* is the sole comprehensive study of New York revues, with a list of revues on Broadway from 1903 to 1945. Mander and Mitchenson's *Revue: A Story in Pictures* is an entertaining summary of the revue era with a focus on England, however. The only book-length study of the Hippodrome (1905-1939) is by Norman Clarke, *The Mighty Hippodrome,* altho~gh essays by John Byram ("Famous American Theatres") and David Ewen ("Down Falls the Hippodrome") are useful, brief supplements. Of the Ziegfeld studies, the most accurate is Randolph Carter's *The World of Flo Ziegfeld,* although both Marjorie Farnsworth (*The Ziegfeld Follies*) and Charles Higham (*Ziegfeld*) cover much the same ground. All three contain magnificent illustrations and together form a reasonably good picture of the "Follies." Patricia Ziegfeld's book, *The Ziegfelds' Girls,* is a curious and sometimes interesting inside view of Ziegfeld written by his daughter. The autobiographies of Billie Burke, Ziegfeld's last wife, can be useful as well (*With a Feather on My Nose* and *With Powder on My Nose*). Also of interest is Anna Held's *Memoires* (in French). Eddie Cantor's *Ziegfeld the Great Glorifier,* compiled from essays in *Collier's,* provides good insight into the personality and tactics of Ziegfeld as told by one of his most famous performers. Cantor's *My Life is in Your Hands* also contains comments on Ziegfeld. Lady Lucile Duff-Gordon's *Discretions and Indiscretions,* though limited in factual information, is a good memoir of a Ziegfeld costume designer; Jan Sherman's "A Denishawn Dancer with the Ziegfeld Follies" discusses Ziegfeld's "Tab" shows; Bernard Sobel's "This Was Ziegfeld" delves into Ziegfeld's relationship with performers and business associates; Ziegfeld's own essay, "Picking Out Pretty Girls for

the Stage," delineates the different types of show girls used by him; and
Joseph Urban's *Theatres* focuses on the architecture of the Ziegfeld Theatre.
Other sources which include material on Ziegfeld's "Follies" are discussed
below in the paragraph on biographies and autobiographies, and in the next
section on other revues or revue in general.

Other major revues have received less coverage than the "Follies" of
Ziegfeld. Alice Crowley includes a chapter on "The Grand Street Follies"
in *The Neighborhood Playhouse,* and Margaret Knapp expertly discusses
the tone, subject matter, performers, and history of the same revue series in
a more scholarly and incisive manner in "Theatrical Parody in the Twentieth-
Century American Theatre." John Murray Anderson and Hugh Abercrombie Anderson's *Out Without My Rubbers,* the autobiography of John M.
Anderson (1886-1954), the producer of the "Greenwich Village Follies,"
includes a brief history of the revue and frequent allusions to the better-
known producers of revues. Allen Churchill in *The Theatrical Twenties* is
quite good on the revues of that era. In "Vive la Folie!" e.e. cummings
analyzes the revue in general and debunks the American form in comparison
to the Parisian revue. Vernon Duke in *Passport to Paris* covers not only
his career as a composer with Ziegfeld but with the Shuberts and other
producers of musicals in the 1930s and 1940s. Priscilla Flood's "The Follies,
Scandals, and Delights of Erté," which includes an impressive colored
portfolio of Erté's designs, is a useful source on this revue designer, as is
Charles Spencer's *Erté.* Frances Hackett's "The Follies" is an interesting
and early attack on the revue form as "ostentatious and boring." A point
of view quite opposite to Hackett can be found in Joseph Wood Krutch's
"Of Revues" and "Bigger and Better," although in "Prodigal Enough"
he finds the form becoming "boring" himself. Ken Murray's *The Body
Merchant* is ostensibly the life of Earl Carroll but only deals indirectly with
his "Vanities." George Jean Nathan's *The Popular Theatre* and *The
Entertainment of a Nation* are worth attention for this critic's analysis of
Ziegfeld in 1918 and the decline in the 1940s of the revue form. Another
respected critic's assessment of the form can be found in Ward Morehouse's
"The Ziegfeld Follies—A Formula with Class." Bernard Sobel's *Broadway
Heartbeat* provides good coverage of the revue with chapters on Carroll
and Ziegfeld, as well as discussions of burlesque and vaudeville. Finally,
an attempt to come to grips with the origin of the term "revue" and its
various theatrical usages can be found in Thomas H. Gressler's "A Review
of the Term Revue," and a good overview of the form (and the Shubert
produced "The Passing Show" series, including a checklist of 104 shows
between 1906 and 1943) is in Sally Banes's edited issue of *The Passing
Show.* Stephen M. Vallillo's recent essay, "Broadway Revues in the Teens
and Twenties," explores sex and nudity in the revue form.

Of the dozens of biographies and autobiographies of performers and producers who participated in revue (and some in musical comedies), in addition to those already mentioned, the following are suggested: Eddie Cantor, *Take My Life;* Irene Castle, *Castle in the Air;* Earl Conrad, *Billy Rose: Manhattan Primitive;* Homer Croy, *Our Will Rogers;* Donald Day (editor), *The Autobiography of Will Rogers* and Day's *Will Rogers: A Biography;* P. J. O'Brien, *Will Rogers: Ambassador of Good Will, Prince of Wit and Wisdom;* Michael Freedland, *Jolson;* Pearl Sieben, *Immortal Jolson;* Al Jolson, "If I Don't Get Laughs and Don't Get Applause—The Mirror Will Show Me Who Is To Blame"; Norman Katkov, *The Fabulous Fanny: The Story of Fanny Brice*; and Harry Richman, *A Hell of a Life.* The black performer Bert Williams, a star of the Ziegfeld "Follies," has received a great deal of attention, especially in the last several years. Among the more perceptive and useful sources on this unique and somewhat tragic entertainer are the following: Ann Charters, *Nobody: The Story of Bert Williams* (a rather undistinguished biography overall); Max Morath, "The Vocal and Theatrical Music of Bert Williams and His Associates"; Sandra L. Richards's "Bert Williams: The Man and the Mask"; Mabel Rowland, editor, *Bert Williams: Son of Laughter* (a collection of tributes); William McFerrin Stowe, Jr., "Damned Funny: The Tragedy of Bert Williams"; Booker T. Washington, "Bert Williams"; and Williams's own "The Comic Side of Trouble," an astute observation on comedy and racial discrimination.

A fascinating study of the Las Vegas strip and its entertainment palaces, from an architectural point of view, is *Learning From Las Vegas* by Robert Venturi, Denise Scott Brown, and Steven Izenour. A recent History of Radio City Music Hall and its modern-day revues is Charles Francisco, *The Radio City Music Hall: An Affectionate History of the World's Greatest Theater.* A very useful source on the modern Las Vegas revue and its technical demands is the special issue of *Theatre Crafts* (1976) devoted to the modern revue and the following specific essays: "Costumes: Baubles, Bangles, and Bright Shiny Beads"; Peter Foy, "Special Effects Casebook: Problem Solving in Las Vegas"; "Lighting: Glitter and Glamorize"; Patricia MacKay, "Las Vegas Spectacular"; "Setting: See Moscow burn; Witness the Great Flood." Attempts to revive the traditional revue, including televised versions, are discussed in the following: Max Liebman, "A Broadway Revue Every Week"; Leonard Sillman, "Who Said the Revue Is Dead?"; and Derek and Julia Parker, *The Natural History of the Chorus Girl,* most useful for its illustrations.

Of the numerous studies, biographies, and autobiographies of major figures in the early development of the American musical, there is only space to mention a select few of the more useful ones. Rudolph Aronson's

Theatrical and Musical Memoirs is especially good on the New York Casino of the 1880s and 1890s. Gerald Bordman's *Jerome Kern: His Life and Music* is a loving look at the composer by an admittedly biased admirer. Agnes de Mille's *Speak to Me, Dance with Me* is an excellent autobiography by the choreographer of *Oklahoma*! and other landmark musicals. George and Ira Gershwin have received a good deal of attention, including in David Ewen's *The Story of George Gershwin, The George and Ira Gershwin Songbook,* Edward Jablonski and Lawrence D. Stewart's *The Gershwin Years,* and Robert Kimball and Alfred Simon's *The Gershwins.* Also of interest is Ira Gershwin's *Lyrics on Several Occasions.* Hugh Fordin's *Getting to Know Him* provides an adequate chronicle of the career of Oscar Hammerstein II; Hammerstein's *Lyrics* is an interesting compilation up to 1949 with an explanatory introduction. The earlier Oscar Hammerstein (the first), musical and theatrical impresario, has been given an adequate biography in Vincent Sheean's *The Amazing Oscar Hammerstein I: The Life and Exploits of An Impresario.* The life of Harold Arlen, with a list of his works, has been told by Edward Jablonski in *Harold Arlen: Happy With the Blues.* Cole Porter's work is examined in Robert Kimball's *Cole* and Charles Schwartz's *Cole Porter, A Biography,* the latter including an excellent bibliography of previously published sources. Richard Rodgers's *Musical Stages* is a superb autobiography by the dean of the American musical. *Time Magazine*'s essay "He Sent Them Away Humming" is a worthy tribute to Rodgers written on his death in 1979. P. G. Wodehouse and Guy Bolton's careers (1914 to 1950s) are told in their *Bring on the Girls.* A dated but useful sketch of twenty-three early musical-comedy stars is recorded in Lewis Clinton Strang's *Celebrated Comedians of Light Opera and Musical Comedy in America.*

The collaboration of America's first important black musical theater creators, Noble Sissle and Eubie Blake, is attractively presented with numerous illustrations by Robert Kimball and William Bolcom in *Reminiscing with Sissle and Blake.* Also of interest is Max Morath's "The Ninety-Three Years of Eubie Blake" and Al Rose's *Eubie Blake.* Excellent sources on the evolution of black musicals are James Weldon Johnson's *Black Manhattan,* Henry T. Sampson's *Black in Blackface,* and Tom Fletcher's *100 Years of the Negro in Show Business.*

An attractive and informative history of musical theater from *Strike Up the Band* to *Dubarry Was a Lady* is *Ring Bells! Sing Songs! Broadway Musicals of the 1930s* by Stanley Green; *Show Boat* has received a full-length study in Miles Kreuger's *Show Boat: The Story of a Classic American Musical,* in some ways more useful on the phenomenon of the showboat than on the musical. The history of the rise and fall of the Shubert empire and its contributions to the musical stage is adequately related by Jerry

Stagg in the only full-length study of the brothers, *The Brothers Shubert. A Half-Century of Show Business.* In this context it should be noted that the archives of the Shubert Foundation are currently in the process of being catalogued and organized in their repository in the Lyceum Theater in New York. Although this collection, a gold mine on the early musical and the revue, is not yet available to the public, its contents are discussed in the Archive's publication, *The Passing Show.* Especially useful is the issue edited by Ginnine Cocuzza, "Musicals in the Shubert Archives." Finally, the most recent of the many musical discographies is Gordon W. Hodgins's *The Broadway Musical: A Complete LP Discography.*

For periodicals on musical theater, the researcher should begin with the major theater serials, especially those discussed in chapter 8. Of more specialized interest are *Dance Research Journal,* published by the Committee on Research in Dance at New York University, and the Shubert Archive's *The Passing Show* (234 West 44th Street, New York, N.Y. 10036). The Archives, should they become available, will prove to be one of the more valuable resources for the study of early musicals and revue. Also useful is the collection in the Library of the Performing Arts at Lincoln Center in New York and the Hoblitzelle Theatre Collection at the University of Texas in Austin. Most major theater collections, however, should be investigated. The Songwriters Hall of Fame Museum in Times Square is dedicated to the art of the American songwriter and contains interesting displays of memorabilia but is not a particularly notable research facility at present. The Committee on Research in Dance at New York University and The Sonneck Society (American Music) are both interested in research that relates to the American musical theater. There is no major organization to my knowledge dedicated exclusively to the musical theater.

BIBLIOGRAPHY

Anderson, John Murray, and Anderson, Hugh Abercrombie. *Out Without My Rubbers: The Memoirs of John Murray Anderson.* New York: Library Publishers, 1954.

Aronson, Rudolph. *Theatrical and Musical Memoirs.* New York: McBride, Nast and Co., 1913.

Banes, Sally, ed. "Revues." *The Passing Show* 3 (Winter 1979):1-12.

Baral, Robert. *Revue: The Great Broadway Period.* New York: Fleet Press, 1962.

Bargainnier, Earl F., ed. "In Depth: Musical Theatre." *Journal of Popular Culture* 12 (Winter 1978):404-571.

Barker, Barbara M. "The Case of Augusta Sohlke vs. John DePol." *Educational Theatre Journal* 30 (May 1978):232-39.

———. "Maria Bonfanti and *The Black Crook,* New Orleans, 1872." *Theatre Journal* 31 (March 1979):88-97.

Barlow, Robert L. "Under My Skin." *Yale University Library Gazette* 42 (October 1967):51-76.

Barzun, Jacques. *Music in America.* Garden City, N.Y.: Doubleday and Co., 1956.

Bordman, Gerald. *American Musical Theatre: A Chronicle.* New York: Oxford University Press, 1978.

_____. *Jerome Kern: His Life and Music.* New York and Oxford: Oxford University Press, 1980.

_____. *American Operetta: From H.M.S. Pinafore to Sweeney Todd.* New York and Oxford: Oxford University Press, 1981.

Burke, Billie, with Cameron Shipp. *With a Feather on My Nose.* New York: Appleton-Century, 1949.

_____. *With Powder on My Nose.* New York: Coward-McCann, 1959.

Burton, Jack. *Blue Book of Broadway Musicals.* Rev. ed. Watkins Glen, N.Y.: Century House, 1974.

Byram, John. "Famous American Theatres." *Theatre Arts* 41 (December 1957): 74-75, 92.

Cantor, Eddie, with Jane Kesner Ardmore. *Take My Life.* Garden City, N.Y.: Doubleday and Co., 1957.

_____, as told to David Freedman. *My Life is in Your Hands.* Foreword by Will Rogers. New York: Blue Ribbon, 1932.

_____, and Freedman, David. "Ziegfeld and His Follies." *Collier's,* 13 January 1934, pp. 7-9; 20 January 1934, pp. 22, 26, 47-48; 27 January 1934, pp. 24-25, 45-56; 3 February 1934, pp. 18-19, 32; 17 February 1934, pp. 22, 38, 40.

_____. *Ziegfeld the Great Glorifier.* New York: Alfred King, 1934.

Carter, Randolph. *The World of Flo Ziegfeld.* New York and Washington, D.C.: Praeger, 1974.

Castle, Irene, as told to Bob and Wanda Duncan. *Castles in the Air.* Garden City, N.Y.: Doubleday and Co., 1958.

Charters, Ann. *Nobody: The Story of Bert Williams.* New York: Macmillan Co., 1970.

Churchill, Allen. *The Theatrical Twenties.* New York: McGraw-Hill, 1975.

Clarke, Norman. *The Mighty Hippodrome.* New York and South Brunswick, N.J.: A. S. Barnes and Co., 1968.

Cocuzza, Ginnine, ed. "Musicals in the Shubert Archives." *The Passing Show* 3 (Summer 1979):1-10.

Cohan, George M. *Twenty Years on Broadway; And the Years It Took to Get There.* New York: Harper and Bros., 1924.

Cohen, Barbara Naomi. "The Dance Direction of Ned Wayburn: Selected Topics in Musical Staging, 1901-1923." Ph.D. dissertation, New York University, 1980.

Comer, Irene Forsythe. "*Little Nell and the Marchioness*: Milestone in the Development of American Musical Comedy." Ph.D. dissertation, Tufts University, 1979.

Conrad, Earl. *Billy Rose; Manhattan Primitive.* Cleveland: World Publishers, 1968.

"Costumes, Baubles, Bangles, and Bright Shiny Beads." *Theatre Crafts* 10 (March-April 1976):10-13, 42, 44.

Crowley, Alice L. *The Neighborhood Playhouse.* New York: Theatre Arts Books, 1959.

Croy, Homer. *Our Will Rogers.* New York: Duell, Sloan, and Pearce, 1953.

cummings, e.e. "Vive la Folie!" In *E.E. Cummings: A Miscellany Revised,* edited by George J. Firmage. New York: October House, 1965.

Day, Donald, ed. *The Autobiography of Will Rogers.* Boston: Houghton Mifflin Co., 1949.

_____. *Will Rogers: A Biography.* New York: David McKay Co., 1962.

Day, Susan Stockbridge. "Productions at Niblo's Garden Theatre, 1862-1868, During the Management of William Wheatley." Ph.D. dissertation, University of Oregon, 1972.

de Mille, Agnes. *Speak to Me, Dance with Me.* Boston: Little, Brown and Co., 1973.

Duff-Gordon, Lady Lucile. *Discretions and Indiscretions.* New York: Frederick A. Stokes Co., 1932.

Duke, Vernon. *Passport to Paris.* Boston and Toronto: Little, Brown and Co., 1955.

Engel, Lehman. *The American Musical Theatre. A CBS Legacy Collection Book.* New York: Macmillan Co., 1967.

_____. *Words With Music.* New York: Macmillan Co., 1972.

_____. *The Words Are Music: The Great Theater Lyricists and Their Lyrics.* New York: Crown Publishers, 1975.

Ewen, David. "Down Falls the Hippodrome." *Theatre Guild Magazine* 7 (April 1930):39-41.

_____. *The Story of George Gershwin.* New York: Henry Holt and Co., 1943.

_____. *The Life and Death of Tin Pan Alley.* New York: Funk and Wagnalls, 1964.

_____. *The Story of America's Musical Theatre.* Rev. ed. New York and Philadelphia: Chilton Book Co., 1968.

_____. *New Complete Book of the American Musical Theatre.* New York: Holt, Rinehart and Winston, 1970.

_____. *Great Men of American Popular Song.* Englewood Cliffs, N.J.: Prentice-Hall, 1970.

Farnsworth, Marjorie. *The Ziegfeld Follies.* New York: Bonanza Books, 1956.

Fletcher, Tom. *100 Years of the Negro in Show Business.* New York: Burdge and Co., 1954.

Flood, Priscilla. "The Follies, Scandals, and Delights of Erté." *Horizon* 17 (Summer 1975):20-31.

Fordin, Hugh. *Getting to Know Him: A Biography of Oscar Hammerstein II.* Introduction by Stephen Sondheim. New York: Random House, 1977.

Foy, Peter. "Special Effects Casebook: Problem Solving in Las Vegas." *Theatre Crafts* 10 (March-April 1976):24-25.

Francisco, Charles. *The Radio City Music Hall: An Affectionate History of the World's Greatest Theater.* New York: E. P. Dutton Co., 1979.

Freedland, Michael. *Jolson.* New York: Stein and Day, 1972.

Freeman, Graydon La Verne. *The Melodies Linger On: Fifty Years of Popular Song.* New York: Century House, 1951.

Friedman, Robert. "The Contributions of Harry Bache Smith (1860-1936) to the American Musical Theatre." Ph.D. dissertation, New York University, 1976.

Gershwin, George, and Gershwin, Ira. *The George and Ira Gershwin Songbook.* Foreword by Ira Gershwin. New York: Simon and Schuster, 1960.

Gershwin, Ira. *Lyrics on Several Occasions.* New York: Viking Press, 1974.

Goldberg, Isaac. *Tin Pan Alley: A Chronicle of the American Popular Music Racket.* Introduction by George Gershwin. New York: John Day Co., 1930.

Gottfried, Martin. *Broadway Musicals.* New York: Harry N. Abrams, 1979.

Green, Stanley. *The World of Musical Comedy.* 4th ed. San Diego, Calif.: A. S. Barnes, 1980.

———. *Ring Bells! Sing Songs! Broadway Musicals of the 1930s.* New York: Galahad Books, 1971.

———. *Encyclopaedia of the Musical Theatre.* New York: Dodd, Mead and Co., 1976.

Gressler, Thomas H. "A Review of the Term Revue." *Players, The Magazine of American Theatre* 48 (June-July 1973):224-29.

Hackett, Frances. "The Follies." *New Republic,* 7 July 1917, p. 278.

Hall, Roger Allan. "Nate Salsbury and His Troubadors: Popular American Farce and Musical Comedy, 1875-1887." Ph.D. dissertation, Ohio State University, 1974.

———. "The Brook: America's Germinal Musical." *Educational Theatre Journal* 27 (October 1975):323-29.

Hamm, Charles. *Yesterdays: Popular Song in America.* New York and London: W. W. Norton, 1979.

Hammerstein, Oscar II. *Lyrics.* New York: Simon and Schuster, 1949.

Held, Anna. *Memoires.* Preface by Jacques-Charles. Paris: La Nef de Paris, 1954.

"He Sent Them Away Humming: Richard Rodgers, 1902-1979." *Time,* 14 January 1980, p. 83.

Higham, Charles. *Ziegfeld.* Chicago: Henry Regnery Co., 1972.

Hodgins, Gordon W. *The Broadway Musical: A Complete LP Discography.* Metuchen, N.J. and London: The Scarecrow Press, 1980.

Jablonski, Edward. *Harold Arlen: Happy With the Blues.* Garden City, N.Y.: Doubleday and Co., 1961.

———, and Stewart, Lawrence D. *The Gershwin Years.* Garden City, N.Y.: Doubleday and Co., 1958.

Jackson, Allan S. "Edward Everett Rice and Musical Burlesque." *Players, The Magazine of American Theatre* 51 (Summer 1976):154-66.

———. "Evangeline: Forgotten American Musical. *Player's Magazine* 44 (October-November 1968):20-25.

Jackson, Arthur. *The Best Musicals From Show Boat to a Chorus Line: Broadway, Off-Broadway, London.* Foreword by Clive Barnes. New York: Crown Publishers, 1977.

Johnson, James Weldon. *Black Manhattan.* New York: Alfred A. Knopf, 1940.

Jolson, Al. "If I Don't Get Laughs and Don't Get Applause—The Mirror Will Show Me Who Is To Blame." *American Magazine* 87 (April 1919): 18-19, 154-58.

Kahn, E. J., Jr. *The Merry Partners: The Age and Stage of Harrigan and Hart.* New York: Random House, 1955.

Katlov, Norman. *The Fabulous Fanny: The Story of Fanny Brice.* New York: Alfred A. Knopf, 1953.

Kimball, Robert, ed. *Cole.* New York: Holt, Rinehart and Winston, 1971.

_____, and Balcom, William. *Reminiscing With Sissle and Blake.* New York: Viking Press, 1973.

_____, and Simon, Alfred. *The Gershwins.* Foreword by Richard Rodgers. Introduction by John S. Wilson. New York: Atheneum, 1973.

Knapp, Margaret M. "Theatrical Parody in the Twentieth-Century American Theatre: The Grand Street Follies." *Educational Theatre Journal* 27 (October 1975):356-68.

Kreuger, Miles. *Show Boat: The Story of a Classic American Musical.* New York: Oxford University Press, 1977.

Krutch, Joseph Wood. "Of Revues." *Nation,* 13 January 1926, pp. 40-41.

_____. "Bigger and Better." *Nation,* June 1926, p. 616.

_____. "Prodigal Enough." *Nation,* 19 October 1932, pp. 365-76.

Laufe, Abe. *Broadway's Greatest Musicals.* Rev. ed. New York: Funk and Wagnalls, 1977.

Lerche, Frank Martin. "The Growth and Development of Scenic Design for the Professional Musical Comedy Stage in New York from 1866 to 1920." Ph.D. dissertation, New York University, 1969.

Lewine, Richard, and Simon, Alfred. *Encyclopedia of Theatre Music.* New York: Random House, 1961.

_____. *Songs of the American Theater: A Comprehensive Listing of More Than 12,000 Songs, Including Selected Titles from Film and Television Productions.* Introduction by Stephen Sondheim. New York: Dodd, Mead and Co., 1973.

Liebman, Max. "A Broadway Revue Every Week." *Theatre Arts* 37 (May 1953): 75-77.

"Lighting: Glitter and Glamorize." *Theatre Crafts* 10 (March-April 1976):14-17, 46, 48.

Lubbock, Mark. *The Complete Book of Light Opera.* With an American section by David Ewen. New York: Scholarly Press, 1962.

McCabe, John. *George M. Cohan: The Man Who Owned Broadway.* Garden City, N.Y.: Doubleday and Co., 1973.

MacKay, Patricia. "Las Vegas Spectacular." *Theatre Crafts* 10 (March-April 1976):28-31, 34, 36-44.

Mander, Raymond, and Mitchenson, Joe. *Musical Comedy: A Story in Pictures.* Foreword by Noel Coward. New York: Taplinger Publishing Co., 1970.

_____. *Revue: A Story in Pictures.* Foreword by Noel Coward. New York: Taplinger Publishing Co., 1971.

Marks, Edward Bennett. *They All Sang: From Tony Pastor to Rudy Vallee.* New York: Viking Press, 1934.

_____. *They All Had Glamour: From the Swedish Nightingale to the Naked Lady.* New York: J. Messner, 1944.

Mates, Julian. *The American Musical Stage Before 1800.* New Brunswick, N.J.: Rutgers University Press, 1962.

_____. "The Black Crook Myth." *Theatre Survey* 7 (May 1966):31-43.

_____. "American Musical Theatre: Beginnings to 1900." In *The American Theatre: A Sum of Its Parts,* edited by Henry B. Williams. New York: Samuel French, 1971.

Mattfeld, Julius. *Variety Music Cavalcade: Musical-Historical Review, 1620-1969.* 3d ed. New York: Prentice-Hall, 1971.

Moody, Richard. *Ned Harrigan: From Corlear's Hook to Herald Square.* Chicago: Nelson-Hall, 1980.

Morath, Max. "The Ninety-Three Years of Eubie Blake." *American Heritage* 27 (October 1976):56-65.

_____. "The Vocal and Theatrical Music of Bert Williams and His Associates." In *American Popular Entertainment,* edited by Myron Matlaw. Westport, Conn. and London: Greenwood Press, 1979.

Mordden, Ethan. *Better Foot Forward: The History of American Musical Theatre.* New York: Grossman Publishers (a division of the Viking Press), 1976.

Morehouse, Ward. *George M. Cohan: Prince of the American Theatre.* Philadelphia: J. B. Lippincott, 1943.

_____. "The Ziegfeld Follies—A Formula with Class." *Theatre Arts* 40 (May 1956):66-69, 87.

Moses, Marilyn A. "Lydia Thompson and the 'British Blondes' in the United States." Ph.D. dissertation, University of Oregon, 1978.

Murray, Ken. *The Body Merchant: The Story of Earl Carroll.* Pasadena: Ward Ritchie Press, 1976.

Nathan, George Jean. *The Popular Theatre.* 2d ed. 1923. Reprint. Rutherford, N.J.: Fairleigh Dickinson University Press, 1971.

_____. *The Entertainment of a Nation: Or, Three Sheets in the Wind.* 1942. Reprint. Rutherford, N.J.: Fairleigh Dickinson University Press, 1971.

O'Brien, P. J. *Will Rogers: Ambassador of Good Will, Prince of Wit and Wisdom.* Philadelphia: John C. Winston Co., 1935.

Olin, Reuel Keith. "A History and Interpretation of the Princess Theatre Musical Plays, 1915-1919." Ph.D. dissertation, New York University, 1979.

Parker, Derek, and Parker, Julia. *The Natural History of the Chorus Girl.* Indianapolis and New York: Bobbs-Merrill, 1975.

Richards, Sandra L. "Bert Williams: The Man and the Mask." *Mime, Mask & Marionette* 1 (Spring 1978):7-24.

Richman, Harry, with Richard Gehman. *A Hell of a Life.* New York: Duell, Sloan, and Pearce, 1966.

Rodgers, Richard. *Musical Stages: An Autobiography.* New York: Random House, 1975.

Rose, Al. *Eubie Blake.* New York: Schirmer Books (a division of Macmillan Co.), 1979.

Rowland, Mabel, ed. *Bert Williams: Son of Laughter.* 1923. Reprint. New York: Negro Universities Press, 1969.

Sampson, Henry T. *Blacks in Blackface: A Source Book on Early Black Musical Shows.* Metuchen, N.J. and London: The Scarecrow Press, 1980.

Schoettler, Eugenia. "From a Chorus Line to *A Chorus Line:* The Emergence of Dance in the American Musical Theatre." Ph.D. dissertation, Kent State University, 1979.

Schwartz, Charles. *Cole Porter, A Biography.* New York: Dial Press, 1977.

Senelick, Laurence. "George L. Fox and American Pantomime." *Nineteenth Century Theatre Research* 7 (Spring 1979):1-25. Abbreviated version in *American Popular Entertainment,* edited by Myron Matlaw. Westport, Conn. and London: Greenwood Press, 1979.

"Setting: See Moscow Burn; Witness the Great Flood." *Theatre Crafts* 10 (March-April 1976):18-23, 44-46.

Sheean, Vincent. *The Amazing Oscar Hammerstein I: The Life and Exploits of an Impresario.* New York: Simon and Schuster, 1956.

Sherman, Jan. "A Denishawn Dancer with the Ziegfeld Follies." *Dance Magazine* 48 (June 1975):32-37.

Sieben, Pearl. *Immortal Jolson: His Life and Times.* New York: Frederick Fell, 1962.

Sillman, Leonard. "Who Said the Revue is Dead?" *Theatre Arts* 46 (March 1961): 16-19, 76.

Slout, William L. "The Black Crook: First of the Super Nudies." *Players, The Magazine of American Theatre* 50 (Fall-Winter 1975):16-19.

Smith, Cecil. *Worlds of Music.* 1952. Reprint. Westport, Conn.: Greenwood Press, 1973.

_____, and Litton, Glenn. *Musical Comedy in America.* Rev. ed. New York: Theatre Arts Books, 1980.

Sobel, Bernard. "This Was Ziegfeld." *American Mercury* 60 (January 1945):96-102.

_____. *Broadway Heartbeat: Memoirs of a Press Agent.* New York: Hermitage House, 1953.

Sommer, Sally Roberson. "Loie Fuller: From the Theatre of Popular Entertainment to the Parisian Avant Garde." Ph.D. dissertation, New York University, 1979.

Spaeth, Sigmund. *A History of Popular Music in America.* New York: Random House, 1948.

Spencer, Charles. *Erté.* New York: Charles N. Potter, 1970.

Spurrier, James J. "The Integration of Music and Lyrics with the Book in the American Musical." Ph.D. dissertation, Southern Illinois University, 1979.

Stagg, Jerry. *The Brothers Shubert. A Half-Century of Show Business and the Fabulous Empire of the Brothers Shubert.* New York: Random House, 1968.

Stambler, Irwin. *Encyclopedia of Popular Music.* New York: St. Martin's Press, 1965.

Stowe, William McFerrin, Jr. "Damned Funny: The Tragedy of Bert Williams." *Journal of Popular Culture* 10 (Summer 1976):5-13.

Strang, Lewis Clinton. *Celebrated Comedians of Light Opera and Musical Comedy in America.* 1901. Reprint. New York: Benjamin Blom, 1972.

Theatre Crafts 10 (March-April 1976), Issue devoted to the revue.

Urban, Joseph. *Theatres.* New York: Theatre Arts, 1929.

Vallillo, Stephen M. "Broadway Revues in the Teens and Twenties." *The Drama Review* 25 (March 1981):25-34.
Venturi, Robert; Scott Brown, Denise; and Izenour, Steven. *Learning From Las Vegas.* Rev. ed. Cambridge, Mass.: M.I.T. Press, 1977.
Washington, Booker T. "Bert Williams." *American Magazine* 70 (May-October 1910):600-604.
Whitton, Joseph. *"The Naked Truth!" An Inside History of The Black Crook.* Philadelphia: H. W. Shaw, 1897.
Wilder, Alec. *American Popular Songs, The Great Innovators 1900-1950.* Edited with introduction by James T. Machee. New York: Oxford University Press, 1972.
Williams, Bert. "The Comic Side of Trouble." *American Magazine* 85 (January 1918):33-35, 58-61.
Wodehouse, P. G., and Bolton, Guy. *Bring on the Girls: The Improbable Story of Our Life in Musical Comedy.* New York: Simon and Schuster, 1953.
Ziegfeld, Florenz, Jr. "Picking Out Pretty Girls for the Stage." *American Magazine* 88 (December 1919):120-22, 125-26, 129.
Ziegfeld, Patricia. *The Ziegfelds' Girls.* Boston: Little, Brown and Co., 1964.

JOURNALS

Dance Research Journal. New York, 1969- .
The Passing Show. New York, 1977- .

CHAPTER II

Stage Magic

HISTORICAL SUMMARY

Despite our presumed sophistication and our technological know-how, stage magic is as popular today as ever. As an entertainment pursuit it is probably number one if all the amateur magicians in the United States were to be counted. Certainly no other performance form can boast of as many current organizations and publications. And although considered here as one of the most popular of all variety acts, stage magic has existed on many levels: as one act in a vaudeville bill, as a turn in a circus, as street entertainment, as close-up or parlor amusement, as television and Las Vegas spectaculars, and as complete stage shows. The great success of *The Magic Show* on Broadway with Doug Henning and the 1979-1980 tour of Harry Blackstone, Jr.'s recent magic show attest to magic's endurance as an entertainment. Like the circus, stage magic's enormous success, especially since mid-nineteenth century, is due in no small measure to its exportability, for like the circus, language is rarely a barrier. Although numerous magicians have succeeded partially because of their clever or mystifying patter, a good magic act need not depend on language for its ultimate effectiveness. Also like the circus, magic in the United States developed its own rich and variegated history and tradition.

Nowhere were magicians more popular than in vaudeville. According to Milbourne Christopher in his *The Illustrated History of Magic,* more than four thousand magicians played on vaudeville bills around the world between the 1890s and the 1930s. With vaudeville's constant search for novelty, magic's potential for the unusual provided a natural source for vaudeville acts. The inherent fascination of the magician's art appealed to virtually everyone. In addition, during vaudeville's heyday, despite the presentation of tricks and illusions that seemed almost miraculous, stage magic gave the patron a certain amount of reassurance in human powers in an age when the encroachment of science and technology threatened and frightened the average working-class patron.

Vaudeville may have represented the ultimate exposure for stage magicians in America, but it certainly did not mark the beginning of magic or the end of its history. More so than most entertainment forms, the history of magic is inextricably tied to the careers of its performers.

Magicians were among the first performers to appear in the American colonies. Several traveling magicians are known to have been seen during the seventeenth and early eighteenth centuries; there is evidence that a traveling magician was operating in the Boston area as early as 1687. Among the earliest named magicians were Joseph Broome, a German who appeared in New York in 1734; a Mr. Bayly who was first seen in New York in 1767; Hymen Saunders, a very active eighteenth-century magician; Signor Falconi and Peter Gardiner, both puppeteer-magicians; Isaac Levy; and other itinerant entertainers. These early magicians were forced to adapt their acts to suit whatever locale and performance space they might find, from a tavern to a legitimate theater. In order to survive, the performers had to be mobile and versatile; that is, capable of supplementing their magical acts with other talents—tight-rope or slack-rope walking, puppetry, fire-eating, pantomime, acrobatics, ventriloquism, and other acts.

The first American-born magician to establish himself as a successful conjuror was Richard Potter, the successor of John Rannie, a magician who had first appeared in the United States in 1801. Potter's debut was in 1811 in Boston, and during his time America continued to see many prominent European-born magicians, including Day Francis and Colonel Eugene Leitensdorfer. As the nineteenth century progressed, magicians were seen more and more in regular theaters, presenting full-length performances or supplying entr'acte entertainment between the acts of legitimate plays.

The names of wonder workers who appeared in America reads like the "who's who" of magic. During the first half of the nineteenth century there were Signor Antonio Blitz, Jonathan Harrington and John Wyman, Jr., who were both magicians and ventriloquists (Wyman appeared four times before Abraham Lincoln), Lionel Goldschmidt, and many others. In 1851 the great John Henry Anderson, known as "The Caledonian Conjuror" or "The Great Wizard of the North," first appeared in New York.

Other international stars followed in quick succession: Carl Herrmann, who first appeared in this country in New Orleans in 1861; his younger brother Alexander (1844-1896), who settled in the United States and became the established leading magician in this country by 1880; and his wife

Adelaide, who kept the Herrmann name alive until 1928. Alexander was one of the first magicians to exploit vaudeville's great possibilities for magic. As large theater buildings and vaudeville circuits became commonplace, a great demand for magician-illusionists became apparent. No longer could small magic suffice. Herrmann, who was a satanic-looking man and to many still the archetypical magician, evolved an act that combined sleight-of-hand and large stage illusions with a humourous style, which audiences found endearing.

Herrmann was succeeded by Harry Kellar (1849-1922), who was known as the "King of American Magic." Born in Erie, Pennsylvania, Kellar was, unlike Herrmann, a meticulous performer who created an air of mystery with his magic. Kellar's success is certainly indicative of the progress made by the American stage magician. In Philadelphia during the 1884-1885 season he performed 267 times at his own Kellar's Egyptian Hall; in 1886-1887 he gave 179 consecutive shows at the Comedy Theatre in New York.

When Kellar retired, his show was purchased by Howard Thurston (1869-1936), a native of Ohio. Thurston's intention was not to perform with Kellar's apparatus but to gain through the purchase the designation of successor to Kellar. Thurston, who began as a card manipulator, turned to elaborate stage shows and became known for his dignified, dramatic presentation of illusions. For twenty-eight years he remained the greatest illusionist on the American stage. During his period of greatness, American audiences, many at vaudeville shows, saw most of the great magicians of the time—Horace Goldin, Servais LeRoy, Talma, Carl Hertz, Arnold De Biere, Leon Bosco, Carter the Great, Nicola, The Great Raymond, and numerous lesser-known performers. Goldin represents the hallmark of vaudeville magicians. He was an especially innovative showman who began in dime museums, giving as many as twenty-five performances a day for ten dollars per week. As a headliner in vaudeville, Goldin developed a silent act and thus began a new trend in stage magic. His mottos were "Silence is Goldin" and "Blink your eyes and you miss a trick," referring to his pattern of presenting a dozen illusions in the same time it took most contemporaries to perform one. Goldin was a true trendsetter in magic, not only as a performer but as an important magical inventor, including the classic "Sawing a Lady in Half."

The best-known of all American magicians and the most popular of them all on the vaudeville stage was Ehrich Weiss, better known as Harry Houdini (1874-1926). Though born in Europe, he moved to the United States at an early age. Houdini began his career as a platform performer in a dime museum, doing card manipulations, graduated with his wife Bess to the Welsh Bros. Circus in 1895, and appeared with a medicine show in 1897. By 1900 Houdini was a headliner in vaudeville and was known principally as a man who could get out of anything—an escapologist, as he billed himself. As a vaudevillian, though best known for his escapes, he perfected an illusion called "Metamorphosis" and featured two well-known mysteries, the "Hindu Needle Trick" (he would swallow loose needles and thread and then bring the needles out of his mouth threaded) and the "Chinese Water Torture Cell" (his feet would be locked in stocks, he would then be lowered head first into a tank of water, the stocks would be padlocked to the tank, and, after covering the tank with a cabinet, he would escape).

Since the days of Thurston and Houdini, the American entertainment scene has continued to see numerous magicians: Harry Blackstone, The Great Leon, William Neff, The Great Virgil, Cardini, John Calvert, Dante, Joseph Dunninger, Protul, Okito (Theodore Bamberg), and others.

The phenomenal interest in amateur magic today in the United States was undoubtedly spurred on by the popularity of magicians on vaudeville circuits, in chautauqua and tent shows, and through major tours by the great magicians of the day. But unlike many entertainments, magic, because of its adaptability, made it possible for small shows, like those of the medicine showman, to travel to the hinterlands and bring the wonders of magic to the smallest of hamlets and rural areas. Magic dealers and writers of "how to" books began to cater largely to the growing number of amateur magicians in the United States. As a hobby, magic has been a major stepping-stone for many American performers, such as Dick Cavett and Johnny Carson.

The professional magician in America has experienced a renaissance in the last decade; today magicians are performing not only on stages but on television and as major attractions in Las Vegas. Among present-day performers of note, the following are worthy of reputations equal to the best of the past: Milbourne Christopher, Mark Wilson, Doug Henning, Sid Lorraine, Harry Blackstone, Jr., Siegfried and Roy, David Copperfield, Abb Dickson, Bev Bergeron, Karrel Fox, Frank Garcia, Jeff Sheridan (who has returned to the streets for his stage), Celeste Evans, Dorothy Dietrich, and Shelley Carroll. World conjurors are busier today than they have been since the days of vaudeville. Milbourne Christopher's conclusion to his monumental 1973 history of magic seems more apropos today than it was almost ten years ago: "There is ample evidence that the new generation of mystifiers will intrigue future audiences as their predecessors have for five thousand years past."

SURVEY OF SOURCES

Stage magic, as has been discussed in the historical survey, was a prominent feature of vaudeville and virtually every other form of variety entertainment; it also developed into a form of popular stage entertainment in its own right. The literature on magic is enormous, and interest in magic has recently burgeoned, producing reprints of standard "how to" books and an assortment of guides to the art and hobby of magic. Likewise, the fiftieth anniversary of Houdini's death in 1976 prompted publishers to exploit this event with numerous books for the popular market. Space in this guide does not allow a discussion of the hundreds of books on performing magic. If, however, the user of this guide wishes to pursue the art of magic performance, an excellent beginning place would be Harlan Tarbell's seven volume "how to" work covering virtually every aspect of the art and practice of magic entitled *The Tarbell Course in Magic.* Another suggestion would be the works of Lewis Ganson on Dai Vernon, a modern wizard known as "The Professor." Of his eight books on Vernon the most highly recommended is *The Dai Vernon Book of Magic.*

Since this guide can only indicate a few of the thousands of books on magic and since magic is one of the few entertainment forms with numerous bibliographical guides, the more useful ones should be mentioned. The most recent, compiled by the outstanding circus bibliographer Raymond Toole-Stott, is the two volume *A Bibliography of English Conjuring, 1581-1876.* Although the focus is on English conjuring, the international nature of magic makes this a useful guide to well over one thousand sources, keyed to their locations. Toole-Stott's *Circus and Allied Arts* (discussed in chapter 3) also should be consulted. A useful one-volume annotated bibliography, although not compiled by a recognized authority on magic, is Robert Gill's *Magic as a Performing Art: A Bibliography of Conjuring,* which, unlike most magic bibliographies, attempts to describe contents of sources and to assess their value. Among the other standard bibliographical reference sources, the following are recommended: Sidney W. Clarke and Adolphe Blind, *The Bibliography of Conjuring and Kindred Deceptions* (two thousand works plus a checklist of periodicals published up to 1920); Henry Ridgely Evans, *Some Rare Old Books on Conjuring and Magic of the 16th, the 17th, and the 18th Century* (on rarities of early magical literature); James B. Findlay, *Collectors Annuals* (nine in all), one of the more comprehensive bibliographies on general magic up to 1973; Trevor H. Hall, *A Bibliography of Books on Conjuring in English from 1580 to 1850* and *Old Conjuring Books: A Bibliographical and Historical Study* (both with limited but scholarly coverage); Harry Price, *Short Title Catalogue ... From Circa 1450 A.D. to 1939 A.D.* and *Supplement to Short Title Catalogue... From 1472 A.D. to the Present Day* (both keyed to the Harry Price Collection at the University of London and focused on spiritualism and psychic phenomena rather than stage magic); Jack Potter, *The Master Index to Magic in Print,* an impressive bibliography in fourteen volumes of practical conjuring/magic up to 1964 with the complete files of over seventy magic periodicals; and James B. Alfredson and George L. Daily, Jr., *A Short Title Checklist of Conjuring Periodicals in English.*

The most readable history of magic, with a superb bibliography and excellent illustrations, is Milbourne Christopher's *The Illustrated History of Magic,* considered by most magic authorities the one indispensible source on magic's annals and performers. Christopher, both a magic historian and performer, has published a number of additional recommended studies. His *Panorama of Prestidigitation: Magic Through the Ages in Pictures,* although susperseded by later works, is still a useful, brief history; the same is true of *Panorama of Magic,* although still a good history; his essay "Magic in Early Baltimore" is an informative study of Signior Falconi in 1787; and his books on Houdini are among the best available, especially *Houdini: The Untold Story* (the more recent *Houdini—A Pictorial Life* does contain some new information, although it is largely pictorial).

The best early history of magic in America, and the only scholarly, documented account, is Charles Pecor's *The Magician on the American Stage, 1752-1874,* which should be consulted by any serious student of magic in this country. In addition to Christopher, a useful survey (through the early 1900s) is Sidney W. Clarke's *The Annals of Conjuring: From the Earliest Times to the Present Day,* originally published as a serial in the *Magic Wand* (1924-1927), although English conjuring received the greatest attention. A recent index to the serialized version, and unfortunately not the one-volume edition, has recently appeared, compiled by Peter Warlock *(Index to The Annals of Conjuring by Sidney Wrangel Clarke).*

Other works with some historical attention or focus on famous conjurors that can be recommended include the following: Charles Bertram, *Isn't It Wonderful* and *A Magicican in Many Lands;* H. J. Burlingham, *Leaves From Conjurers' Scrap Books* (survey of prominent nineteenth-century magicians) and *Herrmann the Magician* (with coverage of both Carl and Alexander Herrmann); a more up-to-date biography of the Herrmanns, though more appropriate for younger readers, is I. G. Edmonds's *The Magic Brothers;* Burlingham's *Magician's Handbook* also includes useful material on the Herrmanns; Edward Claflin and Jeff Sheridan, *Street Magic. An Illustrated History of Wandering Magicians and Their Conjuring Arts,* despite its poorly reproduced illustrations, is a useful history that touches on the entire history of the street entertainer; David Devant, *Woes of a Wizard and My Magic Life* (autobiographies of a late nineteenth- and early twentieth-century magician); Edwin A. Dawes, *The Great Illusionists,* a recent study by an English scholar with frequent references to American magicians; Henry Ridgely Evans, *Magic & Its Professors, The Old and the New Magic, Adventures in Magic* (especially useful on Okito), *History of Conjuring and Magic: From the Earliest Times to the End of the Eighteenth Century*, and *Cagliostro: A Sorcerer of the Eighteenth Century;* J. B. Findlay, *Anderson and His Theatre* (on John Henry Anderson): Ottokar Fischer, *Illustrated Magic* (including a good chapter on Harry Kellar); Thomas Frost, *The Lives of the Conjurers* (the first full-length history of conjuring and still a classic); Arnold Furst, *Famous Magicians of the World* (mostly twentieth century); Walter Brown Gibson, *The Master Magicians—Their Lives and Most Famous Tricks* (one of many books by a prolific writer on magic); Herman Hanson and John U. Zweers, *The Magic Man* (life of Hanson, an early twentieth-century magician); Douglas and Kari Hunt, *The Art of Conjuring,* an introduction to the art largely told through the men who did it; Ward W. Konkle, ''Thurston Was the Best,'' a recent survey of Thurston's career told by an ardent fan; John Mulholland, *Quicken Than the Eye—The Magic & The Magicians of the World, John Mulholland's Story of Magic,* and *The Early Magic Shows,* dated histories by a major performer/historian of magic; and Bill Severn, *Magic and Magicians,* with adequate coverage of such magicians as Robert-Houdin, Herrmann, Kellar, Houdini, and Thurston.

The study of nineteenth-century English conjuring, useful as background to the annals of American conjuring, receives treatment in the following recommended sources: Olive Cook, ''Victorian Magicians'' (on the use of the magic lantern); George A. Jenness, *Maskelyne and Cooke: Egyptian Hall, 1873-1904;* Geoffrey Frederick Lamb, *Victorian Magic* (rather super-ficial treatment, as is true of his survey, *Pegasus Book of Magic and Magicians*); and Jasper Maskelyne, *White Magic: The Story of the Maske-lynes.*

Houdini, as one would expect, has received more attention than all other magicians combined. In addition to Christopher's books on Houdini, the best biographical studies are William L. Gresham's *Houdini: The Man Who Walked Through Walls,* a lively and thorough biography, and Harold Kellock's *Houdini: His Life Story,* compiled from documents and recollec-tions of Beatrice Houdini. Beryl Williams and Samuel Epstein's *The Great Houdini: Magician Extraordinary* is not a distinguished biography but pro-vides a fair sense of Houdini's personality. A number of the largely illustrated coffee-table books published to mark the fiftieth anniversary of Houdini's death are surprisingly useful and complete, especially the following: *The Original Houdini Scrapbook* compiled by Walter Gibson; Doug Henning with Charles Reynolds, *Houdini, His Legend and His Magic;* and The Amazing Randi and Bert Randolph Sugar, *Presenting Houdini: His Life and Art.* Other Houdini studies of varying degrees of usefulness and reliability include: John Cannell, *The Secrets of Houdini* (which includes a biographical sketch); Walter Brown Gibson and Morris N. Young, *Houdini on Magic* and *Houdini's Fabulous Magic;* Bernard C. Meyer, *Houdini: A Man in Chains,* a questionable psychoanalytic portrait of Houdini; and Art Ronnie, ''Houdini's High-Flying Hoax,'' on Houdini's filming of *The Grim Game* in 1919. The most recent biography of Houdini, Raymund Fitzsimons's *Death and the Magician,* deals most effectively with Houdini as a scholar of magic, and exposer of charlatans, and a tortured man in private life.

Houdini's own book, *The Unmasking of Robert-Houdin,* a controversial attack on his former idol (and the source of his professional name), and Maurice Sardina's *Where Houdini Was Wrong,* a response to Houdini and a defense of the French magician's integrity, are intriguing historical documents. In order to comprehend Houdini's fascination with Robert-Houdin one must read Robert-Houdin's memoirs. Recommended is the edition edited by Milbourne Christopher called *King of Conjurors: Memoirs of Robert-Houdin.*

Among more recent surveys of famous magicians, Hyla M. Clark's *The World's Greatest Magic* and Wendy Rydell and George Gilbert's *The Great Book of Magic* are among the most complete. Of guides to collecting magic (books, apparatus, and so forth) and the art of the magician, William Doerflinger's *Magic Catalogue: A Comprehensive Guide to the Wonderful World of Magic* is a superb resource; *Bill Severn's Guide to Magic As a Hobby* is a useful introduction as well. Charles and Regina Reynolds's *100 Years of Magic Posters* is a magnificent collection of full-color posters with informative text.

The following miscellaneous sources should not be omitted from any list of basic magic books: Henry Hay's *Cyclopedia of Magic;* Marvin Kaye's *The Stein & Day Handbook of Magic;* Professor Hoffman's *Modern Magic: A Practical Treatise on the Art of Conjuring,* one of the most influential texts on magic and considered by many the bible of the conjuror; John Northern Hilliard's *Greater Magic,* considered by many to be the greatest single work on performing magic in English; Geoffrey Lamb's *Illustrated Magic Dictionary,* the most recent dictionary of terms, apparatus, techniques, and men of magic; and Nevil Maskelyne and David Devant's *Our Magic,* a classic work and the first to treat magic as a valid dramatic art. Julian M. Olf's useful summary of the similarities between the art of the actor and the magicians ("The Actor and the Magician") offers an interesting perspective. Finally, Peter Warlock's *Magicians' Pseudonyms* provides an exhaustive list of magicians and their pseudonyms used as writers and performers.

Although few magic periodicals deal extensively with magic history, they still are major sources of information on all aspects of magic. The major and most useful current publications are *Bulletin for Friends of Magic History, Genii, Houdini's Magic Magazine, The Linking Ring* (published by the International Brotherhood of Magicians), *Magic, Unity, and Might (M.U.M.)* (published by the Society of American Magicians), *Magic Circular* (published by the International Brotherhood of Magicians in England), *Magicol, The New Tops,* and *The American Museum of Magic*

Newsletter. Of the older periodicals, now suspended, the following are suggested: *The Conjurers' Monthly Magazine* (published and edited by Houdini), *Magician Monthly* (England), *Mahatma,* and *Sphinx,* the latter edited for many years by John Mulholland and containing numerous essays on magic history.

Of the various collections and museums devoted to magic, the following are repositories of note: American Museum of Magic in Marshall, Michigan; the Egyptian Hall Museum of Magical History in Brentwood, Tennessee; Flosso Hornmann Magic Company in New York; The H. Adrian Smith Collection in North Attleboro, Massachusetts; the Messmore Kendall Collection (gathered by Houdini) in the Hoblitzelle Theatre Arts Library of the University of Texas at Austin; Houdini Magical Hall of Fame in Niagara Falls, Ontario; the International Magician's Hall of Fame in Galveston, Indiana; the Library of Congress (John J. and Hanna M. McManus Collection, Morris N. and Chesley V. Young Collection, and the Harry Houdini Collection); The Magic Castle in Hollywood; The Magic Cellar in San Francisco (Earthquake McGoon's Saloon); The Magic Circle Library in London; the Carl Waring Jones Collection in the Princeton University Library; and the Society of American Magicians Hall of Fame in Hollywood. Most major theater collections in the United States hold useful primary materials or rare magic books as well.

The major magicians' organizations are The International Brotherhood of Magicians, the Academy of Magical Arts & Sciences (a private club connected to The Magic Castle in Hollywood), The Magic Circle in London, The Magic Collectors Association, and the Society of American Magicians.

BIBLIOGRAPHY

BOOKS AND ARTICLES

Alfredson, James B., and Daily, George L., Jr. *A Short Title Checklist of Conjuring Periodicals in English.* Lansing, Mich.: Privately printed, 1976.
Bertram, Charles. *Isn't It Wonderful.* London: Swan Sonnenschein and Co., 1896.
_____. *A Magician in Many Lands.* New York: E. P. Dutton and Co., 1911.
Burlingham, H. J. *Leaves From Conjurers' Scrap Books.* Chicago: Donohue, Henneberry and Co., 1891.
_____. *Hermann the Magician.* Chicago: Laird and Lee, 1897.
_____. *Magician's Handbook.* 1897. New ed. Chicago: Wilcox and Follet, 1942.
Cannell, John Clucas. *The Secrets of Houdini.* 1931. Reprint. Detroit: Gale Research Co., 1974.
Christopher, Milbourne. "Magic in Early Baltimore." *Maryland Historical Magazine* 38 (December 1943):323-30.
_____. *Panorama of Prestidigitation: Magic Through the Ages in Pictures.* New York: By the author, 1955.
_____. *Panorama of Magic.* New York: Dover Publications, 1962.
_____. *Houdini: The Untold Story.* New York: Thomas Y. Crowell Co., 1969.

_____. *The Illustrated History of Magic*. New York: Thomas Y. Crowell Co., 1973.

_____. *Houdini—A Pictorial Life*. New York: Thomas Y. Crowell Co., 1976.

Claflin, Edward, and Sheridan, Jeff. *Street Magic. An Illustrated History of Wandering Magicians and Their Conjuring Arts*. Garden City, N.Y.: Doubleday and Co., 1977.

Clark, Hyla M. *The World's Greatest Magic*. Photographs by Paul Levin. New York: Tree Communications Edition (Crown Publishers), 1976.

Clarke, Sidney W. *The Annals of Conjuring: From the Earliest Times to the Present Day*. London: George Johnson, 1929.

_____, and Blind, Adolphe. *The Bibliography of Conjuring and Kindred Deceptions*. London: George Johnson, 1920.

Cook, Olive. "Victorian Magicians." In *The Saturday Book 27,* edited by John Hadfield. Boston and Toronto: Little, Brown and Co., 1967.

Dawes, Edwin A. *The Great Illusionists*. Seacaucus, N.J.: Chartwell, 1979.

Devant, David [David Wighton]. *Woes of a Wizard*. London: S. H. Bousfield and Co., 1903.

_____. *My Magic Life*. London: Hutchinson and Co., 1931.

Doerflinger, William. *The Magic Catalogue: A Comprehensive Guide to the Wonderful World of Magic*. New York: E. P. Dutton and Co., 1977.

Edmonds, I. G. *The Magic Brothers: Carl & Alexander Herrmann*. New York: Elsevier/Nelson Books, 1979.

Evans, Henry Ridgely. *Magic & Its Professors*. New York: George Routledge and Son, 1902.

_____. *The Old and the New Magic*. 1906. Rev. ed. London: Kegan Paul, 1909.

_____. *Adventures in Magic*. New York: Leo Rullman, 1927.

_____. *History of Conjuring and Magic: From the Earliest Times to the End of the Eighteenth Century*. Rev. ed. Kenton, Ohio: William W. Durbin, 1930.

_____. *Cagliostro: A Sorcerer of the Eighteenth Century*. New York: Masonic Bibliophiles, 1931.

_____. *Some Rare Old Books on Conjuring and Magic of the 16th, the 17th, and the 18th Century*. Kenton, Ohio: IBM, 1943.

Findlay, James B. *Collectors Annuals*. 9 vols. Isle of Wight, England: Shanklin, 1949-1975.

_____. *Anderson and His Theatre*. Isle of Wight, England: Shanklin, 1967.

Fischer, Ottokar. *Illustrated Magic: [With] An Unpublished Chapter by the Late Harry Kellar*. Translated and edited by Fulton Oursler and J. B. Mussey. New York: Macmillan Co., 1931 and 1955.

Fitzsimons, Raymund. *Death and the Magician*. New York: Atheneum, 1981.

Frost, Thomas. *The Lives of the Conjurers*. 2d ed. 1881. Reprint. Detroit: Singing Tree Press, 1970.

Furst, Arnold. *Famous Magicians of the World*. Los Angeles: Genii, 1957.

Ganson, Lewis. *The Dai Vernon Book of Magic*. 1957. Reprint. Bideford, England: Supreme Magic Co., 1971.

Gibson, Walter Brown. *The Master Magicians—Their Lives and Most Famous Tricks*. Garden City, N.Y.: Doubleday and Co., 1966.

_____. *The Original Houdini Scrapbook*. New York: Corwin Sterling Publishing Co., 1976.

_____, and Young, Morris N. *Houdini on Magic*. New York: Dover Publications, 1953.

_____. *Houdini's Fabulous Magic*. New York: Bell Publishing Co., 1961.

Gill, Robert. *Magic as a Performing Art: A Bibliography of Conjuring*. London and New York: Bowker, 1976.

Gresham, William L. *Houdini: The Man Who Walked Through Walls*. New York: Henry Holt and Co., 1949.

Hall, Trevor H. *A Bibliography of Books on Conjuring in English From 1580 to 1850*. Minneapolis: Carl Waring Jones, 1957.

_____. *Old Conjuring Books: A Bibliographical and Historical Study*. New York: St. Martin's Press, 1973.

Hanson, Herman, and Zweers, John U. *The Magic Man*. Cincinnati: Haines House of Cards, 1974.

Hay, Henry. *Cyclopedia of Magic*. 1949. Reprint. New York: Dover Publications, 1973.

Henning, Doug, with Charles Reynolds. *Houdini, His Legend and His Magic*. New York: Times Books (a division of Quandrangle-New York Times Book Co.), 1977.

Hilliard, John Northern. *Greater Magic*. London: Carl Waring Jones, 1938.

Hoffman, Professor [Angelo John Lewis]. *Modern Magic: A Practical Treatise on the Art of Conjuring*. London: Routledge, 1876.

Houdini, Harry. *The Unmasking of Robert-Houdin*. New York: Publishers Printing Co., 1908.

Hunt, Douglas, and Hunt, Kari. *The Art of Conjuring*. Folkestone, England: Bailey Bros. and Swinfer Ltd., 1975.

Jenness, George A. *Maskelyne and Cooke: Egyptian Hall, 1873-1904*. London: By the author, 1967.

Kaye, Marvin. *The Stein & Day Handbook of Magic*. Edited by John Salisse. New York: Stein and Day, 1973.

Kellock, Harold. *Houdini: His Life Story*. London: Heinemann, 1928.

Konkle, Ward W. "Thurston Was the Best." *Yankee* 45 (February 1981):87-91, 122, 124.

Lamb, Geoffrey Frederick. *Pegasus Book of Magic and Magicians*. London: Dobson, 1968.

_____. *Victorian Magic*. London, Henley, and Boston: Routledge and Kegan Paul, 1976.

_____. *Illustrated Magic Dictionary*. New York: Elsevier/Nelson Books, 1979.

Maskelyne, Jasper. *White Magic: The Story of the Maskelynes*. London: Stanley Paul, 1936.

Maskelyne, Nevil, and Devant, David [David Wighton]. *Our Magic*. 2d ed. Berkeley Heights, N.J.: Fleming Book Co., 1946. Reissue. Bideford, England: Supreme, 1971.

Meyer, Bernard C. *Houdini: A Man in Chains. A Psychoanalytic Portrait*. New York: E. P. Dutton and Co., 1976.

Mulholland, John. *Quicker Than the Eye—The Magic & The Magicians of the World*. Indianapolis: Bobbs-Merrill Co., 1932.

———. *John Mulholland's Story of Magic*. New York: Loring and Mussey, 1935.

———. *The Early Magic Show*. New York: By the author, 1945.

Olf, Julian M. "The Actor and the Magician." *The Drama Review* 18 (March 1974):53-58.

Pecor, Charles. *The Magician on the American Stage, 1752-1874*. Washington, D.C.: Emerson and West, 1977.

Potter, Jack. *The Master Index to Magic in Print*. 14 vols. Calgary, Alberta, Canada: Micky Hades, 1967-75.

Price, Harry. *Short Title Catalogue . . . From Circa 1450 A.D. to 1939 A.D*. London: National Laboratory of Psychical Research, 1929.

———. *Supplement to Short Title Catalogue . . . From 1472 A.D. to the Present Day*. London: University of London Council for Psychical Research, 1935.

Randi, The Amazing, and Sugar, Bert Randolph. *Presenting Houdini: His Life and Art*. New York: Grosset and Dunlap, 1976.

Reynolds, Charles, and Reynolds, Regina. *100 Years of Magic Posters*. New York: Grosset and Dunlap, 1976.

Robert-Houdin, Jean Eugene. *Memoirs of Robert-Houdin*. 1859. Translation by Lascelles Wraxall, with introduction by Milbourne Christopher. *King of Conjurors: Memoirs of Robert-Houdin*. New York: Dover Publications, 1964.

Ronnie, Art. "Houdini's High-Flying Hoax." *American Heritage* 23 (April 1972):106-9.

Rydell, Wendy, and Gilbert, George. *The Great Book of Magic*. New York: Harry N. Abrams, 1976.

Sardina, Maurice. *Where Houdini Was Wrong*. Edited and translated by Victor Farelli. London: Magic Wand, 1950.

Severn, Bill. *Magic and Magicians*. New York: David McKay Co., 1958.

———. *Bill Severn's Guide to Magic As a Hobby*. New York: David McKay Co., 1979.

Tarbell, Harlan. *The Tarbell Course in Magic*. 7 vols. New York: Louis Tannen, 1941-1972.

Toole-Stott, Raymond. *Circus and Allied Arts, A World Bibliography*. 4 vols. Derby, England: Harpur, 1958-1971.

———. *A Bibliography of English Conjuring, 1581-1876*. 2 vols. Derby, England: Harpur and Sons, 1976-1978.

Warlock, Peter. *Index to the Annals of Conjuring by Sidney Wrangel Clarke*. Wallington, Surrey, England: By the author, 1979.

———. *Magicians' Pseudonyms*. Wallington, Surrey, England: By the compiler, 1980.

Williams, Beryl, and Epstein, Samuel. *The Great Houdini: Magician Extraordinary*. New York: Julian Messner, 1954.

SELECT PERIODICALS AND SERIALS

The American Museum of Magic Newsletter. Marshall, Michigan, 1977- .

Bulletin for Friends of Magic History. Toledo, Ohio.

The Conjurers, Monthly Magazine. New York, 1906-1908.

Genii. Los Angeles, Calif., 1936- .
Houdini's Magic Magazine. Englewood Cliffs, N.J., 1977-
The Linking Ring. Palatine, Illinois, 1922- .
Magic, Unity, and Might (M.U.M.) Lynn, Mass., 1911- .
Magic Circular. London, 1906- .
Magician Monthly. London, 1904-1939.
Magicol. Chicago, Illinois, 1950- .
Mahatma. New York, 1895-1906.
The New Tops. Colon, Michigan.
Sphinx. Chicago (later New York), 1902-1953.

CHAPTER 12

Variety on Floating Palaces and in Traveling Tent Theaters

HISTORICAL SUMMARY

A guide to variety entertainment would not be complete without a brief look at two major and uniquely American traditions, the showboat and the tent theater. Both featured all kinds of amusement from minstrel shows to popular drama, and from medicine shows to musical comedy. Since limitation of space excludes all but essential mention of popular drama in this guide, it is important to underscore here that the presentation of popular drama in tents, on showboats, in "opera houses," and other small-town entertainment centers was an essential ingredient of American grassroot theatrical circuits. For the sake of brevity, however, major focus on popular drama must be omitted from this present volume.

The development of the showboat is inextricably associated with frontier expansion. Just as flour, textiles, lantern oil, and other goods, inaccessible by land, were delivered to settlers by means of the river, so eventually was entertainment. As a result of bad roads and poor facilities, adventurous performers had to find not only a way of transporting themselves to amusement-starved pioneers but also had to seek out a place to present their shows. The showboat, or floating theater, a natural amalgam of boat and stage, was a predictable solution. Whatever the patrons craved the showboat supplied, revamping both the vehicle and the entertainment to adjust to the demands. With the development of overland travel, providing adequate access to rural areas, the showboat declined in popularity.

William Chapman and his family pioneered the first "floating theater" in 1831, at a time when the Ohio-Mississippi river basin had begun to attract millions of inhabitants, pioneers in need of entertainment to provide release from the rigors of their arduous existences. Chapman's vessel, originating out of Pittsburgh on the Ohio River, was a simple flatboat with a primitive rectangular theater perched on top. Chapman, an Englishman trained in the legitimate theater, emphasized reputable drama in this early showboat but offered variety entertainment as well. Because it was a family operation, the unsavory reputation of existing river entertainment was avoided, and the geniality of the showboat was established at hundreds of landings, where people had never seen live entertainment. The Chapmans began their annual tour in Pittsburgh, drifted down the Ohio and lower Mississippi rivers (with occasional side-trips up the Arkansas and White rivers) to New Orleans. There the boat would be sold for firewood and the family would return to Pittsburgh to build a new one. In 1836 the prosperity of the Chapmans facilitated the purchase of a small steamboat, fitted with a stage and less primitive accoutrements. Now they could make the return trip upstream and add heretofore inaccessible territory to their itinerary. In 1841 William Chapman, Sr. died in Cincinnati, where he was planning an even larger steamboat theater. The boat was completed in 1842 and operated by his wife as "Chapman's Floating Palace." Mrs. Chapman sold out in 1847, ending the brief history of America's first showboat pioneers.

The Chapmans established a trend of river entertainment that was imitated by many, though few followed the Chapman's emphasis on legitimate drama. During the 1840s and 1850s makeshift shows swarmed the rivers of the Middle West, most frequently offering some form of variety entertainment; there were boats featuring every amusement fad of the day: medicine boats, menagerie boats, museum boats, and even revival boats. Larger operations, such as that of G. R. Spalding, a major name in the history of the early American circus, helped to counter the unsavory reputation of the more primitive showboats. Spalding's "Floating Circus Palace" traveling the Ohio and Mississippi rivers and stopping at larger centers of population until 1862, measured 200 by 35 feet and consisted not only of an arena, but also of a museum off the main theater and an elegant concert saloon on the assisting towboat.

After the Civil War previously objectionable elements (such as saloon atmosphere and shady operations), which had menaced river entertainment were lessened. During the Reconstruction years, new major showboats began to appear, beginning in 1878 with A. B. French's "New Sensation," a small flatboat vehicle that emphasized family entertainment. After building a second larger and more elaborate boat in 1886, Captain French and his wife Callie took their wholesome entertainment to the outskirts of civilization. Their profits brought them three more boats over the next fifteen years and established the trend toward floating palaces. Their last showboat, measuring 140 by 42 feet, could accommodate almost one thousand patrons in comfortable seats and surrounded by ornate fixtures, including incandescent electric lights. French's operation and that of his major rival, E. A. Price, clearly indicate the trends in showboat entertainment at the turn of the century. As land-based entertainment facilities increased and improved, the showboat attempted to compete under this increasing pressure.

Captain Price bought French's fifth "New Sensation" in 1907 and another elaborate showboat called the "New Grand Floating Palace," which he renamed the "Greater New York." For the next ten years Price presented traditional variety shows on the "New Sensation" and a combination of musical comedy and legitimate drama on the "Greater New York." Serious melodrama proved to be extremely popular, and Price's reversion to legitimate drama, spawned by the precedent established by the "Eisenbarth-Henderson Floating Theater," indicated that the showboat could compete, at least for a short period, as a popular theater, thus compensating for the flagging interest in variety entertainment.

The rise of the floating palaces during the first fifteen years of this century also marked the slow decline of this distinctive institution. The first decade of the twentieth century witnessed marked changes in land entertainment. The advent of the automobile, better roads, and an increase in railroad connections made previously isolated regions more accessible. Road shows and movie houses attracted a broad spectrum of spectators. Only the most remote of rural areas were without some form of entertainment, and as we will see shortly, enterprising land-locked showmen soon found a solution to this problem as well. The showboat, with its limited facilities and second-rate performers, could no longer compete on an equal footing with land-based forces. Even the once noble melodramas appeared comic and stuffy to patrons who could see films of high living and easy morals. By 1925 audiences nurtured on picture shows found it impossible to embrace the conventions of showboat productions and variety entertainment.

After 1925 the showboat entered a period of rapid decline because it was unable to meet the needs of a worldly and mobile society, as Bruce Pettit illustrated in his 1945 essay. Only a few showboats were able to survive the depression, and then only by burlesquing their own programs. Billy Bryant, for example, extended his career through World War II with productions such as *Hamlet and Yeggs*. The most magnificent of all the showboats, "The Goldenrod," tied up at St. Louis in 1943 and for years offered burlesqued melodramas.

For several decades, then, a large section of America would have been deprived of live performance had it not been for the showboat, and, although the typical showboat fare consisted of a popular melodrama or a light and innocent comedy, variety entertainment was almost always presented as well, if not as the main attraction, then as the conclusion to the evening's entertainment, known as the "olio," in which members of the dramatic company performed their variety specialities.

The escapist yet thoroughly moral diversion offered by the showboat to hard-working middle-Americans—farm hands, small-town merchants, and others—was the key to the success of the more prominent river entrepreneurs. So it was with entertainment in all rural areas of America well into the twentieth century.

As has been noted, the increase of railroad mileage after the Civil War opened up previously inaccessible areas to showmen, who no longer were limited to river transportation. During the last thirty years of the century, small mid-American towns became important and profitable stops for touring theater and variety companies. Nearly every village and hamlet began to construct a local "opera house" to accommodate traveling entertainments, creating a vast theatrical network known as "the road." If an "opera house" or "academy of music" was unavailable, traveling shows turned to existing courthouses, schools, town halls, churches, or other large halls.

Like the showboat, companies playing to these average American audiences offered both legitimate drama and variety specialties. The most enduring form of theater that appealed to the common people and reflected their desires, needs, and tastes was the melodrama, just as it was on the showboat. The melodrama dominated the popular stage during its 1850 to 1920 heyday. Although much of this popular fare—called 10-20-30 melodrama after its admission prices—was poorly written, its formula was such that it could accommodate any setting, time, or character, and the simplistic dramatis personae were immediately identifiable to the audience. To a public that found its traditional values exalted, melodrama was more real than reality. Although melodrama rarely dealt with social issues or problems, several of the more prominent examples were significant exceptions: *Uncle Tom's Cabin,* ostensibly against slavery but popular because of its emotionally moving, melodramatic scenes and its spectacle, gave rise to dozens of touring companies called *Tommers* or *Tom shows* that toured the nation well into the twentieth century; *Ten Nights in a Barroom* and *The Drunkard,* temperance plays, created patronage for the theater from people who had condemned playgoing as immoral.

The thirst for a nostalgic look at the American past and a reminder of simpler, nobler times, as well as the need for the reinforcement of older values that were rapidly changing, gave melodrama writers fertile ground for creation. The themes ranged from Denman Thompson's 1876 study of rural America, *The Old Homestead,* to William F. Cody's mythic creations of genuine western heroes in both drama and Wild West shows, to Civil

War dramas that ignored the broad issues and the causes of the suffering and the divisiveness in the 1880s.

In time small towns were invaded by too many touring companies, each doing much the same thing. During the season of 1900, 340 theatrical companies were touring; by 1920 the number had dwindled to less than fifty. As the new century began, a trend developed toward outdoor entertainment; tent show repertoire became very much a part of the movement, although its beginnings date from the last half of the nineteenth century. Like the showboat, tent shows brought entertainment, primarily during the summer months, to thousands of small rural towns in all parts of the country. The development of what became known as tent "repertoire," as opposed to its big city cousin's "repertory," was related to many popular entertainment forms of the earlier part of the century, including the circus, vaudeville, touring musical and theatrical companies, and the chautauqua. The adoption of the tent theater was a predictable solution to otherwise insurmountable problems, much as the flatboat had been a solution for river showmen. As repertoire companies found themselves squeezed out of many opera houses and permanent theaters, in part because of the control of established houses by theatrical trusts and the closing or conversion of others due to the new motion picture craze, managers looked toward more remote areas where one-night stand companies never appeared, and where, as William Lawrence Slout points out in *Theatre in a Tent,* audiences could not compare entertainment values, and obscurity was a protection against tightened copyright enforcement. The solution for many was the canvas pavilion used by the circus, medicine shows, and other forms of variety entertainment.

Ironically, the movement was encouraged by cultural and religious organizations, first the Millerites in 1842 and the most popular of the movements, the chautauqua. Chautauqua was a movement in the United States that began in New York State during the summer of 1874 as a tent meeting on the shores of Lake Chautauqua. In a short time, there were chautauqua tents all over the country, traveling established circuits, usually in the summer months. Within a short time show business crept into the brown tents of chautauqua (brown canvas was used to distinguish their tent from the white top of the circus and thus became a symbol of its cultural inspiration), and a good chautauqua act, because of the extensive circuits (by 1912 there were over 1,000 independent chautauquas), could sustain itself for several years. A typical chautauqua program would combine elements of vaudeville and dramatic sketches (plus the usual lectures and other "cultural" attractions). The acceptance of chautauqua was transferred, in part, to the more commercial tent repertoire operations, especially during the first quarter of the twentieth century when both prospered. Between 1900 and 1910 there were well over one hundred repertoire companies under canvas. Slout estimates that by the mid-1920s there were at least 400 tent shows traveling primarily by truck, trailer, or touring car. By the summer of 1921, faced with a recession, the golden years of tent repertoire ended; its final decline dates from the years immediately following the depression.

Like the permanent opera house, tent theaters offered a wide assortment of entertainments other than legitimate drama: musical extravaganzas, minstrel shows, concerts, comic operas, vaudeville, and other enter- tainments. Even more so than the small-town opera house operation, the tent show was designed to appeal to rural audiences. During the peak years, a tent repertoire company's bill advertised a combination of plays and vaudeville. The performer in a tent rep company invariably was required to "double in brass," that is, not only act but also play a musical instrument or present a specialty or variety act. Hundreds of companies operated in their own limited territories, especially in the South and Southwest, during the summer months, playing in tents especially designed with a stage at one end of the tent (originally companies performed in circus tents with center poles obstructing the patron's view of the stage). Some of the more suc- cessful companies performed in permanent opera houses during the winter months. Year after year the same company would return to the same towns, usually staying no longer than a week in each locale and each evening offer- ing a different program consisting of three or four melodramas or comedies with vaudeville between the acts. Some tent rep companies offered, for ad- ditional money, a "concert," which in rep terms meant either several vaudeville acts or a one-act farce given after the main performance.

Although variety acts remained a major staple of tent rep throughout its history, the major contribution of the tent tradition was the emergence of one of the last of the native stock characters in American theater. From the earliest days of the American theater, a popular fare dominated much of the best of native productions, and much of its popularity was possible because of identifiable native characters, beginning with the stage Yankee, Jonathan, in Royall Tyler's *The Contrast* (1787). As more common people found their way into theaters, the popularization of drama became a necessity. Native actors gained prominence in plays with native themes and types: for example, James Hackett as the Yankee with his common sense and rustic manners; Joseph Jefferson III, as Rip Van Winkle, providing the audience a momentary escape into a world of fantasy and freedom; Frank Mayo as the idealized American hero, Davy Crockett; Frank Chanfrau as the Irish volunteer fireman from the Bowery, "Mose the Fire Bhoy." By the late nineteenth century, some versions of all the most popular plays began to reach small-town America. The earlier stock resident company gave way to "combination" traveling companies, bringing more elaborate productions of the most popular of these plays. For the more rural areas, many of these plays with native characters did not reflect their agrarian society; consequently a new group of identifiable characters evolved that would more successfully capture rural local color and could cater to rural tastes and belief in virtue, mother, home, and heaven, coupled with a suspicion of change and urban immorality. Emerging as the dominant character was Toby, followed closely by his female counterpart, Sis Hopkins or Susie, and complemented by a full range of stock characters from the gossip and fallen woman to the local pastor and the shrewd town eccentric.

Toby, a redheaded, freckle-faced, rustic country boy, became a nightly fixture and feature attraction with many tent rep companies. Although the role was tailored for the rural audience, he was clearly a descendant of the traditional line of theatrical rustics dating back to Shakespeare and even earlier; in the tent show tradition, however, he was as American as Iowa corn, inspired most directly from the Tobe Haxton part in the 1911 tent-repertoire play, *Clouds and Sunshine* (which, in turn, was based on *Out of the Fold* by Langdon McCormick featuring the part of Toby Tompkins,) When he finally emerged in about 1915 as a stock-in-trade of most tent companies, Toby was invariably portrayed as a country boy, dressed in rural attire, and at various times, brash, sly, shrewd, natively bright, stupid, industrious, and lazy. The enthusiastic acceptance of the character is most clearly reflected in the actors who specialized in the role, so much so that scores of Toby comedians became known to their followers only as Toby, both on and off stage. Also distinctive was the flexibility of the part. An actor playing the part could take on the manners of the region in which he was appearing without missing a beat and could improvise his way into almost any play or style, depending on the audience's wishes.

As tent rep companies began to lose all momentum in the 1930s and attempted to alter their offerings to attract more patrons, they at the same time diminished in quality. Tent show fare began to lose its relevancy for rural audiences, and Toby became so exaggerated as to lose identity with them. Thus a final chapter in American native drama and popular theater fell into an irreversible decline. While it lasted, however, tent rep was energetic, vital, immensely entertaining, and successful and truly belonged to the people. Indeed, the combined yearly attendance at tent shows during its heyday exceeded that of the New York stage, despite the frequently makeshift, shabby quality of the performances. In 1927, for example, a total of some 18 million people attended performances given by some 400 shows operating under canvas.

Like virtually every form of amusement examined in this guide, the tent show was ultimately taken over by films that could be brought into America's heartland inexpensively and with a minimum of effort.

SURVEY OF SOURCES

This bibliographic section will focus on tent shows and showboats, although a few selected basic sources on popular theater have been discussed as well in order to provide a more complete overview. Popular theater and drama, not a central emphasis of this guide, encompasses the largest body of sources of any form of stage entertainment, primarily because of its scripted nature and its overlap with mainstream theater forms. Virtually all American theater histories deal with various aspects of popular theater, such as nineteenth-century melodrama, Tom shows, Toby and Susie shows, equestrian drama, tent theater and touring troupes, mining camp theater, and other topics that use mainstream theater structures and techniques. In order to restrict the present guide, sources on popular drama have been excluded, other than material on Tom shows and Toby shows. Only select sources in the general area of popular theater are indicated, concentrating on theater presented outside of the major theater centers.

The wealth of material on popular theater has been more accessible in the last decade or so as a result of several useful, detailed bibliographies and indexes. The following are especially recommended as important supplements to this limited assessment: Carl F.W. Larson, *American Regional Theatre History to 1900,* a listing of 1,481 sources; Ronald Lee Moyer, *American Actors, 1861-1910,* 363 annotated sources; Stephen M. Archer, *Actors and Actresses,* a guide to over 3,000 sources on American performers; J. P. Wearing, *American and British Theatrical Biography: A Directory;* Jeb H. Perry, *Variety Obits,* an index to obituaries in *Variety* from 1905 through 1978; Walter J. Meserve, *American Drama to 1900,* a useful guide to sources on playwrights; Richard Stoddard, *Stage Scenery, Machinery, and Lighting* and *Theatre and Cinema Architecture,* two valuable guides to the physical theater in America; and Don B. Wilmeth, *The American Stage to World War I,* a guide to almost 1,500 sources, and *American and English Popular Entertainment,* an annotated listing of almost 2,500 sources. Though not as current or reliable, two older bibliographies are still useful: Clarence Gohdes's *Literature and Theater of the States and Regions of the U.S.A.* (1967) and Carl J. Stratman's *Bibliography of the American Theatre, Excluding New York City* (1965). Wilmeth's *American Stage* includes annotated listings of other useful bibliographies, as well as major histories of the American stage not mentioned in this guide.

An excellent overview of popular theater is included in Robert C. Toll's *On with the Show,* along with a good selective bibliography. Toll, though offering nothing new, is especially effective in his analysis of native themes and characters dealt with in American drama. Arthur H. Quinn's *A History of the American Drama from the Beginning to the Present Day,* though dated, remains a standard survey of specific plays and playwrights. Walter Mcserve's projected multivolume history of American drama should supersede Quinn when completed (the first volume, *An Emerging Entertainment,* covers the early period to 1828). Though a disappointing historical survey, Garff B. Wilson's *Three Hundred Years of American Drama and Theatre* is the only history of the American stage currently in print. Essays on specific performers of the popular theater can be found in William C. Young's *Famous Actors and Actresses on the American Stage,* an uneven but nonetheless useful collection by or about 225 performers. Sources on popular theater in New York City and other basic sources relevant to this section are discussed in chapter 1.

For drama, the most important developments in the late-nineteenth century took place in small-town America, where versions of most of the popular plays of the day were presented. Basic formulas evolved that virtually guaranteed success. Specific sources on these genres can be found in the bibliographies listed above. A few major sources on identifiable, native American characters that figure prominently in the evolution of popular theatre are: Francis Hodge, *Yankee Theatre,* the definitive history and analysis of this stage character; Willis Turner, "City Low-Life on the American Stage to 1900": Richard Dorson, "Mose the Far-Famed and World Renowned," an excellent essay on Mose the Fire Bhoy, as is the recent essay "F. S. Chanfrau's Mose: The Rise and Fall of an Urban Folk-Hero" by David L. Rinear; Duane J. Fike, "Frank Mayo: Actor, Playwright, and Manager," on the Davy Crockett specialist; Arthur E. Waterman, "Joseph Jefferson as Rip Van Winkle"; and Richard Moody's recent biography of Edward Harrigan discussed in chapter 10. Consult the bibliographies by Wilmeth and Meserve for additional sources.

Uncle Tom's Cabin, one of the world's most successful plays (in its many versions), has received considerable attention. Of the numerous sources available, the following should be noted: Harry Birdoff, *The World's Greatest Hit—Uncle Tom's Cabin,* the only full-length study of "Tommers" and derivatives from the original novel; Elizabeth F. Corbett, "A Foot Note to 'THE DRAMA' " and "Uncle Tom is Dead," assessments of the play's history; J. Frank David, "Tom Shows," on the structure and content of Tom shows; J. C. Furnas, *Goodbye to Uncle Tom,* a Canadian's analysis; Ralph Lund, "Trouping with Uncle Tom," on touring companies of the play; Cordelia Howard MacDonald, "Memoirs of the Original Little Eva"; John H. McDowell, "Original Scenery and Documents for Productions of *Uncle Tom's Cabin*" and "Scenery and Staging of *Uncle Tom's Cabin*"; Richard Moody, "Uncle Tom, The Theater and Mrs. Stowe" and, with A. M. Drummond, "The Hit of the Century: *Uncle Tom's Cabin*"; I. Blaine Quarnstorm, "Early Twentieth-Century Staging of *Uncle Tom's Cabin*"; Frank Rahill (author of numerous articles and books on melodrama), "America's Number One Hit"; and Wesley Winans Stout, "Little Eva is Seventy-Five." Sources discussed in chapter 7 under the minstrel show should be consulted also.

The story of the "trouper" and the evolution of traveling companies, culminating in repertoire tent shows, is effectively and comprehensively told in William L. Slout's *Theatre in a Tent,* also an excellent source on operational practices of the tent show, as is his essay, "Tent Rep: Broadway's

Poor Relation.'' An excellent introduction to the entertainment business in small-town America, although not well documented, is Harlowe Hoyt's *Town Hall Tonight.* Philip Lewis's *Trouping: How the Show Came to Town* is a pleasant but not too reliable history of the same subject. A more scholarly analysis of touring systems, specifically in California from 1849 to 1859, is Douglas McDermott's fine essay, ''Touring Patterns on California's Theatrical Frontier, 1849-1859.'' Also recommended is his essay, ''The Development of Theatre on the American Frontier, 1750-1890,'' an excellent framework for the study of frontier theater.

Much of the atmosphere and climate for popular theater and variety is reflected in early western theater and amusements in the mining frontiers of Arizona, Oregon, California, and Nevada, in particular. This aspect is well covered in the following studies: Allen J. Adams, ''Mining Theatre History''; Luke Cosgrave, *Theater Tonight*; Ronald L. Davis, ''They Played for Gold: Theater on the Mining Frontier'' and ''Sopranos and Six Guns: The Frontier Opera House as a Cultural Symbol''; Jefferson De Angelis and Alvin F. Harlow, *Vagabond Trouper;* Edmond McAdoo Gagey, *The San Francisco Stage;* William Ransome Hogan, ''The Theatre in the Republic of Texas''; George R. MacMinn, *The Theater of the Golden Era in California;* William N. Monson, ''Frontier Theatre Town'' (Visalia, California); Constance Rourke, *Troupers of the Gold Coast, or the Rise of Lotta Crabtree;* Pat M. Ryan, ''Tombstone Theatre Tonight''; George R. Stewart, Jr., ''The Drama in a Frontier Theater'' (Nevada City); Margaret Watson, *Silver Theatre, Amusements of the Mining Frontier in Early Nevada, 1850-1864;* and Clair Eugene Willson, *Mimes and Miners: A Historical Study of the Theater in Tombstone.* Extensive sources on the small-town opera house can be found in the bibliographies listed at the beginning of this section.

The American showboat, which included not only floating theaters but circus and medicine showboats, has been most fully explored by Philip Graham in *Showboats,* which includes an excellent bibliography. George Ford's *These Were Actors* is an enjoyable, if somewhat fanciful, account of the Chapmans, one of the earliest showboat families, and should be consulted, but with caution. Other sources on the showboat, which supplement Graham, include: William J. Aylward, ''Steamboating Through Dixie,'' on early floating theaters; Hamilton Basso, ''Cotton Blossom, the South from a Mississippi Showboat,'' useful for atmosphere; Harold E. Briggs, ''Floating Circuses,'' on showboats at Cairo, Illinois; Billy Bryant, *Children of Ol' Man River: The Life and Times of a Show-Boat Trouper;* Ben Lucian Burman, *Big River to Cross,* good on showboat operations in the 1930s; Thoda Cocroft, ''The Floating Theatre Thrives,'' principally on Captain Menke's ''Golden Rod''; Kyle Crichton, '' 'Showboat' 'Round the Bend','' a study of Captain Reynold's ''Majestic''; Frank Donovan, *Riverboats of America,* a thorough history of riverboats, including showboats; Jan and Cora Gordon, "Two English Tourists on a Showboat"; Graham's "Showboats in the South," a useful complement to his book; John Marvin Hunter, "Mollie Bailey, Great Showwoman," on showboat performers on the Mississippi around 1866; "Doctor" Judd, "The Water Days of the Drama," on Butler's showboat in the 1830s; Rose B. Knox, *Footlights Afloat,* a fictional story based on French's "New Sensation": Miles Kreuger, *Show Boat,* a history of the Kern-Hammerstein II musical with a fair summary of showboat history; West Lathrop, *River Circus,* A fictional account of a showboat; Pete Martin, "River Singer," the story of the Hughes's "Floating Enterprise," a minor showboat on the Ohio; W. Frank M'Clure, "A Floating Theatre," a brief discussion of a showboat at the turn of the century; Paul Bruce Pettit, "The Showboat Theatre," a useful summary and analysis covering the period 1817 to 1937; Willard Price, *The Amazing Mississippi,* including a review of showboats in the early 1960s; Duane Eldon Reed, "A History of Showboats on the Western Rivers"; Joseph S. Schick, "Early Showboat and Circus in the Upper Valley," most useful on the Spalding and Rogers floating circus; Sidney Snook, "The Showboat Drifts Downstream," a summary survey; Raymond S. Spears, "The Mississippi Boat Theatres" (as of 1909); and Hopper Striker, "Cruising Theatres of Long Age," a review of the floating theaters of the mid-1800s.

In addition to the work of William Slout, the major sources on tent theater include Jere C. Mickel's *Footlights on the Prairie,* a full history of tent show groups that traveled Midwestern small towns from the mid-1850s to World War II, and Marian McKennon's *Tent Show,* based on fact but written in a fictional form. Other sources on tent shows include the following: Clifford Ashby, "Trouping Through Texas: Harley Sadler and His Own Show"; Charles Harris Bell, III, "An Ohio Repertoire-Tent Show Family: The Kinsey Komedy Kompany and the Madge Kinsey Players, 1881-1951"; Herbert Walter Channell and Velma E. Lowry, *Fifty Years Under Canvas;* Harry L. Dixson, "Doff Your Hat to the Tent Shows"; Frank Emmett, "Trouping Under Canvas"; "End of an Era"; Vance Johnson, "Hits in the Tall Corn" (On the Schaffner Players, the Madge Kinsey Players, and the Harley Sadler Co.); Robert Dean Klussen, "The Tent-Repertoire Theatre: A Rural American Institution" (a useful scholarly study); Maurice L. Kusell and M. S. Merritt, *Marquee Ballyhoo* (fictional account); Carlton Miles, "Doubling in Brass" (status in 1926); Zelda F. Popkin, "The Tent Show Turns to Sex"; Caroline Schaffner, "Trouping with the Schaffners"; W. L. Wilson, "The Tented Theatre"; and L. B. Yates, "Hittin' The Grit."

The chautauqua movement has been chronicled most completely in Theodore Morrison's *Chautauqua,* which examines in detail its role in American society. Other major sources include Charles F. Horner's *Strike*

The Tents, Marian Scott's *Chautauqua Caravan,* Harry P. Harrison's *Culture Under Canvas* (a recounting of the traveling tent shows by the manager of the Redpath Chautauqua), Victoria Case and Robert Ormond's *We Called It Culture: The Story of Chautauqua,* R. Alan Hedges's "Actors Under Canvas: A Study of the Theatre of the Circuit Chautauqua, 1910-1933," David Mead's "1914: The Chautaqua and American Innocence," and James S. Smoot's "Platform Theater. Theatrical Elements of the Lyceum—Chautauqua." Other suggested sources on chautauqua include the following: Allen D. Albert, "Tents of the Conservative"; Bruce Bliven, "Mother, Home, and Heaven" and "Nearest the Hearts of Ten Millions"; Albert Britt, *Turn of the Century;* Marian Johnson Castle, "Chautauqua; the Intellectual Circus"; James W. Conlin, "The Merom Bluff Chautauqua"; Karl W. Detzer, "Broadway, R.F.D.: The Rejuvenated Chautauqua is Bigger and Better Than Ever"; Alma and Paul Ellerbe, "The Most American Thing in America"; Joseph E. Gould, *The Chautauqua Movement;* Fred High, "The Circus and the Chautaqua" and "Chautauqua's Growth"; Randall R. Howard, "Chautauqua Invades the West"; "An Inveterate Chautauqua Fan" (a defense of its conservatism); Alfreda L. Irwin, *The Chautauqua Story;* Gay MacLaren, *Morally We Roll Along* (which includes a useful chapter on "Talent"); Melvin H. Miller, "The Chautauqua in Lansing" (Michigan); Hugh Anderson Orchard, *Fifty Years of Chautauqua* (on two pioneers, Keith Vawter and M. Roy Ellison); Frances Perry-Cowen, *Chautauqua to Opera;* Lucien Price, "Orpheus in Zion: An Idyl of Chautauqua"; Henry F. Pringle, "Chautauqua in the Jazz Age"; Rebecca Richmond, *Chautauqua, An American Place* (with little on entertainment); Arthur William Row, "Acting in Tents in Chautauqua"; L. Verne Slout, "The Chautauqua Drama"; Truman H. Talley, "The Chautauqua, an American Achievement"; Harrison J. Thornton, "Chautauqua and the Midwest"; Roy Becker Tozier, "A Short Life-History of the Chautauqua"; Frederick Warde, *Fifty Years of Make Believe;* Edward Weeks, "Chautauqua, the First 100 Years"; L. Jeanette Wells, *A History of the Music Festival at the Chautauqua Institution, 1874-1957;* Edna Erle Wilson, "Canvas and Culture: When Chautauqua Comes to Town"; Evert M. Winks (as told to Robin W. Winks), "Recollections of a Dead Art: The Traveling Chautauqua"; and Gregory Zilboorg, "Chautauqua and the Drama. Impressions of a Travelling Stranger." William Slout's *Theatre in a Tent* also includes a good deal of coverage of chautauqua.

The Lyceum movement, closely aligned to chautauqua, has received less attention and analysis, and, as a rule, Lyceum incorporated less pure entertainment in its programs. Lyceum, in contrast to chautauqua, functioned during the fall and winter months and utilized town halls or other permanent facilities for their presentations. A few excellent sources, however, should be mentioned. David Mead's *Yankee Eloquence in the Middle West* is the best study to date of this social and cultural institution, although Charles F. Horner's *The Life of James Redpath and the Development of the Modern Lyceum* provides an adequate but superficial survey of Lyceum presentations, and Fred W. Lorch's *The Trouble Begins at Eight* is a fascinating study of Lyceum and Mark Twain's dealings with James Redpath. Cecil B. Hayes's *The American Lyceum* incorporates all the essential factual material on the Lyceum and its educational aims.

A survey of sources on tent repertoire would be incomplete without a discussion of principal sources on the stock character Toby, who has been the subject of several scholarly investigations, in particular those by Larry Clark ("Toby Shows"), Sherwood Snyder ("The Toby Shows"), and Jere C. Mickel ("The Genesis of Toby" and *Footlights on the Prairie*). William L. Slout's *Theatre in a Tent* is also a major source. Neil E. Schaffner and Vance Johnson's *The Fabulous Toby and Me,* the story of Neil Schaffner, the last of the well-known tent repertoire showmen, is an entertaining and sometimes revealing look at the tag end of an American tradition. Other recommended sources include: Larry Clark's "The Toby Show: A Rural American Harlequinade"; Dolores Dorn-Heft's "Toby: The Twilight of a Tradition"; Robert Downing's "Toby" and "Folding of Last of Toby Troupes Ends Another Show Biz Tradition" (Schaffner Players); Joe Alex Morris's "Corniest Show on the Road" (Schaffner Players); Hobe Morrison's "Last of the 'Toby' Tenters" (on the Schaffner Players and the Museum of Repertoire Americana); Carol Pennepacher's "A Surviving Toby Show" (Bisbee's Comedians in Tennessee and Kentucky); Omar Ranney's "Forever Toby"; "Rose Melville—The Feminine Denman Thompson" (a famous Sis Hopkins); and "Rural Invasion."

Serious research into the tent theater movement is impossible without close attention to the coverage provided in *Billboard* and in *Bill Bruno's Bulletin,* the latter a publication that largely specialized in tent show coverage from 1929 until its founder's death in 1940. Articles can be found also in most of the show business publications listed in chapter 8 of this guide, including *Variety* and the *New York Clipper*. In the past few years, two repositories for materials on the tent show have been established. The Museum of Repertoire Americana was founded by The National Society for the Preservation of Tent, Folk and Repertoire Theatre, with the urging of Caroline Schaffner, and established in Mount Pleasant, Iowa (Route 1, zip code 52641), by the Midwest Old Settlers and Threshers Association. This collection, which contains many play manuscripts, also includes what was known as "House Rep," that is, touring companies that played tents in the summer and regular theaters during the other months of the year. More recently Texas Tech University has established The Tent Show Collection as part of their Southwest Collection (Box 4090, Lubbock, TX 79409). Since

1976 this collection has been gathering the papers of the tent showman Harley Sadler, the notes and papers of Jere C. Mickel, play scripts, and other material relating to the tent show. Unfortunately, there is no similar collection for the American showboat.

BIBLIOGRAPHY

Adams, Allen J. "Mining Theatre History." *Players, The Magazine of American Theatre* 44 (December-January 1969):62-64.

Albert, Allen D. "Tents of the Conservative." *Scribner's Magazine* 72 (July 1922): 54-59.

Archer, Stephen M., ed. *Actors and Actresses: A Guide to Information Sources.* Detroit: Gale Research Co., 1982.

Ashby, Clifford. "Trouping Through Texas: Harley Sadler and His Own Show." In *American Popular Entertainment,* edited by Myron Matlaw. Westport, Conn. and London: Greenwood Press, 1979.

Aylward, William J. "Steamboating Through Dixie." *Harper's Magazine* 131 (September 1915):512-22.

Basso, Hamilton. "Cotton Blossom, the South from a Mississippi Showboat." *Sewanee Review* 40 (October 1932):385-95.

Bell, Charles Harris, III. "An Ohio Repertoire-Tent Show Family: The Kinsey Komedy Kompany and the Madge Kinsey Players, 1881-1951." Ph.D. dissertation, Bowling Green State University, 1978.

Birdoff, Harry. *The World's Greatest Hit—Uncle Tom's Cabin.* New York: S. F. Vanni, 1947.

Bliven, Bruce. "Mother, Home, and Heaven." *New Republic,* 9 January 1924, pp. 172-75.

_____. "Nearest the Hearts of Ten Millions." *Collier's,* 8 September 1923, pp. 6-7.

Briggs, Harold Edward. "Floating Circuses." *Egyptian Key* 3 (September 1951): 19-23.

Britt, Albert. *Turn of the Century.* Barre, Mass.: Barre Publishers, 1966.

Bryant, Billy. *Children of Ol' Man River: The Life and Times of a Show-Boat Trouper.* New York: L. Furman, [1936].

Burman, Ben Lucian. *Big River to Cross.* New York: John Day Co., 1940.

Case, Victoria, and Ormond, Robert. *We Called It Culture: The Story of Chautauqua.* Garden City, N.Y.: Doubleday and Co., 1948.

Castle, Marian Johnson. "Chautauqua, the Intellectual Circus." *Forum* 87 (June 1932):369-74.

Channell, Herbert Walter, and Lowry, Velma E. *Fifty Years Under Canvas.* Hugo, Okla.: Acme Publishing Co., 1962.

Crichton, Kyle. "'Showboat' 'Round the Bend'." *Collier's,* 15 July 1939, pp. 19, 40-41.

Clark, Larry D. "Toby Shows: A Form of American Popular Theatre." Ph.D. dissertation, University of Illinois, 1963.

_____. "The Toby Show: A Rural American Harlequinade." *Central States Speech Journal* 19 (Summer 1968):91-95.

Cocroft, Thoda, "The Floating Theatre Thrives." *Bookman* 66 (December 1927): 396-98.

Conlin, James W. "The Merom Bluff Chautauqua." *Indiana Magazine of History* 36 (March 1940):23-28.

Corbett, Elizabeth F. "A Foot Note to 'THE DRAMA'." *Drama* 16 (May 1926): 285-86.

_____. "Uncle Tom Is Dead." *Theatre Guild Magazine* 18 (January 1931):16-20.

Cosgrave, Luke. *Theater Tonight.* Hollywood: House-Warven, 1952.

David, J. Frank. "Tom Shows." *Scribner's Magazine* 77 (April 1925):350-60.

Davis, Ronald L. "They Played for Gold: Theater on the Mining Frontier." *Southwest Review* 51 (Spring 1966):169-84.

_____. "Sopranos and Six Guns: The Frontier Opera House as a Cultural Symbol." *American West* 7 (November 1970):10-17.

DeAngelis, Jefferson, and Harlow, Alvin F. *Vagabond Trouper.* New York: Harcourt, Brace and Co., 1931.

Detzer, Karl W. "Broadway R.F.D.: The Rejuvenated Chautauqua is Bigger and Better Than Ever." *Century Magazine* 116 (July 1928):311-17.

Dixson, Harry L. "Doff Your Hat to the Tent Shows." *Billboard,* 20 March 1926, pp. 9, 13, 218-20.

Donovan, Frank. *Riverboats of America.* New York: Thomas Y. Crowell, 1966.

Dorn-Heft, Dolores. "Toby: The Twilight of a Tradition." *Theatre Arts* 42 (August 1958):52-55, 80.

Dorson, Richard M. "Mose the Far-Famed and World Renowned." *American Literature* 15 (November 1943):288-300.

Downing, Robert. "Toby." *Theatre Arts* 30 (November 1946):651-54.

_____. "Folding of Last of Toby Troupes Ends Another Show Biz Tradition." *Variety,* 16 May 1962, pp. 61, 67.

Ellerbe, Alma, and Ellerbe, Paul. "The Most American Thing in America." *World's Work* 68 (August 1924):440-46.

Emmett, Frank. "Trouping Under Canvas." *Billboard,* 9 December 1911, pp. 24, 97.

"End of an Era." *Newsweek,* 27 August 1962, p. 54.

Fike, Duane Joseph. "Frank Mayo: Actor, Playwright, and Manager." Ph.D. dissertation, University of Nebraska, 1980.

Ford, George D. *These Were Actors: The Story of the Chapmans and the Drakes.* New York: Library Publishers, 1955.

Furnas, J. C. *Goodbye to Uncle Tom.* New York: William Sloane Associates, 1956.

Gaer, Joseph, ed. *Theater of the Gold Rush Decade in San Francisco.* 1935. Reprint. New York: Burt Franklin, 1970.

Gagey, Edmond McAdoo. *The San Francisco Stage.* New York: Columbia University Press, 1950.

Gohdes, Clarence. *Literature and Theater of the States and Regions of the U.S.A.: An Historical Bibliography.* Durham, N.C.: Duke University Press, 1967.

Gordon, Jan, and Gordon, Cora. "Two English Tourists on a Showboat." *Literary Digest,* 29 December 1928, pp. 38-41.

Gould, Joseph E. *The Chautauqua Movement: An Episode in the Continuing American Revolution.* New York: State University of New York, 1961.

Graham, Philip. *Showboats. The History of an American Institution.* 1951. Reprint. Austin: University of Texas Press, 1969.

_____. "Showboats in the South." *Georgia Review* 12 (Summer 1958): 174-85.

Harrison, Harry P., as told to Karl Detzer. *Culture Under Canvas: The Story of Tent Chautauqua.* New York: Hastings House, 1958.

Hayes, Cecil B. *The American Lyceum: Its History and Contributions to Education.* Washington, D.C.: Office of Education Bulletin No. 12, 1932.

Hedges, R. Alan. "Actors Under Canvas: A Study of the Theatre of the Circuit Chautauqua, 1910-1933." Ph.D. dissertation, Ohio State University, 1976.

High, Fred. "The Circus and the Chautauqua." *Billboard,* 22 December 1917, pp. 14-15.

_____. "Chautauqua's Growth." *Billboard,* 20 March 1920, pp. 16-17, 204.

Hodge, Francis. *Yankee Theatre: The Image of America on Stage 1825-1850.* Austin: University of Texas Press, 1964.

Hogan, William Ransom. "The Theatre in the Republic of Texas." *Southwest Review* 19 (July 1934):374-401.

Horner, Charles F. *The Life of James Redpath and the Development of the Modern Lyceum.* New York and Newark, N.J.: Barse and Hopkins, 1926.

_____. *Strike the Tents: The Story of the Chautauqua.* Philadelphia: Dorrance and Co., 1954

Howard, Randall R. "Chautauqua Invades the West." *Sunset* 40 (May 1918): 49-50.

Hoyt, Harlowe. *Town Hall Tonight.* New York: Bramhall House, 1955.

Hunter, John Marvin. "Mollie Bailey, Great Showwoman." *Frontier Times* 27 (April 1950):183-93.

"An Inveterate Chautauqua Fan." *Scribner's Magazine* 74 (July 1923):119-20.

Irwin, Alfreda L. *The Chautauqua Story: Three Taps of the Gavel.* Westfield, N.Y.: The Westfield Republican, Inc., 1970.

Johnson, Vance. "Hits in the Tall Corn." *Collier's,* 20 August 1949, pp. 16-17, 72-73.

Judd, "Doctor," "The Water Days of the Drama." *Theatre Magazine* 3 (August 1903):202-4.

Klussen, Robert Dean. "The Tent-Repertoire Theatre: A Rural American Institution." Ph.D. dissertation, Michigan State University, 1970.

Knox, Rose B. *Footlights Afloat.* Garden City, N.Y.: Doubleday, Doran and Co., 1937.

Kreuger, Miles. *Show Boat: The Story of a Classic American Musical.* New York: Oxford University Press, 1977.

Kusell, Maurice L., and Merritt, N. S. *Marquee Ballyhoo.* Los Angeles: Overland-Out West Publications, 1932.

Lathrop, West. *River Circus.* New York: Random House, 1953.

Larson, Carl F. W. *American Regional Theatre History to 1900: A Bibliography.* Metuchen, N.J. and London: The Scarecrow Press, 1979.

Lewis, Philip C. *Trouping: How the Show Came to Town.* New York: Harper and Row, 1973.

Lorch, Fred W. *The Trouble Begins at Eight. Mark Twain's Lecture Tours.* Ames: Iowa State University Press, 1968.

Lund, Ralph Eugene. "Trouping with Uncle Tom." *The Century* 115 (January 1928):329-37.

M'Clure, W. Frank. "A Floating Theatre." *Scientific America,* 9 January 1904, p. 24.

McDermott, Douglas. "Touring Patterns on California's Theatrical Frontier, 1849-1859." *Theatre Survey* 15 (May 1974):18-28.

_____. "The Development of Theatre on the American Frontier, 1750-1890." *Theatre Survey,* 19 (May 1978):63-78.

MacDonald, Cordelia Howard. "Memoirs of the Original Little Eva." *Educational Theatre Journal* 8 (December 1956):267-82.

McDowell, John H. "Original Scenery and Documents for Productions of *Uncle Tom's Cabin.*" *Revue d'Histoire du Theatre* 15 (January-March 1963):71-79.

_____. "Scenery and Staging of *Uncle Tom's Cabin:* Selected Scenes." *The Ohio State University Theatre Collection Bulletin,* no. 10 (1963), pp. 19-30.

McKennon, Marian. *Tent Show.* New York: Exposition Press, 1964.

MacLaren, Gay. *Morally We Roll Along.* Boston: Little, Brown and Co., 1938.

MacMinn, George R. *The Theater of the Golden Era in California.* Caldwell, Idaho: Caxton Printers, 1941.

Martin, Pete. "River Singer." *Saturday Evening Post,* 16 August 1947, pp. 30-31, 50, 52-54, 56; 23 August 1947, pp. 28, 104-6, 108; August 1947, pp. 26, 70, 73-74.

Mead, David. *Yankee Eloquence in the Middle West: The Ohio Lyceum 1850-1870.* 1951. Reprint. Westport, Conn.: Greenwood Press, 1977.

_____. "1914: The Chautauqua and American Innocence." *Journal of Popular Culture* 1 (Spring 1968):339-56.

Meserve, Walter J. *An Emerging Entertainment: The Drama of the American People to 1828.* Bloomington and London: Indiana University Press, 1977.

_____, ed. *American Drama to 1900: A Guide to Information Sources.* Detroit Gale Research Co., 1980.

Mickel, Jere C. "The Genesis of Toby. A Folk Hero of the American Theater." *Journal of American Folklore* 80 (October-December 1967):334-40.

_____. *Footlights on the Prairie.* St. Cloud, Minn.: North Star Press, 1974.

Miles, Carlton. "Doubling in Brass." *Theatre Arts* 10 (October 1926):685-88.

Miller, Melvin H. "The Chautauqua in Lansing." *Michigan History* 40 (September 1956):257-74.

Monson, William Neil. "Frontier Theatre Town. An Historical Study of Some Paratheatrical Activities in Visalia, California, 1852 to 1889." Ph.D. dissertation, University of Oregon, 1976.

Moody, Richard. "Uncle Tom, The Theater and Mrs. Stowe." *American Heritage* 6 (October 1955):29-33, 102-3.

_____, and Drummond, A. M. "The Hit of the Century: *Uncle Tom's Cabin.*" *Educational Theatre Journal* 4 (December 1952):315-22.

Morris, Joe Alex. "Corniest Show on the Road." *Saturday Evening Post,* 17 September 1955, pp. 30-31, 60-62, 66, 70.

Morrison, Hobe. "Last of the 'Toby' Tenters." *Variety,* 4 January 1978, p. 180.

Morrison, Theodore. *Chautauqua.* Chicago: University of Chicago Press, 1974.

Moyer, Ronald Lee. *American Actors, 1861-1910: An Annotated Bibliography of Books, Published in the United States in English from 1861 through 1976.* Troy, N.Y.: Whitston, 1979.

Orchard, Hugh Anderson. *Fifty Years of Chautauqua: Its Beginnings, Its Development, Its Message and Its Life.* Iowa: Torch Press, 1923.

Pennepacher, Carol. "A Surviving Toby Show: Bisbee's Comedians." *Tennessee Folklore Society Bulletin* 30 (June 1964):49-52.

Perry, Jeb H. *Variety Obits: An Index to Obituaries in Variety. 1905-1978.* Metuchen, N.J. and London: The Scarecrow Press, 1980.

Perry-Cowen, Frances. *Chautauqua to Opera.* Hicksville, N.Y.: Exposition Press, 1978.

Pettit, Paul Bruce. "The Showboat Theatre." *Quarterly Journal of Speech* 31 (April 1945):167-75.

Popkin, Zelda F. "The Tent Show Turns to Sex." *Outlook and Independent,* 24 September 1930, pp. 128-30, 157.

Price, Lucien. "Orpheus in Zion: An Idyl of Chautauqua." *Yale Review* 19 (December 1929):303-24.

Price, Willard. *The Amazing Mississippi.* New York: John Day Co., 1963.

Pringle, Henry F. "Chautauqua in the Jazz Age." *American Mercury* 17 (January 1929):85-93.

Quarnstrom, I. Blaine. "Early Twentieth-Century Staging of *Uncle Tom's Cabin.*" *The Ohio State University Theatre Collection Bulletin,* no. 15 (1968), pp. 32-42.

Quinn, Arthur Hobson. *A History of the American Drama From the Beginning to the Civil War and...From the Civil War to the Present.* New York: Appleton-Century-Crofts, 1936 and 1943.

Rahill, Frank. "America's Number One Hit." *Theatre Arts* 37 (August 1953): 73, 95.

Reed, Duane Eldon. "A History of Showboats on the Western Rivers." Ph.D. dissertation, Michigan State University, 1978.

Richmond, Rebecca. *Chautauqua, An American Place.* New York: Duell, Sloan and Pearce, 1943.

Rinear, David L. "F. S. Chanfrau's Mose: The Rise and Fall of an Urban Folk-Hero." *The Theatre Journal* 33 (May 1981):199-212.

"Rose Melville—The Feminine Denman Thompson." *The Theatre* 8 (January 1908):28-29.

Rourke, Constance. *Troupers of the Gold Coast, or The Rise of Lotta Crabtree.* New York: Harcourt, Brace and Co., 1928.

Row, Arthur William. "Acting in Tents in Chautauqua." *Poet-Lore* 36 (Spring 1925):222-31.

"Rural Invasion." *Harper's Magazine* 209 (November 1954):82-84.

Ryan, Pat M. "Tombstone Theatre Tonight." *Smoke Signal* 13 (Spring 1966), pp. 50-76.

Schaffner, Caroline. "Trouping with the Schaffners." In *American Popular Entertainment,* edited by Myron Matlaw. Westport, Conn. and London: Greenwood Press, 1979.

Schaffner, Neil E., with Vance Johnson. *The Fabulous Toby and Me.* Englewood Cliffs, N.J.: Prentice-Hall, 1968.

Schick, Joseph S. "Early Showboat and Circus in the Upper Valley." *Mid-America* 32 (October 1950):211-25.

Scott, Marian. *Chautauqua Caravan.* New York: D. Appleton-Century, 1939.

Slout, L. Verne. "The Chautauqua Drama." *Lyceum Magazine* (April 1923):19-20.

Slout, William Lawrence. *Theatre in a Tent: The Development of a Provincial Entertainment.* Bowling Green, Ohio: Bowling Green University Popular Press, 1972.

_____. "Tent Rep: Broadway's Poor Relation." In *American Popular Entertainment,* edited by Myron Matlaw. Westport, Conn. and London: Greenwood Press, 1979.

Smoot, James S. "Platform Theater. Theatrical Elements of the Lyceum—Chautauqua." Ph.D. dissertation, University of Michigan, 1954.

Snook, Sidney. "The Showboat Drifts Downstream." *South Atlantic Quarterly* 41 (July 1942):321-26.

Snyder, Sherwood III. "The Toby Shows." Ph.D. dissertation, University of Minnesota, 1966.

Spears, Raymond S. "The Mississippi Boat Theatres." *Harper's Weekly,* 4 September 1909, p. 13.

Stewart, George R., Jr. "The Drama in a Frontier Theater." In *The Parriott Presentation Volume,* edited by Hardin Craig. Princeton, N.J.: Princeton University Press, 1935.

Stoddard, Richard, ed. *Stage Scenery, Machinery, and Lighting: A Guide to Information Sources.* Detroit: Gale Research Co., 1977.

_____, ed. *Theatre and Cinema Architecture: A Guide to Information Sources.* Detroit: Gale Research Co., 1978.

Stout, Wesley Winans. "Little Eva is Seventy-Five." *Saturday Evening Post,* 8 October 1927, p. 10.

Stratman, Carl J. *Bibliography of the American Theatre, Excluding New York City.* Chicago: Loyola University Press, 1965.

Striker, Hopper. "Cruising Theatres of Long Ago." *Literary Digest,* 22 July 1916, p. 189.

Talley, Truman H. "The Chautauqua, an American Achievement." *World's Work* 42 (June 1921):172-84.

Thornton, Harrison J. "Chautauqua and the Midwest." *Wisconsin Magazine of History* 33 (December 1949):152-63.

Toll, Robert C. *On with the Show: The First Century of Show Business in America.* New York: Oxford University Press, 1976.

Tozier, Roy Becker. "A Short Life-History of the Chautauqua." Ph.D. dissertation, University of Iowa, 1932.

Turner, Willis L. "City Low-Life on the American Stage to 1900." Ph.D. dissertation, University of Illinois, 1956.

Warde, Frederick. *Fifty Years of Make Believe.* Los Angeles: Times-Mirror, 1923.

Waterman, Arthur E. "Joseph Jefferson as Rip Van Winkle." *Journal of Popular Culture* 1 (Spring 1968):371-78.

Watson, Margaret. *Silver Theatre, Amusements of the Mining Frontier in Early Nevada, 1850-1864.* Glendale, Calif.: Arthur H. Clark Co., 1964.

Wearing, J. P. *American and British Theatrical Biography: A Directory.* Metuchen, N.J. and London: The Scarecrow Press, 1979.

Weeks, Edward. "Chautauqua, The First 100 Years." *Americana* 2 (July 1974):2-7.

Wells, L. Jeanette. *A History of the Music Festival at the Chautauqua Institution, 1874-1957.* Washington, D.C.: Catholic University of America Press, 1958.

Willson, Clair Eugene. *Mimes and Miners: A Historical Study of the Theater in Tombstone.* Tucson: University of Arizona Press, 1935.

Wilmeth, Don B., ed. *The American Stage to World War I: A Guide to Information Sources.* Detroit: Gale Research Co., 1978.

————, ed. *American and English Popular Entertainment: A Guide to Information Sources.* Detroit: Gale Research Co., 1980.

Wilson, Edna Erle. "Canvas and Culture: When Chautauqua Comes to Town." *Outlook,* 9 August 1922, pp. 598-600.

Wilson, Garff B. *Three Hundred Years of American Drama and Theatre.* 2d. ed. Englewood Cliffs, N.J.: Prentice-Hall, 1982.

Wilson, W. L. "The Tented Theatre." *Billboard* (23 March 1912):34, 84.

Winks, Evert M., as told to Robin W. Winks. "Recollections of a Dead Art: The Traveling Chautauqua." *Indiana Magazine of History* 54 (March 1958): 41-48.

Yates, L.B. "Hittin' The Grit." *Saturday Evening Post,* 13 August 1921, pp. 8-9, 92-94.

Young, William C., ed. and comp. *Famous Actors and Actresses on the American Stage.* 2 vols. New York and London: Bowker, 1975.

Zilboorg, Gregory. "Chautauqua and the Drama. Impressions of a Travelling Stranger." *Drama* 12 (October-November 1921):16-18, 40.

Index

ABOUT THE AUTHOR

DON B. WILMETH is Professor of Theatre Arts and English, and Chairman of the Theatre Arts Department at Brown University. He has authored numerous books and articles on the history of American popular entertainment. His biography *George Frederick Cooke* (Greenwood Press, 1980) won the 1981 Barnard Hewitt Theatre History Award of the American Theatre Association. He has been selected as a Guggenheim Fellow for 1982-83.